Bullying

■   ■   ■

A practical guide to coping for schools

Bullying

■ ■ ■

A Practical Guide
to Coping for Schools

Second Edition

Edited by
MICHELE ELLIOTT

FINANCIAL TIMES
PITMAN PUBLISHING

FINANCIAL TIMES

MANAGEMENT

LONDON · SAN FRANCISCO
KUALA LUMPUR · JOHANNESBURG

*Financial Times Management delivers the knowledge,
skills and understanding that enable students,
managers and organisations to achieve their ambitions,
whatever their needs, wherever they are.*

London Office:
128 Long Acre, London WC2E 9AN
Tel: +44 (0)171 447 2000
Fax: +44 (0)171 240 5771
Website: www.ftmanagement.com

A Division of Financial Times Professional Limited

First edition © Longman Group UK Limited 1992
Second edition first published in Great Britain in 1997

© Pearson Professional Limited 1997

Introduction and Chapters 1, 4, 6, 7 and 19 © Michele Elliott 1997
Chapter 2 © Eric Jones 1997
Chapter 3 © Linda Frost 1997
Chapter 5 and 12 © Valerie Besag 1997
Chapter 8 © Wendy Stainton Rogers 1997
Chapter 9 © John Pearce 1997
Chapter 10 © Jane Kilpatrick 1997
Chapter 11 © Andrew Mellor 1997
Chapter 13 © Carolyn Hamilton 1997
Chapter 14 © Hereward Harrison 1997
Chapter 15 © Francis Gobey 1997
Chapter 16 © Astrid Mona O'Moore 1997
Chapter 17 © Peter Stephenson and David Smith 1997
Chapter 18 © Ludwig Lowenstein 1997

The right of Valerie Besag, Michele Elliott, Linda Frost,
Francis Gobey, Carolyn Hamilton, Hereward Harrison,
Eric Jones, Jane Kilpatrick, Ludwig Lowenstein, Andrew Mellor,
Astrid Mona O'Moore, John Pearce, David Smith,
Wendy Stainton Rogers and Peter Stephenson to be identified
as Authors of this Work has been asserted by them in accordance
with the Copyright, Design, and Patents Act 1988.

ISDN 0 273 62692 2

British Library Cataloguing in Publication Data
A CIP catalogue record for this book can be obtained from the British Library

10 9 8 7 6 5 4 3 2

Printed and bound in Great Britain by Redwood Books, Trowbridge, Wiltshire

The Publishers' policy is to use paper manufactured from sustainable forests.

Contents

■ ■ ■

Contributors

■ ■ ■

Valerie Besag is one of the UK's leading experts on bullying. She is qualified as a teacher and has taught every age group from infants to teenagers. She worked in various parts of the country before taking a degree in Educational Psychology. She now works as an educational psychologist in Gateshead and is the author of *Bullies and Victims in Schools*. Valerie also works with Home Start.

Michele Elliott is the Director of the children's charity Kidscape which deals with the prevention of bullying and child abuse. She is a teacher, psychologist and the author of several books, including five which deal with bullying. She has chaired World Health Organisation and Home Office Working Groups about the prevention of child abuse and is a Winston Churchill Fellow.

Linda Frost is the head teacher of a junior school in North London, where she has taught since 1971. She has previously had articles published on child safety.

Francis Gobey lectured in Literature at the University of Ghana, and taught in Belgium, Zambia and London. In 1988 he went on the Enterprise Allowance Scheme as a full-time writer. He is now a drama consultant and combines education work with theatres, workshops, freelance editing and writing poems.

Carolyn Hamilton is Director of the Children's Legal Centre, a national charity which promotes the rights of children. It operates a national legal advice line, produces *Childright* and carries out research, policy and campaigning work. She is also a Senior Lecturer in the Department of Law at the University of Essex. She is the author of *Family, Law and Religion* and *Family Law in Europe* as well as numerous articles in the field of child law, family law, children's rights and evidence law. She was recently commissioned to write one of the study papers, 'Children's Rights and Humanitarian Law', for the UN Study on the Impact of Armed Conflict on Children headed by Graca Machel.

Hereward Harrison is the Director of Children's Services at ChildLine UK. He is a trained social worker and psychotherapist with 25 years' experience in the helping professions. He has specialised in clinical work, the supervision of mental health professionals and teaching. Before joining ChildLine he was Principal Social Worker (Teaching) at Guy's Hospital, where he specialised in paediatric social work and child abuse.

Eric Jones spent eight years in motor insurance in the City before training as a teacher at Westhill College, Birmingham University, in the 1960s. He has spent his entire career in the inner city of London at schools in Brixton, Tooting and Camberwell, only returning to Birmingham to gain an honours degree in Education in the 1970s. He was the deputy head of a London school until he took supposed early retirement. Unable to stay away from education, he is now working in a secondary school in charge of drama production. He produced and directed the first production to go into the new Globe theatre, using children from his secondary school. He has also written books for the Boys' Brigade.

Jane Kilpatrick is the Assistant Director of Kidscape, the children's safety charity. She has written *How to Stop Bullying: A Kidscape Training Guide* with Michele Elliott and has developed practical advice booklets on coping with bullying for parents and teenagers. She also coordinates Kidscape's schools training programme.

Dr L.F. Lowenstein is Chief Examiner in Advanced Educational Psychology, College of Preceptors, London. He is also a Visiting Professor, the University of Khartoum, Sudan, and was formerly a chief educational psychologist in Hampshire. Dr Lowenstein pioneered research on bullying in the UK in the early 1970s. He is the author of numerous books and hundreds of articles, and is currently Director of Allington Manor School and Therapeutic Community.

Andrew Mellor is Principal Teacher of Guidance at Dalry School in Galloway, Scotland, where he has spent all 23 years of his teaching career. His interest in bullying comes from a personal dissatisfaction with existing remedies. In 1987 he was one of two Scottish teachers who attended the European Teachers' Seminar on Bullying in Stavanger, Norway. This experience inspired him to carry out the first ever research project on bullying in Scottish schools. The publication of its findings early in 1990 caused considerable interest in the Scottish press. Between 1993 and 1995, he was seconded to the Scottish Council for Research in Education as the Scottish Anti-bullying Development Officer.

Astrid Mona O'Moore is a Norwegian who has lived and worked in the UK and Ireland. She is qualified in Child Psychology and has a PhD in Special Education, having specialised in the integration and segregation of children with physical handicaps. She is the author of the Council of Europe's Report *Bullying in Schools*. Mona is at present Lecturer in Developmental and Educational Psychology and Special Education at Trinity College, Dublin.

John Pearce is a qualified doctor and has worked in the field of child and adolescent psychiatry at the Maudsley Hospital, Guy's Hospital and the University of Leicester. He is currently Professor of Child and Adolescent Psychiatry at the University of Nottingham. His current research interests include emotional disorders in children. He has written several practical guides for parents (including *Fighting, Teasing and Bullying*) and has appeared on radio and TV speaking on child care issues.

Wendy Stainton Rogers graduated in psychology in 1967, and then spent three years teaching science in secondary schools. After a period working in market research and supply teaching she was appointed by the Open University as a lecturer, first in Psychology and subsequently in Health and Social Welfare. She is providing training for the Children Act 1989 and related legislation, having completed the production of a distance learning course on Child Abuse and Neglect. She edited *Child Abuse and Neglect: Facing the Challenge* and has written and lectured extensively in the areas of child protection and children's rights.

David Smith is the Principal Educational Psychologist with Durham County Council. He trained as a primary teacher and then went on to undertake an MEd in Educational Psychology, subsequently working mostly in the north of England. David's interest in bullying dates from the early 1980s when, with Peter Stephenson, he undertook a number of studies on the subject in Cleveland schools. Since then he has contributed to various seminars and undertaken in-service work for individual schools, as well as organised courses for head teachers and senior management.

Peter Stephenson initially qualified in law but went on to become a teacher and child educational psychologist. For the past 15 years he has been working as a psychologist in Cleveland. From 1982, together with David Smith, he has carried out research on bullying and presented seminars and papers on the subject. He is currently producing guidelines on dealing with bullying at the request of the Cleveland Education Authority. He is currently working with four education boroughs.

Introduction

■ ■ ■

Why a book on bullying?

'Bullying has been around since time began. It equips kids to deal with life. Why on earth do we need a book about how to cope with it?' Fortunately, the attitude of this person is not shared by the majority of teachers. In fact, most teachers are concerned to stop bullying and want practical ideas on how to cope with it. Children who are worried about being bullied have a hard time concentrating on learning. Children who are bullies are seldom our best pupils. The effects of bullying can go on for years. The following, written by a 50-year-old man, is an excerpt from one of thousands of letters Kidscape has received about bullying:

Dear Kidscape

As a former sufferer of severe children bullying, I hope my story may help to stop this happening to other children. I was born severely cross-eyed and was very small for my age. I was also patient and rather self-effacing. It made me vulnerable to attack by 'hyper-macho' boys. I am able to write this calmly because I am undergoing therapy and coming to terms with myself and my nightmare childhood.

It began on my first day of school. The teacher left the classroom for some reason. I was instantly surrounded by a mob of kids all laughing, pushing and shouting at me. I was totally terrified and bewildered and broke a pencil I was holding. The teacher came back, and found me in the centre of chaos. Then a girl told her I had broken a pencil and I was made to stand in the corner for being a bad boy! From then on I was the object of continual bullying. Hell of a responsibility being a teacher, that kind of mistake can ruined a kid's life for years. Still, she is forgiven now.

It seemed that the whole mob constantly chased and tormented me. I was alone and became what I now know was withdrawn and virtually paranoid. Not surprising when I did not imagine the hostility. What really hurt was never knowing why they did it, when I was always 'nice' to everyone. I couldn't figure why the teachers didn't stop it – they must have known.

The early attacks were because I 'looked funny' to other young children. The later ones happened because I became withdrawn and 'seemed funny' because they were so awful to me that I did not want anything to do with them. Talk about a 'no win' situation. If I read a story about child bullying, it sets off my bad memories and I am overwhelmed with anger, rage and tears, as though it was happening all over again, even 45 years later.

Your work is most important in preventing children going through what I did. Please tell adults involved in your work to never tell a child to 'take no notice'. If a child complains, he or she is absolutely desperate and only adult intervention can help. Yours sincerely

No child deserves to be bullied. Perhaps by using some of the suggestions in this second edition of *Bullying: A Practical Guide to Coping for Schools*, we will prevent children from becoming embittered, unhappy and unfulfilled.

Bullies, too, have a miserable future in front of them. One study found that bullies were much more likely as adults to be violent and to have difficulty with relationships than children who are not bullies. A Kidscape study (Chapter 10) found that the vast majority of young people in institutions for young offenders we visited had been involved in bullying while at school. Many said they thought that being allowed to get away with bullying had led them into a life of crime. So we do bullies no favours by ignoring their behaviour.

Coming back to the points my friend raised at the beginning: Yes, bullying has gone on for years – that doesn't make it right. We stuffed children up chimneys and down mines for years – that wasn't right either and we changed it. We can change the attitudes which allow bullying as well. No, it doesn't equip people for life. It can lead to self-destruction and a pretty miserable society.

We needed the first edition of this book as a starting point to understanding the problem. This second edition goes further – it not only includes the commonsense ideas of teachers and head teachers working on the coalface, it gives more practical suggestions for dealing with the problem of bullying. Having been a teacher myself and being married to a teacher, I know that using the ideas in this book will improve your lives as teachers and make the children more confident and more open to learning.

If you have any suggestions for the third edition, please do contact me at the Kidscape address listed in the back of the book. (Don't be surprised at our charity's address – the Queen lives at one end of Buckingham Palace Road, we live at the other end in a basement by the Coach Station.)

Michele Elliott
Editor

Acknowledgements

■ ■ ■

The poem 'Friends' by Nicholas English in Chapter 5 is reproduced with the kind permission of the English family.

The 'What if' questions in Chapter 18 are reproduced with the kind permission of Kidscape.

Kidscape and the author of Chapter 10 would like to thank the Governor and staff of HMYOI Onley and the Governor and staff of HMYOI Glen Parva for allowing us to talk to inmates. We are especially grateful to Senior Officer Tony Coleman at HMYOI Onley and Johanna Hilton of HMYOI Glen Parva – without their help the study would not have been possible. We would also like to thank all the young offenders who answered our questionnaire and who spoke to us so frankly.

1

■ ■ ■

Bullies and victims

MICHELE ELLIOTT

Nine-year-old Mark was walking home from school when a gang of bullies set upon him. His arm was broken, his money stolen and his books were destroyed. His self-confidence was also destroyed – he became withdrawn, hated to go to school and eventually had counselling to help him through the trauma. He knew the boys who attacked him, but refused to tell who they were. He was frightened of what they would do if he told.

Fourteen-year-old Sarah was cornered on the playground by a gang of ten boys and girls. She was stripped to the waist and had to beg on her knees to get her clothes back. She was pushed, punched and had her hair pulled. 'Tell and you'll get worse' was the parting shot from one of the girls. Sarah didn't tell until they did it again and took photographs. When her mother confronted the school, she was told it was only 'horseplay'. Sarah, who had attempted suicide after the latest incident, was transferred to another school in which she is now thriving.

In a similar case, 13-year-old Theresa was held down by a gang of nine girls, physically assaulted and then stripped in front of a group of boys. Her distraught father rang the Kidscape helpline because the school advised him that he should not go to the police. He was also advised that the gang of girls would be leaving the school within weeks so the school were not taking any further action, having given the girls detention.

Twelve-year-old Simon was bullied over two years by three boys at his boarding school. He was beaten, locked out of his room, shoved outdoors in his underwear on a freezing January night and constantly subjected to taunts about his weight. Simon ran away from the school and had a nervous breakdown.

The extent of bullying

Isolated cases of bullying or just the tip of the iceberg? Most studies show that bullying takes place in every type of school.

The first UK nationwide survey of bullying was conducted by Kidscape from 1984 to 1986 with 4000 children aged 5 to 16. The survey revealed that 68 per cent of the children had been bullied at least once; 38 per cent had been bullied at least twice or had experienced a particularly bad incident; 5 per cent of the students felt it had affected their lives to the point that they had tried suicide, had run away, refused to go to school or been chronically ill (Elliott and Kilpatrick, 1996). Subsequent studies have found very similar results. A Department of Education funded project found that 27 per cent of the pupils who took part in the project in junior and middle schools in Sheffield were bullied; 10 per cent indicated that they were bullied once a week (Whitney and Smith 1993). Researchers at Exeter University questioned 5500 children aged 13 and found that 26 per cent of boys and 34 per cent of girls had been afraid of bullies sometimes, often or very often (Balding, 1996).

ChildLine, the national telephone helpline for children, last year received nearly 13 000 calls from children and young people who are worried about bullying (see Chapter 14). Kidscape receives calls from over 6000 parents a year who say their children are being bullied. Bullying affects not only the child, but also the entire family.

Bullying is not only a UK problem – it happens throughout the world. Dan Olweus, the world-renowned expert, has been researching the problem of bullying in Norway since 1973. He has estimated that one in seven students in Norwegian schools has been involved in bully/victim problems (Olweus, 1993). Similar findings in other countries indicate that if adults are willing to listen and investigate, children will tell them that bullying is one of the major problems children face during their school years.

What is it?

Bullying takes many forms. It can be physical, like a child being pushed, beaten or thumped with knuckles. It can involve a weapon and threats. One seven-year-old boy had a knife pulled on him in the playground. Bullying can also be verbal and emotional, racial or sexual. A 13-year-old girl was told she was dirty and ugly by one group of girls. She used to wash two or three times a day to try to win their approval, which was never forthcoming. An Asian boy was taunted with racist remarks and eventually played truant rather than face his tormentors. An 11-year-old girl found herself the victim of continuous sexist remarks because she was beginning to develop physically – she tried to tape her breasts so the comments would stop.

From the cases we have assembled, it would seem that boys are more likely to be physical in bullying, while girls tend to be cruel verbally. Research by Dan Olweus (Olweus, 1993) indicates that girls are more often exposed to harassment such as slandering, the spreading of rumours and exclusion from the group rather than physical attacks. Olweus says it must be emphasised that these gender differences are general and that in some schools girls are also exposed to physical bullying. Recently there have been cases in the UK in which girls have violently and aggressively attacked other girls, as happened to Sarah and Theresa mentioned at the beginning of this chapter. There has been a death caused by young teenage girl bullies beating up a 13-year-old girl, who was trying her best to stop a fight. It cost her her life. The incidence of girls being violent does seem to be increasing and is a trend that must be viewed with concern.

Bystander attitude

If a child is bullied, peer pressure sometimes makes it difficult for the victim to rally support from other children. As one girl told me: 'I don't like it that Gill is bullied, but I can't do anything about it or they will turn on me, too.' This 'bystander attitude' also hurts the children who feel that they can't help the victim. In several schools teachers report that children who had witnessed bullying were badly affected by what they saw. Some of them felt anger, rage and helplessness. Several had nightmares and were worried that they might be the next victims. Most felt guilty that they did not stop the bully, but really did not know how to help the victim.

The tell-tale signs

A child may indicate by signs or behaviour that he or she is being bullied. Sometimes this is the only clue adults have about what is happening because of the code of silence so often maintained about bullying.

Children or young people may:

- be frightened of walking to or from school;
- be unwilling to go to school and make continual excuses to avoid going;
- beg to be driven to school;
- change their route to school everyday;
- begin doing poorly in their school work;
- regularly have clothes or books or school work torn or destroyed;
- come home starving (because dinner money was taken);
- become withdrawn;
- start stammering;
- start hitting other children (as a reaction to being bullied by those children or others);

- stop eating or be obsessively clean (as a reaction to being called 'fatty' or 'dirty');
- develop stomach troubles and headaches due to stress;
- attempt suicide;
- cry themselves to sleep;
- begin wetting the bed;
- have nightmares and call out things like 'leave me alone';
- have unexplained bruises, scratches, cuts;
- have their possessions go 'missing';
- ask for money or begin stealing money (to pay the bully);
- continually 'lose' their pocket money;
- refuse to say what's wrong;
- give improbable excuses to explain any of the above.

If a child is displaying some of these symptoms, bullying is a likely cause, though obviously not the only possibility.

Chronic bullies

In the Kidscape studies two kinds of bullies emerged. One was the spoilt brat – over-indulged by doting parents who felt their child could do no wrong. This kind of bully was completely selfish and hit out if anyone got in his or her way. The second kind of bully was the victim of some sort of abuse or neglect. He or she had been made to feel inadequate, stupid and humiliated.

Children who are nurtured and loved can cope with being vulnerable and dependent, and with making mistakes or not doing everything properly. This is a normal part of growing up. Some children are punished or humiliated for things they cannot help, like accidentally wetting the bed, not being hungry when adults decide it is time to eat, spilling a drink, falling over and getting hurt or putting on a jumper back to front.

The adults expect impossible things from the child and make it clear that being dependent and vulnerable are not acceptable. Being strong and humiliating others are the acceptable ways to behave. Indeed, this is the only way to behave if the child is to survive.

The child comes to deny and hate this vulnerable self. It is linked with weakness and being weak is associated with pain. When this child perceives that another child is weak in any way, he or she attacks. But the sad fact is that the bully is really attacking his or her own self – it is self-hatred that makes a bully.

Bullies need help, but usually reject any attempt to provide it. Realistic firm guidelines and rules may help them to control their reactions and lashing-out behaviour. Also trying to help them achieve some success can make a difference.

One boy was nurtured by a teacher who helped him to learn skills in woodworking. He began to produce beautiful boxes which the teacher made sure were prominently displayed and admired. The boy found a part of himself that he could like and stopped bullying others. Unfortunately, the 'success' that most bullies achieve is by being a bully and other children need help to cope with the problem.

John Pearce gives an excellent background and suggestions about how children become bullies and how to help them in Chapter 9.

Victims

Many children are one-off victims of bullying. They just happen to be at the wrong place at the wrong time. They become victims of bullying because, unfortunately, the bully chooses them to torment. If no one stops the bully, these victims start to think that they are to blame for the bullying. The reality is that the bully needs a victim. Kidscape has found that often these children get along quite well in one school, but are victimised continually at another. This may be because of the particular mix of children at the schools, but more likely it is because of the policy one school has evolved towards bullying, while the other school takes firm action.

A small minority of children seem to be perpetual victims. They are bullied no matter where they go and it even carries on into adult life. Several people have contacted Kidscape to say that they had been bullied at school from an early age. Subsequently they were bullied all their lives – at work, in marriage and in all relationships. They have developed a victim mentality and are unable to stand up for themselves.

In one study Kidscape found that the children who were chronic victims were intelligent, sensitive and creative, but they were also lacking in humour. They had good relationships with their parents and families, but were inclined to be intense and very serious. The everyday 'give and take' of life was not easy for them. A small group of the chronic victims seemed almost to seek out being bullied. These children were often victims of some other kinds of abuse and actually had much in common with the chronic bullies. Some had been both victim and bully.

Children first need to know that there are some situations which might be impossible to deal with – a gang of bullies attacking one child or a bully with a weapon. Since the child's safety is the primary concern, advise them that money or anything else is not worth getting badly hurt over. Sometimes it is better to give the bully what he or she asks for and get away and tell an adult.

Some adults feel it is best to just give as good as you get. If a child reports being bullied, the response is 'hit back or you will continue to be bullied'. While this tactic can work, it places the often smaller, weaker victim in an impossible situation. And bullies are most likely to choose this kind of victim.

In Chapter 11, Andrew Mellor gives some effective suggestions for dealing with the victims of bullying.

Suggestions for dealing with bullying

The children who always seem to be bullied need as much help as possible. The first thing to do is to examine the child's behaviour to find out if he or she is acting and feeling like a victim. Perhaps the child needs to learn to walk in a more confident manner or learn to express feelings of anger and become more self-assertive.

One family helped their son by practising walking, which also increased his self-confidence. They first had the child walk like he was frightened, head down and shoulders hunched. They then discussed how it felt inside. 'Scared', replied the child. They then had him practise walking with head held high, taking long strides and looking straight ahead. Asked about what it felt like, the boy said, 'strong'.

It was a simple way to begin to help him understand how the bully might be looking at him. It is best to repeat this kind of exercise over weeks and involve other family members or friends, giving the child lots of praise. It should not be done if it creates tension or if it becomes a form of bullying, which would only make the child feel worse.

Coping

If a child is tied into knots by a difficult situation such as bullying, help them get the anger out and express those feelings. Drawing, keeping a diary and using plasticine are three good ways to do this. For example, it is therapeutic to make a plasticine model of the bully and act out inner frustrations. This can lead to more open discussion and help you to develop strategies with the child about how to cope and what to do.

Coping might include getting other children to help, if possible, as in the school situation mentioned below. One little girl practised saying no in front of the mirror for a month, learned to walk in a more assertive way and her mother arranged for another child to walk with her to school. When the bully did approach, the girl looked her right in the eye, said 'leave me alone' very loudly and firmly and walked away. The bully started to follow and the girl and her friend turned around and shouted 'get away from us'. The bully left.

One mother was more direct. She went to school, sought out the groups which had been terrorising her daughter and told them: 'I don't care if you don't like my daughter – that's your right. But heaven help you if I find that you go near her or talk to her or even look at her. Is that clear?' She fixed them with such a stare that they meekly nodded. The mum made it her business to be around for a week after that.

The girls turned to a new victim. One without an assertive mother, no doubt! Although some people would not agree with her approach, in this case it did solve the problem. Her daughter told me that she was at first embarrassed, but then really proud that her mum cared enough to try to protect her.

When a child has been part of a group that turns and starts to bully him or her, it is particularly difficult. Sometimes it is one of those temporary phases where one or another of the group is in or out of favour. Other times it becomes a real vendetta, usually led by one of the old gang. When this happens, the only choice may be to find a new group – often very difficult – or to try to stop the victimisation and get back into the group.

One mother successfully helped her son to break the cycle by inviting two of the boys and their families around for a barbecue. It broke the group's desire to bully this boy. It also eventually led to a parents' group which worked on the general problem of bullying in the neighbourhood. Part of their strategy was to say to their children that it was alright to tell if they are being bullied – that is it is not telling tales.

But if children tell, adults must be prepared to try to help, as these parents did. Bullying then becomes unacceptable behaviour within the community and the children feel comfortable supporting one another.

Teachers of younger children might suggest that parents invite over one or two children in the bullying group, who are not ringleaders. By ensuring that there is a lot to do and that a good time is had, it becomes much more difficult for the children to want to bully the victim. Gradually increase the size of the group so that the 'victim's' home becomes a focal point and somewhere that the children want to go. This is extra work, but it is usually worth it. Better to spend energy creating a positive situation than trying to pick up the pieces of a bullied child. See Chapter 4 about younger children.

Cooperation

Teachers have a major role to play in the prevention of bullying. Kidscape suggests that lessons on cooperation and how to cope with bullying be part of the normal school curriculum. All of the Kidscape programmes, which range from age 3 to age 16, include lessons about the problem of bullying and how to develop strategies. The students roleplay situations, discuss the issues and decide how to best tackle the problem. Again, peer pressure is a formidable force and should be used. See Chapter 6 for information about anti-bullying exercises in schools.

A slightly more controversial approach which Kidscape initiated in some schools is the bully 'court'. It can be easily set up, but only in the right school context where a policy has been established and there is solid backing from parents and teachers. The 'courts' are a way of getting children constructively involved in citizenship and in taking responsibility for one another (*see* Chapter 7).

Of course the problem of bullying is best addressed by a joint approach between parents, teachers, playground supervisors and children. The prevention of bullying then becomes a priority. In the Kidscape programmes, bullying is one of the most important lessons dealt with because it is one that concerns everyone. The children usually respond to this lesson so well that some schools report that bullying is reduced to a minimum, although no one claims to have stopped it altogether.

Cowardly behaviour

The reduction in bullying happened because the children learned that bullying was cowardly, that they could not be bystanders and that everyone had a responsibility to stop this kind of behaviour. The bully was quite often left without victims to bully and sometimes became a positive member of the group.

Bullying will never go away completely, but by condemning bullying and acting to stop it, we can prevent thousands of children suffering. As I said in the Introduction, we used to shove children up chimneys and stuff them down mines. Now, that would seem totally unacceptable. Perhaps in ten years the idea of bullying will seem equally unacceptable.

References

Balding, J. (1996) *Bully Off: Young People Who Fear Going to School*, Schools Health Education Unit, Exeter University.

Elliott, M. and Kilpatrick, J. (1994) *How to Stop Bullying: A Kidscape Training Guide*, Kidscape.

Olweus, D. (1993) *Bullying at School: What We Know and What We Can Do*, Oxford, Blackwell.

Whitney, I. and Smith, P.K. (1993) 'A survey of the nature and extent of bullying in junior/middle and secondary schools', *Educational Research*, Vol. 35, No. 1, pp. 3–25.

2
■　■　■

Practical considerations in dealing with bullying – in secondary school

ERIC JONES

There is a joke which occasionally does the rounds and which our profession finds amusing, even if it is a little cruel and barbed towards those who work with people in a social setting. The story is of a social worker, teacher or priest (suit yourself), who comes across the bruised and battered victim of a mugging, stoops down to look at the damage and exclaims, 'My goodness, I bet the person who did this has got some problems!' . . .

As professionals in teaching, we are as concerned as anyone with underlying causes and reasons for the behaviour of the bully. We are interested in prevention and this chapter will outline some of the strategies already found useful in preventing outbreaks of bullying. But, in addition, we are technicians, operatives in the school situation, and as such find ourselves having to act when bullying has occurred, responding to both victim and culprit. We have to sanction and control. Strategies for operating in the situation, at the 'chalk-face', are our concern.

Context

The context in which this piece was written is an inner-city comprehensive school. Nearly 50 per cent of the mixed population come from single parent homes. The school is surrounded by poor housing, unemployment, and there is considerable disenchantment on the part of many pupils and parents. The 'establishment' includes teachers. The law and the police are not always looked upon with great favour.

The advantages of an education are not always acknowledged. Less than academically successful parents do not tend to breed wildly enthusiastic scholars. Parents who cannot read at all pose a particular problem. Well over half of the yearly intake arrives with a reading age two or more years behind their chronological age. Attracting teachers to fill vacancies takes up a distorted proportion of the working week and providing extra help for the seriously disadvantaged, academically or socially, is a logistical nightmare.

Many of these parents and children have been bullied already, by the society in which they find themselves, by the demands made of them and the restrictions placed upon them, all of which some find extraordinarily difficult to handle. There is a lot of bullying going on – by officials enforcing regulations, by the comfortably-off towards the hard-up, by those in employment towards those who seek to work, by the literate towards those who find it hard to learn, and by whites who were born in Britain towards young blacks who were also born in Britain, and vice versa.

Nevertheless there is success. Many achieve commendable results in GCSEs. Some achieve outstanding success. Nearly every pupil gains some graded results in some subjects. The results do not always please the media or the education statisticians, but teachers are exhausted and pleased when the entire fourth year can go out on work experience and when the entire fifth year population leaves school with comprehensive records of their achievements. And when boys and girls in their first year pull up their reading age by well over a year in the first few months it is at enormous cost, deserving of no little acclaim.

There is also success in dealing with the problem of bullying. Outlining the context was necessary in order to see how some of these anti-bullying strategies might be appropriate, and usable. Looking at one's own education environment is essential.

Defining the bully/victim

We shall almost certainly fall short of a universally acceptable definition, but here goes. The bully is someone who is responsible for premeditated, continuous, malicious and belittling tyranny. The victim is on the receiving end, repeatedly, defencelessly and typically without a champion.

Is everything that gets labelled 'bullying' really that, or is it bullying because the victim says it is? Teachers should, and do, try to deal with all the problems, but these are not all *bullying*, in the 'career' sense. The worry is that quite often, teachers, parents and pupils talk about bullying when they ought to be talking about something else – rather like all headaches, to some people, come to be called migraines. That is not to say that there aren't any migraines, or that headaches are not serious in themselves. Everything needs to be dealt with for what it is.

None of us like children who make fun, and giggle, pointing fingers at others for their idiosyncracies, but they are not career bullies who pick out a weaker victim and repeatedly use strategies to make them feel small; they are children growing up and doing what children do, rather cruelly, but predictably. We seek to teach them better attitudes and we try to solve the problems that they cause.

Nobody likes children who steal money or sweets from others, but beware of giving them the notoriety of being called bullies. They are thieves. We seek to teach them better attitudes and the law. Bullies tend to extort money from a weak victim, or victims, systematically and repeatedly. This may be prompted by greed, but primarily it is an act of power.

Teachers get remarkably fed up with children who fight or scrap with one another. But they are not bullies because they fight, and the one who wins is most certainly not a bully because he or she wins. The mindless and degrading violence of the strong against the weak may be bullying, but fighting, by definition, is not.

Here, there is the risk of offending people if it is said that some of the so-called bullying is part of growing up and learning to cope. It does not excuse the bully, but some of the behaviour of both the victim and the bully is predictable and may even be unavoidable. As children move into their own circles and grow out of full-time adult supervision they make the most dreadful mistakes in the way they treat each other. Perhaps it should be called the development of peer structures. They learn from it and before the rot of megalomania or dire timidity sets in teachers should seek to direct the lessons they learn from it. Responsible adults must teach and guide. They must not allow unbridled nastiness and exploitation, but must allow the children to grow up and learn from real situations how to handle life itself. Both the strong and the weak must be monitored.

Some children thrive on attention from older pupils. It can be healthy, but sometimes it is not. Young leaders can be a power of great good. The very best of prefectorial systems and uniformed youth organisations can vouch for this. Strong youngsters can also be a cancer in a young society. We often find that young victims, perhaps because they have no better example or model, go back for more, and are treated unmercifully, abused and exploited. It is a fact, however, that not all such peer structures and relationships are bad *per se*.

Prevention

Having said all that, and having to keep it all in mind, here are some strategies that have worked.

Prepare the ground

Teachers must talk about the possibilities of being bullied to youngsters as they arrive at secondary school, even before they arrive. On Induction Day (a day in the summer term when primary school children can come and spend a day at their new secondary school) don't brush the subject aside. Bring it up, even if it does not arise naturally (as it well might) among the questions. During the first week in the new school talk about it alongside where the toilets are, dinner queues, what happens if you are late. Let children know that sometimes there are bullies abroad, and that we do not tolerate them. Above all do not try to pretend that there used to be bullies and now there aren't.

Drama and tutorial work

If there is active tutorial work (and if not, why not?) use it to discuss the topic. Mention it in assemblies. Use the perfect safety of drama lessons, or a dramatic piece in an assembly (created and composed by youngsters themselves, of course), to enact how to rebuff the bully attempt, or how to say 'No' to the thief, or how to 'Go and tell'. Laugh at it, but be sure to prompt sensible discussion about what happens to the bully as well as the victim. Children can be very cruel towards the 'nasties' and perhaps they must face the ideas of forgiveness and responsibility to each other.

Don't kid the parents

It is essential that teachers do not convey the impression that, somehow, one school has cracked it, and that, 'Here in this school, bullies are a thing of the past'. Mention the well-known fact among adults that some children in every generation are nasty to others. Then, teachers are free to inform parents about attitudes of the school towards such pupils and their victims, methods of dealing with them and so on.

Create a contract

It may be proper to tell pupils the school rules but it is even more important that they create their own, a contract, to refer to in their own group. This is a mutually agreed set of guidelines about what we, in Class 7T or 1W, regard as good and bad, acceptable and unacceptable. Everyone signs it, including the teacher, and it stays on the tutor group noticeboard. Of course it includes many things. In fact it takes a while to generate the detail and the full contents, but it ought to include the way we treat others, and what the school thinks of those who exploit and abuse others (see Chapter 18).

Be around

Hopefully it is not too obvious to suggest that bullying might be avoided in some of its manifestations if the opportunities are not there for it to occur. Teachers ought to be in corridors and 'doing their proper duties' if they don't want to spend a lot of time later sorting out what happened when bullies stalked the quiet corners of the playground. Beware the evolution of no-go areas. 'My God,' says one teacher, 'I would never go around there. You'd never get out alive!' That might be funny in the staffroom of a 1950s schoolboy story, but it is not good enough in the present climate.

Testing

Some quick tests might help to take the wind out of the sails of an assailant. Try these ideas to stop him (usually a 'him') in his tracks when he starts to make excuses for his aggressive behaviour.

- Beware the joke that isn't funny. 'It was only a joke' is a phrase we might all have heard at some time in teaching, muttered by the naughty child or the hardened bully. The acid test is whether everyone was laughing. If they were not, then it either was not a joke or it was in very poor taste, and quite obviously directed against somebody. Tripping up, taking property, hitting, pushing into a corner are all very poor jokes indeed. If one person was not party to the humour of it, but was rather the victim of it, then it wasn't a joke. Don't accept it as such.

- Beware the game that not everyone was playing. 'We were only playing.' There it is again, and a very poor excuse it is for leaving somebody bruised and crying. The furious ball game is a poor cover for knocking people over, particularly if the game was just that – a cover. If the person who gets knocked about was not playing, and curiously appears to be the same victim as yesterday, then it was not a game! We do not accept that it was. Incidentally, the reverse of this is the bully who declares that he was playing, but in fact he was joining in someone else's game unwanted and uninvited. Get the facts and put it to him that he was not playing, he was invading the game.

- Beware the non-accidental accident. We have heard this one too, have we not? 'It was an accident.' The victim ends up in a heap at the bottom of the stairs, or in a corridor, or with a torn bag and belongings scattered everywhere, but 'It was an accident.' This, too, has a foolproof test. If you did something accidentally to someone, then you should stay behind and do what people normally do when they accidentally do such things . . . help! If you did not pick up the victim, apologise, assist, collect the belongings, take her to the nurse, etc., etc., then it doesn't count as an accident, and we do not accept it as such.

- 'I found it' is just one more cry from the bully who is in possession of someone else's property. If bullies knew how many times we have heard the 'I found it' excuse and how stupid it sounds they wouldn't use it, but they still do because they think it is acceptable. It is not. As teachers we will never convince the culprit that practically every person we ever speak to in similar circumstances uses the same excuse, but we can ask the simple question, 'Why did you keep it?'

- 'I was only borrowing.' That is a poor excuse for taking money from someone. Always ask the question, instantly, of the bully, 'Right then, what's his name? Where does he live? What class is he in? When's his birthday?' Anything, to prove that the bully knows nothing of the victim and that he had no way, and thus no intention, of returning the cash. Besides, we do not, in our society, go around borrowing money from each other, certainly not from strangers, and from weak, anonymous little strangers. It is unacceptable, and if you do it, it very soon crosses the threshhold from 'borrowing' into mugging.

- The discussion with the alleged culprit might include the question, 'Do you accept that we have a problem?' The chances are he will say, 'Yes'. The allegations and the culprit's own written account, looked at calmly, will reveal that there is something to sort out. The discussion can go on to show that the culprit was in control of what happened. The victim had no choice as to the outcome. What happened, happened *to* him. The alleged bully must face the fact that he could have handled it differently. He could have behaved differently and could have avoided being accused. He is responsible for the current situation which is 'the problem'. We can say, 'You are responsible, and if you are a bully – so be it. We will deal with you. If you are not, then learn from this. Handle it differently next time and remember that all of this is on record.'

- Do not allow the use of the words 'only' or 'just' when listening to or reading an account from somebody accused of bullying behaviour. It's a cop-out. If you do not believe that then try to explain your last motor car accident without using those words! Boys and girls must be encouraged to say 'I hit him' or 'I took the money', not 'I only hit him a bit' or 'I just took the money to see what he'd say'. In a written account cross out these words.

Attitudes and tactics

What happens, and what pupils, parents and teachers *do* in the event of an incident, are the dynamics of these situations.

Children ought never to succumb to the 'stay quiet or else' threat, whether spoken or implied. 'We did not say anything because it would have been worse the next day' is, frankly, crazy. Of course it is difficult for the victim, but the alternative is worse, far worse. It means that a deliberate decision has been taken to let the bully go on bullying as long as he likes. We must help children to 'tell'.

'Telling' is crucial. Not tomorrow, not when you get home, not a month later when it has become intolerable, but **now**. Of course, the advice about 'telling' is fraught with danger. Some victims believe that their reward for telling is to be able to dictate the punishment – 'Is he going to be expelled, Miss?' Also, teachers are frantically busy most of the time, so we must qualify the 'tell now' instruction.

The best way is to have covered the dynamics of 'telling' during the discussions when children arrive, as already mentioned. Remember, too, that one push doesn't make a bullying; one hit does not make a beating. Teachers want to know what is going on, but a brief record and a quick warning ought to be enough in the event of a single incident. Then, stay alert. The victim must be prepared to write it down, with help if need be, perhaps even overnight, and then let us deal with it.

Also, just because the child tells immediately ought not to mean, indeed cannot mean, that there will be instant retribution. 'If it is revenge you want, you've come to the wrong place' is best said in the early days well before incidents take place. On the strength of a reported incident no teacher can drop everything and abandon a class, rushing off to mete out instant and severe punishment to the accused. The trouble with **not** doing that is that the victim invariably goes home and says, 'Miss So-and-so did nothing' and up comes Mum breathing fire. Not everything that is important, even urgent, is a crisis. A fire is a crisis. Bullying is important.

If one confronts the bully in a mood of crisis it will be a lost cause. 'Why did you hit So-and-so?' will almost certainly be rebuffed by 'I didn't' or, worse, 'Who said I did?' to which you have no useful answer. The discussion is doomed. Bide your time. Similarly, if the victim is clearly in distress then the available teacher should deal with the distress or the injury. Deal with the bullying later. Don't rush like a bull into the precarious china shop of negotiations with the bully and his victim.

Ideally the best solution is to sit the child down and get a written report of the incident. That can be hours, even days later, but of course the sooner the better. The problem is then taken on board, not in an air of crisis, but calmly. The written report is on record, the teacher can show the accused and warn him off. He can see the account. He ought even to write his own. If the bullying accusation has no foundation he has nothing to fear. It will die a natural death and never be mentioned again. If it is the start of a 'career', then the facts *and* the warning are on record. If it is the next in a line of career incidents then of course you have a problem. So has the bully.

Bullies like nothing worse than knowing that you know what is going on, and that the record is on file. They can see it if they wish. So can their family. Call their bluff, go public. Tell the assembly what has been going on, and what you have done about it. Mention no names, just make it perfectly plain that you will not tolerate it, and why.

Sometimes that works in reverse. It is possible to announce in an assembly, 'I want to see, after this assembly, the people responsible for such-and-such an incident (but of course, I won't mention your names here!)' After the assembly up they come, never knowing that you didn't actually know who was going to appear. It is a tricky card to play.

Here's one for mums and dads. **Please** do not keep the child victim at home 'until it's sorted out'. First, because we cannot sort out a one-sided affair, on the strength of the story your child has told you and which will, sure as eggs, not be the same story we get from the accused. And second, because we should not lift a finger to sort out a one-sided affair. The accusations will be flying in all directions on the strength of a distraught phone call while little Johnnie (who actually **might** have made it up to get out of Games) will be sitting at home watching the lunchtime edition of another Australian soap. The teacher is lonely, stuck in the middle, bursting blood vessels and accusing people with no real evidence, Mum is fuming at 'that dreadful school', and the alleged culprit is indignant, while Johnnie is dipping his hand into his second packet of crisps.

The victim must come, and Mum, too, if necessary, and we must sort it out face to face. If the appointment cannot be within the day the victim should still be in school, and closely looked after until the interviews take place. It's like falling off a bike; get back on or you might never ride again.

The parents of the accused ought also to be invited, of course. Again, not in an air of crisis, but calmly. Say to parents, 'There is something you ought to know, if possible today. Can you come and pick him up from school? I'll keep him until you get here.' Or, 'Your son is likely to be excluded but, first, can you come and see me straight away, like tomorrow morning?' Put the onus on the parents to come and have some control over their child's destiny. Children are their parents' responsibility, not, in the end, ours.

It is not wrong to confront bully and victim. The idea that victims insist that we punish the nasties but want to be a million miles away when we confront the bullies with the story is nonsense. We cannot say to a bully, 'I've been told that you bullied someone. I believe it and I'm going to punish you. Oh, and by the way I can't tell you who it was that accused you.' If the bully sees that the victim will repeat the accusations in your office he has lost the best weapon he has – the silent victim. Very often the victim is amazed to see how cowed and cowardly the big guy really is. It is also a very useful fact that, quite often, the families of victim and accused will, in school, sort out the problem quite amicably when put face to face.

In the event of an actual bruise, or injury, why not photograph it? The quickest way is to give a child money to go to a photo booth on the way home (along with a brief letter, or a following phone call home to explain what's going on). The accused and his parents are invariably confounded by the evidence of a swollen eye. Dad will be aghast at the fact that his son 'did that', even while the son is pleading accident, joke or game.

It is a good idea to use a simply designed 'incident slip' as a universal way of recording such incidents in school. It needs a space for name, date, form, teacher, the incident and the action taken. Of course there will always be copies of letters, interviews and pupils' accounts but the incident slip, if it is not too big, concentrates the mind of the reporting teacher beautifully. Half an A4 sheet, cut lengthways, is almost perfect. If the school decides to use one colour to report 'good things' and another for 'bad news' so much the better. Some pupil files take on a certain hue when one thumbs through them.

Use the rules and use the law. Punish bullies. Record the punishment and the reasons for it. Show him what you are putting on file and make him pay with whatever time it cost you to sort it out.

Of course, exclusion may be the punishment decided upon. In that case, yet again, be sure to record reasons and everyone's account. Play it by the book, and insist upon a proper interview with parents before readmission. Our concern is to build a relationship between aggressor, family and school, not just to hand out punishment. We are not in the 'eye for an eye' business. The victim should not see the outcome as a kind of victory over the culprit. All concerned should try to achieve an outcome in which the victim feels he has been supported, need fear no more, and in which the bully and his family feel the school has dealt with the situation compassionately, if strictly, for the benefit of all. The culprit is welcomed back, having 'served his time'. Such outcomes are rarely perfect, but are achieveable and should be the objective.

As far as the law is concerned we should not fear to teach, or remind, bullies about common law. The laws concerning assault, threatening behaviour, actual bodily harm and theft apply to them as to every other citizen. Advise victims' families to go to law, and offer to cooperate if they do. If, however, they ask the school to deal with it, as almost invariably they do, then make two things clear to all concerned. One, to the victim and family, that having asked the school to deal with it, they let the school get on with it. Two, to the accused and family, that they should cooperate with the authority of the school because the victim's family have asked it to handle things instead of going to the police.

Finally, as a general rule, we should never teach children to criticise and hate. Some pupils are always swearing at and vilifying other children. Then they run off home yelling 'bully' when they get a smack in the mouth for some of the really nasty things they say. Even if the potential bully is a natural and well-known nasty piece of work, it really is rather pointless to point it out to him. 'My Mum says I'm to keep away from you because you are a rotten bully' is hardly going to gain any child the school peace prize.

The best way to make friends is to be friendly.

A word about the locals

A lady arrived at school late one morning with her daughter, a pupil, and said that her daughter had been attacked on the bus on the way to school. She knew which school the attacker went to and the name of the girl, so she thought that perhaps the school would like to get in touch and . . .

No, not really. If the lady's daughter was the victim of a crime in a public place then she ought to have gone to the police. The school has no more authority over girls from other schools committing crimes on buses than anyone else. If your daughter was mugged in August would you wait until September, the new term, to tell the school? I hope not. This is a very touchy area, but local people, shopkeepers, residents and parents of other children will insist on referring to 'our children'. With respect, they are not; they are their parents' children. Teachers must control what goes on in school, but they are not and cannot possibly be responsible for what goes on outside. They can advise, of course. They can even help. They should not, however, take on the role of parent or police.

It is very sad that a mother can come into school and say that her son was mugged on the way home the previous evening, and that they have not been to the police. They have left it overnight to come and ask the teacher what they should do. Perhaps one should be flattered, but the sadness is overwhelming, especially when one then hears, 'The school did nothing about it.' When the writer's own son was attacked on a bus after school an instant furrow was ploughed between home and the local police station before he'd even finished telling the story.

Once the pupil leaves the premises, even truanting, the parents must take their share of responsibility. Even the security manager of a large London store has been known to telephone, telling the school the name of a shoplifting culprit and asking if someone could come and fetch him. He says, 'Well, we don't want a lot of fuss, or the police involved. We thought the school could sort it out.' Frankly, the school cannot. Apart from usually being short of teachers, how could the school, even with a full complement of staff, release teachers to go on a collecting mission? Is it then expected to punish the child, in school, for what he or she did, criminally, outside? For all we know, shoplifting could be the family business. Such an example is not one of bullying, but it highlights the fact that so many people believe the teacher ought to sort out everything. There are other agencies, not least parents, who are responsible for the children too and must play their part.

And does it all work?

If the school says that these attitudes and strategies have proved useful in dealing with aggressive children, then it does tend to prove that the problem most certainly exists. If the school says that these ideas solve the problem and that there is no bullying, the school will not be believed. Of course it knows there is a problem.

The truth is of course that school is an ongoing, living community. One does not solve anything once and for all. Immunising the girls against rubella one year, no matter how well organised or how pure the vaccine, does not solve the problem forever. Each new intake of pupils has to learn how to behave, as 11-, 13-, 15-year-olds. But it should be possible to create an atmosphere, an ethos, in school in which maltreatment of one's peers is not acceptable and is openly discussed – an atmosphere in which incidents are reported, recorded and dealt with.

The example given of the writer's son was 'solved' by the police warning off the aggressor within a couple of hours. However, the aggressor then tried to make matters worse, by making sure his friends gave my son a hard time *at school*. That was the school's and my problem, so we wrote, put the facts, named names and were delighted with the outcome. The boys were seen and warned and all blew over pretty quickly. Maybe it would not have if we had stayed quiet for fear of reprisal.

Perhaps this is a good moment to refer to the model shown in Figure 2.1. It may not be perfect but it does try to show that the early discussion of the possibility of bullying *could* lead directly to no incidents occurring. At the other extreme, a bully might return again and again to his unacceptable behaviour provoking incidents.

In the inner city there are youngsters suffering from startling disadvantages. Those with stunted growth, bad burn scars, hare-lips as well as non-English-speaking refugees, all are quite likely to become victims of the strong mindless bully, alongside the feeble and the bookworm. The suggestion is, however, that the systems, the discussion and the firmness in handling the potential and the actuality of bullying help to create an atmosphere in which youngsters do not get away with it. The rub is, of course, that the atmosphere is differently perceived by pupils and teachers. The predictable delusion of the deputy head is that he or she thinks they see the truth of what is going on in the playground.

Will the teachers ever see it all? Whatever the answer, they must continue to make proper record of a proven, minor incident, then forgive and promote the relationships involved. Children might then learn to be very wary of what the outcome of a major incident would be. They must then follow their own advice and hope that there are no ongoing, or major, incidents happening about which they know nothing. They have got to make it worthwhile for the children to bring the teachers in, so that they can solve what is possible, report and refer elsewhere what isn't, and never fear to admit that children are sometimes nasty to each other.

Figure 2.1: Dealing with bullying – actions and outcomes

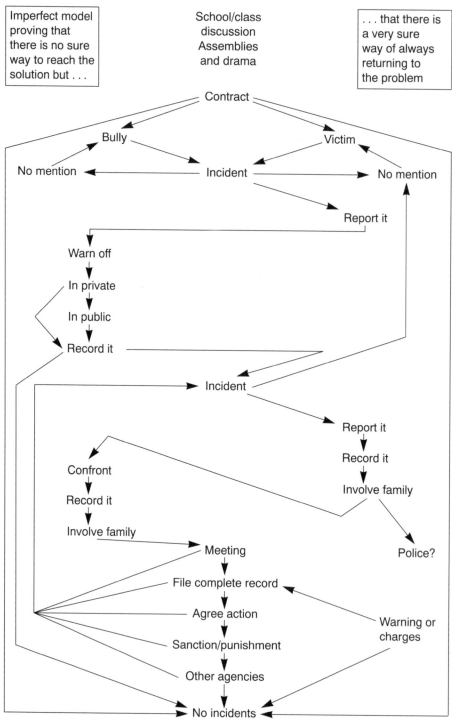

Professional concerns

I began this chapter by putting the teaching situation into an inner-city context. I conclude by putting the teacher and the bully into a teaching perspective. The teacher's professional concern is with the bully and his victim. It cannot, however, with the best will in the world, be the total preoccupation. If what follows appears to be off the subject, I make no apology. The wonder is not that teachers deal quite successfully with some bullying, but that they have time to handle any of it at all.

Twenty years ago teaching might have been considered a fairly straightforward professional task. One prepared, one taught, one marked books and reported on achievement. Pupils were prepared for public examinations, all sat down in June and the papers were sent off. There were sports days, concerts, speech days and prizegivings. There were detentions and the notorious punishment book. These words do not hanker after those days, with all their faults, but so much has happened to the teaching world that many teachers and observers of education are now left breathless at what is expected of the profession. So often, too, demands have been made without the resources being made available to fulfil these demands. The overall task has burgeoned to extremes.

Once each of us in the profession was a teacher. Now, even taking into account the differences that an elevated post may make, it is difficult to tell whether we are teacher, friend, public enemy, social worker, doctor, accountant, personnel manager, counsellor, judge, jury, policeman, lawyer, Father Christmas or Florence Nightingale. Additions to the task load and to the curriculum during recent years have left some fine teachers punch-drunk. Think about it; the public examination season begins now in mid-April and goes on for two months. Much of the marking, and individual testing is done on site by teachers who are unable to teach mainstream classes and who occupy specialist rooms to the detriment of younger pupils for much of that time. Endless moderating meetings are demanded by the boards, taking teachers away from the 'chalk-face' time and time again. The whole concept of negotiating and consulting (with pupils, among ourselves, with the authority and parents) occupies thousands of hours of meetings. What that does to the general atmosphere of schools and learning can only be guessed at. Having a 'stand-in' teacher, sometimes several times a day, no matter if the system pays for it, is not good for pupils, discipline, continuity of courses. Readers who are teachers will know that.

The number of subjects somehow expected to 'appear' on the timetable for teachers to pass on to the next generation has nearly doubled. Some of them are, without doubt, the political flavour of the month: Business Studies, Commerce, Accountancy, Catering, Leisure Pursuits, Computing, Careers – these are some of the more obvious ones. Consider also boys' subjects for girls, and vice versa (adding to the load of both), Consumer Awareness, Industry Links, Work Experience, Aids, Sex Education, Sexism, Child Abuse, Racism,

Alcoholism, Drug Abuse, Health Education, Nutrition, Child Care, Equal Opportunities, Community Care, The Third World, The Elderly, Media Studies – Oh! and Bullying. Add to these the constraints placed upon teachers and heads by new legislation, the additional considerations required by pupil and parent power and the time taken up by records of achievement, continuous assessment and local management (with heads of average secondary schools having to manage some £2 000 000 a year) and we get some idea why pupils in the street don't always know who the six wives of Henry VIII were.

Some secondary school teachers are still teaching 400–500 different children a week. A 60–70 hour week is not uncommon, much of it spent in exasperating negotiations, meetings and continual justification of one's actions. The mental exhaustion has to be experienced to be understood.

A lot of discussion has taken place in recent times about methods of teaching, particularly whether we have children in rows and facing the teacher! Teachers, as always, have been caught in the middle of 'experts' vying with each other for catchy headlines about what's best for our children in schools, and what teachers should be told to do today, tomorrow and the day after! One wonders if the gradual abolition of 'battery-taught' children in rows with narrow discipline and curriculum methods – unsatisfactory though that was in many ways – just might have left little room for 'free-range' bullies.

That is the background against which the teacher operates. The bottom line is that everyone has the right to go home happy at the end of a day (and with the same number of teeth and amount of property that they arrived with!), be they pupils, teachers or parents – whether it be following a normal school day or at the end of a difficult interview. The teacher's onerous task is to see that, as far as possible, it always happens. Even the culprit and his family have the right to go home feeling they have been fairly treated. Which nearly brings us back to our opening 'joke'.

The task is always to open up the field of discussion and put it alongside the life of the school, building relationships in an open and learning atmosphere in which bullying is unacceptable. There are so many pressing and important things for the teacher to do for the benefit of all pupils.

The task must be to deal with bullying if it arises and when it is reported, and to take whatever time it needs to put the situation right. Teachers continue to strive to do just that.

3

■ ■ ■

A primary school approach

LINDA FROST

The problem with bullying, as with education itself, is that almost everyone has had a bad personal experience or has an anecdote they can quote about someone else who has.

Being the emotive subject it is, involved parties hardly ever view bullying with detachment. Opinions are entrenched and polarised from the outset, because it appears to be a clear-cut issue – 'child X bullied Y. What are you going to do about it?'

Initial reaction

My initial response to a bullying incident in school is to talk it through *individually* with the children who are involved. This is often exasperating for the victim and seldom seen as helpful to the bully either, as a bully rarely sees him/herself as being in the wrong, and the ensuing reports seldom combine to form a coherent picture of the incident. What it does serve to achieve, though, is a framework in which children's disagreements are aired, and both sides at least have the opportunity to express an opinion, and feel that someone is listening to them and that their viewpoint matters.

In the course of these discussions, two words are frequently overused by the bully. They are 'just' and 'only' – 'I was just playing with her' and 'I only tapped his ear with my foot'.

It is helpful to tell the children that these two words are *not allowed* in any explanation. They invariably serve only to justify and lessen the offence in the eyes of the perpetrator.

It can also help to keep these time-consuming processes to a minimum if questions are short, sharp and unambiguous. 'What did you do wrong?' leaves little room for needless argument, and requires one of two specific answers, either 'nothing' or an admission of some understanding of how an action or attitude contributed to this negative situation. A 'nothing' answer *might* be accepted after explanation at face value, or amended to one accepting some degree of responsibility for the outcome.

In the school situation, talk is the most powerful weapon in the armoury. We talk to children, we talk to parents, we talk to colleagues. I often wonder if a compulsory dose of laryngitis wouldn't work wonders fulfilling the other aspects covered by the head teacher's job description!

It is also helpful if children answer these specific questions. Often 'What did you do wrong?' gets the response, 'He was rude to me this morning and ...', and this is followed by an immense dissertation on the shortcomings of the other protagonist.

While giving an indication of the degree of resentment of the one child towards the other, it again avoids the issue, and needs redirecting towards *identifying* the specific incidents or attitudes which could be changed to ameliorate the situation.

Talking then is the first line of defence, because it takes the heat out of the situation, allows a forum for views to be expressed, and shows to the other children that the matter is viewed seriously and that adults will listen. This is a most important aspect if children are to have the confidence to trust us and seek our help if they are bullied.

Defining the problem

Before you can hope to deal with bullying, you need to define it. I wouldn't attempt to provide a formal definition of bullying but, *in my school*, I have found that bullying:

- varies from situation to situation and from child to child;
- depends on status in the peer group;
- varies with the degree of personal stress involved;
- can be not only physical but verbal;
- can be conveyed purely by body language;
- can include isolating the victim by influencing the rest of the peer group;
- can be as subtle as a curl of the lip or a cut of the eye;
- can be as obvious as a bloody nose or a kick in the groin.

The following illustrate a number of situations which I would consider involve at least some degree of bullying:

- following someone, or menacing stares;

- mother-cussing, which is when children make derogatory remarks about each other's mother, often implying prostitution or obesity, or being racist in undertone. This can even be stylised down to saying 'M', and is seen as an enormous provocation by some children. I have yet to discover how to sanction appropriately a child who says 'M' to another!
- swearing, bearing malice and 'getting even';
- rubbishing other children's work;
- wilful destruction of someone else's work or property;
- stealing – valued possessions, packed lunches, etc.;
- intimidation and extortion;
- physical violence;
- mental cruelty.

Mental cruelty seems to have a very damaging effect. For example, which is worse, a bully saying, 'Your Mum's new baby is going to be deformed just like you', or the bully giving the victim a punch in the eye? Both bring immediate misery, but the effects of the former may still cause anxiety when the bruise from the latter has faded.

Survey results

Recently, I did a survey with our new first-year intake two weeks after they had started into the school. Only 5 per cent felt that they had never been bullied. Over half felt they had been bullied in their first two weeks. However, on further examination, it seemed that the timescale was confused. Once children had identified someone as a bully the impression and memory remained very strong, even if not reinforced by future experience. Having experienced bullying the perpetrator then remained a person to be feared, and further interaction involving that person was always viewed at best negatively, or sometimes fearfully, hence the bullying persisted in the victim's mind.

I also asked children, in confidence, to identify children they believed to be very bad bullies. Four or five names reappeared continuously, and this was mirrored in responses from children throughout the school.

There were factors which many of these bully figures shared. Often they were the youngest sibling in the family. Each of them felt they were bullied, not bullies, and constantly unfairly picked upon. Most of the parents of these children were unwilling to believe their child's bullying behaviour. Girl bullies often resorted to mental cruelty, whereas boy bullies were more often more physical. This may seem a sexist generalisation, but this was our experience.

Sages

One of the interesting factors which emerged from the survey was that there were a small group of children who claimed they had never been bullied. These were not bullies, but children whose demeanour, behaviour and attitude exempted them from this kind of interaction. I nicknamed this group the 'sages'. They were usually intelligent, non-contentious, seen by other children as fair and generally held in high esteem by their peer group.

Outsiders

Another group I called the 'outsiders'. These shared some characteristics with the sages, but were principally children who 'didn't need anyone', and to a great extent they remained uninvolved in the group dynamics. These children tended to go their own way and had little effect on their peers, either positive or negative.

Victims

Yet another group appeared after discussion with the 'sages'. These were the 'victims'. Often they were children of low prestige in the group. They were often seen as misfits, either for reasons of appearance, lack of friends or other trivial reasons. The basic problem was one of body language. These children almost seemed to invite bullying, by compliance rather than aggression, or by being thoroughly irritating. They had low self-esteem, and didn't tell if victimised. Often they would cry or stamp their feet, but would not follow this up by asking for support. They therefore offered all the excitement of an anguished victim with no fear of repercussions. I asked one child who was identified as a victim why she didn't ask for help when bullied. She responded. 'Bullied? I don't get bullied. It was much worse at my last school. It's better here.'

Bullies

The last groups to emerge were the bullies. Often it was physically impossible to pick them out – they weren't necessarily the biggest or strongest. They had no clearly defined ranking in the peer group order. Some were respected but feared, some had physical or other skills which were admired. One group were outcasts who only managed to keep friends by treats and were socially isolated. Often, like their victims, they suffered from very low self-esteem, but had channelled their weakness offensively rather than accepting their fate compliantly. They saw an aggressive role as one necessary for survival and had built upon it to reinforce their prestige.

Secret bullies

Another group the children identified as bullies were a surprise to me. The behaviour they showed to adults was totally at variance with that they showed to peers. They gave the impression of being class leaders – the most popular children in the class. In effect, their dominance was accepted, and the response of the other pupils was to appease or 'keep on the right side of them'.

A thorough knowledge of the dynamics of the group involved, especially from the children's own viewpoint, can therefore be highly enlightening, and help when planning positive strategies.

Supervision and observation

Bullying flourishes where supervision is minimal. Travelling to school, leaving at some time during lunch breaks and playtimes, moving between classes and 'playing out' after school and at weekends afford the bully the best opportunities.

Merely observing a child's interaction in one of these situations, when he or she is unaware of being watched, can clearly show the number of negative contacts a bully can make in a very short period. If the parents can be persuaded to come into the school without the child knowing, and look at their child at play for half an hour from some vantage point, they are often totally amazed at their child's behaviour and are more willing to cooperate to improve it.

Parental support

Parental support is crucial, if a child's behaviour is to be changed. Sometimes a child feels his parents will be more impressed if he can 'stand up for himself'. Sometimes, parents have different views of their child's 'macho' behaviour, particularly when it is one parent only who bears the lion's share of the responsibility for 'picking up the pieces'. In some cases, this parent's help can be enlisted to persuade the other partner into a frank discussion with the child over a changed set of values to make life more tolerable and less stressful for all concerned.

Living up to a tough image to impress people who matter can be just as precarious and stressful as waiting for the next round of bullying to start.

Anti-bullying policy

It helps if a school has a clear anti-bullying policy from the outset. Ideally, parents and children should sign an agreed behaviour contract on admission. This should accurately reflect the social aims and ethos of the school and delineate the range of sanctions that will be enforced for non-compliance. This contract should be drawn up in consultation with all the involved parties: teachers, parents, children and governors, and be sanctioned by the education authority (*see* Chapter 19).

This approach could be explained in a letter home to parents as follows:

Dear Parents

I should like your help with a matter that concerns us all.

Just recently there have been children involved in isolated incidents of violent behaviour. These concern very few pupils, but are carried over out of school at hometime and are causing great anxiety to the victims and to younger children and their parents.

Our school has a very good reputation in the area. It is one of the most controlled, and the majority of pupils can be relied upon to act in a responsible manner. I am very concerned that the behaviour of a few should not reflect on everyone else, and that a few irresponsible people should not be allowed to get away with intimidating and frightening others.

We spend an enormous amount of time in school sorting out children's problems. We allow 'time out' for children to calm down and avoid incidents, and encourage them to talk about and share problems. Please ask your child not to 'give as good as s/he gets'. This only exacerbates the problem and every child involved in a row always sees him/herself as the victim not the offender.

We hope you will help in the following ways:

- *please let us know if your child has been bullied or threatened, or hurt by another child;*

- *if your child is one who punches first and thinks later, please have a serious talk with him/her.*

I view this as such a serious problem that I intend in future to suspend children who have borne grudges and taken revenge days later, or ganged up with others to pick on one child, or indulge in violent, unprovoked behaviour.

I do hope that you will do all you can to support us in stamping out this undesirable trend towards violence. It is in everyone's interest that such antisocial behaviour should be dealt with most severely.

Yours sincerely

The reaction I received from parents to such a letter was that the majority were reassured and pleased, and a small minority implied this was an unfair device to suspend their child.

Right to be safe

I think the message should be quite simple: children have a right to feel safe and protected in school. Children who recognise they are about to violate this right should be allowed 'time out' to cool down and ask for help to resolve the difficulty. All adults have an obligation to support this principle, and all children should be encouraged to share in the responsibility for the safety and well-being of each other. Children who do not make use of the appropriate channels, and who are consistently guilty of premeditated attacks or violent revenge over long-held grudges, should be suspended.

However, these extreme measures should not be used in isolation. It is vital to build up an ongoing picture of the child's behaviour patterns, keeping close contact with the parents to try to establish reasons for the problems and seeking ways of moderating their negative effects.

Children may turn to bullying when weighed down with inherited anger, or highly stressed by some external social factor. Identifying with a trusted adult may be all that is needed. If the parents are willing to cooperate at an early stage, a two-way diary, stressing the child's positive achievements at home and school, may be adequate to raise self-esteem and counter feelings of persecution which start the spiral of negative behaviour.

Incidents log

Negative incidents should be separately logged, indicating the date, time, place and name of the adult filing the report (see Figure 3.1). It helps if these forms are colour-coded for easy access (e.g. behaviour reports – orange, and parent interviews – bright blue). These reports help to establish any pattern (e.g. playground behaviour significantly worst after a weekend) and also chart if a child's misbehaviour varies according to the approach, status or attitude of the person dealing with the incident. Teachers should contribute to behaviour reports, and all staff concerned with caring for children in school: secretary, support staff, meals supervisors and schoolkeeper – all see a different facet of a child's behaviour. The wider the consensus, the less easy it becomes to blame 'a simple clash of personalities' for the child's problem.

Figure 3.1: Example of an incidents log

SCHOOL

Address:
Head teacher:
Behaviour report on:
Class:
Date: Time: Location:
Suggested action : File for future reference
(please ring as   : Monitor
appropriate   : Sanction
                : Contact parents
                : Further comments

Signed:

Head/Teacher/Helper/Cook/Secretary
(Please ring as appropriate)

Telling

Children should be strongly encouraged to think of 'telling' as positive behaviour, not as 'sneaking'. In this way, the bully cannot be sure of maintaining a conspiracy of silence, and it becomes more difficult for him or her to single out the victim without interference from others. However, one of the difficulties which can result from 'telling' is retaliation.

When an adult intervenes to protect a victim, unless the sanction is very powerful it will only be effective for as long as the situation continues to be closely monitored. As soon as the bully sees the opportunity, he or she will be tempted to seek revenge. The victim is then in an even more vulnerable position and dependent on remaining in proximity to the protecting adult for safety. The victim has therefore sacrificed freedom of movement for what might be temporary sanctuary, unless we ensure that the whole school is safe for all children.

The alternative is to create very clear rules for an institution and, if you wish, support them with draconian sanctions, but what then is the benefit if all you are achieving is to remove the problem from your patch to someone else's?

'Miss, if I kick him will you suspend me?'

'Yes!'

'But what about if I leave him alone in school, but get him when he's walking down the street on Sunday afternoon?' . . .

So, we need to ensure that at least in the school the victim is safe and the bully may have to have his or her freedom restricted. It may not solve the long-term problem but it will provide much needed limits for the bully and relative safety for the victim.

Problems

The first problem is that we have to realise that our sphere of influence is limited to the school environs and the bully's interpretation of our actions may well be that we are the ones who are the biggest bullies of all. In other words, it's a dog-eat-dog world, so keep biting even if you're being bitten because only the biggest dog survives in the end.

The second problem is one of expectation. If children see bullying as endemic, rather like the common cold – you suffer a bout of it, but there's no known cure, so you put up with it and hope it goes away soon – then we never find out how serious and widespread the bullying problem is.

The third problem is one of apathy. Bullying becomes a cheap spectator sport – the 'cheer it on and be glad it's not you' mentality.

Solutions

I believe that the solution to all these problems, and the most effective sanction, must be peer group pressure. Children should be empowered, with the support of adults, to be made accountable for their actions and responsible for each other's safety. It utilises the key groups I have already identified, sages, bullies, victims and outsiders, in a forum such as a bully court.

If each child is given this forum to identify and debate antisocial behaviour towards himself or his peers, then every child assumes the role of protector. The identifying force ceases to be only the victim. It becomes everyone.

In a bully court situation (*see* Chapter 7) the sages assume the role of advocate and improve their perceived status still further. The bullies see the balance of power shifting away from them and their opportunities for retaliation diminished. The outsiders are drawn in as impartial observers. The victim becomes the focus of everyone's concern.

We must look at the problem of bullying dispassionately, and overcome it by employing practical strategies such as bully courts, a whole-school anti-bullying policy and two-way involvement with parents, developing in children the acceptance of telling and sharing problems and encouraging children to have a sense of communal responsibility. The insidious power of the school bully can then eventually be undermined, and a more responsible, positive set of social values can be established as the norm for all children.

4
■ ■ ■
Bullying and the under fives

MICHELE ELLIOTT

'Bullying is part of human nature, something children must learn to cope with if they are to survive the rough and tumble of everyday life.' This can be a hard line to swallow for those who work with tender four- and five-year-olds. Little ones often find the playground jungle a sinister place at first so it is often thought that any distress shown by young children is just natural. In fact, some nursery nurses don't think that bullying affects their charges. One nursery nurse said: 'It was only children playing – it wasn't bullying.' She was dealing with a parent's concern that her child was being consistently punched and pushed by another child. It turned out that the punching child was lashing out not only at school, but at home and just about everywhere else. She was only four, but she knew she was hurting others; she only attacked them when there was no one looking. Yes, she had problems, but she *was* a bully.

The mother of the bullied child also recognised that her child had problems. Sam was having difficulty outside the nursery school as well. His mother said that she took him to the Toy Library where he was pushed over: 'I hadn't even taken off his coat, but it's always like this. Other kids pick on him the whole time, taking his toys, pulling his hair even when I'm there. I can't protect him every second.' Sam is only three and yet he is already a victim of bullying.

It seems surprising that bullying should be an issue for young children, but at Kidscape we have had a 40 per cent increase in the number of cases involving children aged 5 and under. The actual numbers are still low compared with reported cases of older children, but it is a worrying trend.

A father rang to say that his five-year-old daughter had been threatened on the playground by a boy wielding a knife! When he complained that the other child had been readmitted to the school after a brief suspension, he was told that the boy 'had family problems'. He was also five years old. Of course this was quite serious and might not be considered bullying. However, it turned out he had been bullying children since the age of three.

The mother of a four-year-old boy was in great distress after her son came home covered with mud and sporting a black eye. He had been set upon by a group of five-year-olds and told that he had better not tell or they would beat him up again the next day. Fortunately, the nursery school in this case took immediate action and the bullying was nipped in the bud.

If children as young as three or four might become victims and bullies, what can nursery nurses and reception teachers do? Is it best to make a big fuss or to leave children to sort it out? More and more nursery school teachers feel that bullying should be taken seriously and stopped from the earliest age. One teacher commented that the behaviour of children in her nursery school had definitely changed over the past 15 years:

> Children are more likely now to lash out at each other and to act out violence on the playground than they were in the past. I am alarmed that some children are deliberately bullying others and cannot seem to understand the concept of kindness. If we don't stop them bullying now I think we are laying the foundations for short-term misery and later adult aggression. After all, versions of the playground heavies and their victims are re-enacted in sitting rooms and boardrooms daily.

It makes common sense that tackling bullying issues with young children should eliminate a lot of problems for them as they grow up – both for victims and for bullies.

Who bullies?

Probably all young children bully once in a while – brother and sisters, if no one else. Also young children may be so intent on getting what they want that they just bowl over anyone in their way. The child doesn't even realise that she or he is harming someone. Or a young child may go along with the crowd and say or do hurtful things without thinking through what they are doing.

While all children need to learn to get along with others, concern about young bullies should be focused more on the child who deliberately sets out to cause distress to another child or who is a danger to other young children, as with the child who brought the knife to school mentioned above. These are the children who have problems and may share the characteristics outlined in Chapter 1 of this book.

Who are the victims?

The under fives who become victims of bullying are described by their teachers as sensitive, gentle children. They are often not used to conflict, so when bullies come at them they don't know what to do. They frequently ask why someone would want to bully them – they've done nothing to deserve it and they haven't been treated this way before. The sad fact is that, from the bully's viewpoint, they make excellent targets because they are nice and won't fight back. They might even cry, a bonus for the bully. If you could point out one 'fault' of these victims, it would be that they are too nice! In a nursery or playgroup which doesn't tolerate bullying, they have no problems.

There are, however, some children who seem to get bullied everywhere – in school, at parties, during activities, in the local playground, at the toy library – you name a place and they are bullied there. These are the children who seem almost to thrive on the negative attention they get when they are bullied. It is as if the bullying confirms their opinion of themselves that they are worthless and deserve what is happening to them. There may be problems in the lives of these children, or they may have been bullied right from the day when they started nursery school and have never recovered their confidence.

Practical suggestions

Bullies depend for their success on a code of silence. It is based on, of all things, honour ('It's wrong to tell tales') or on fear ('Don't tell anyone or I'll thump you'). Either way, it prevents children from telling when they have been bullied or have seen someone being bullied.

To crack the code of silence, those who work with the under fives may try to:

- become 'telling' schools – the nursery nurses and teachers make it clear that bullying is unacceptable and children have an obligation to *tell* if they are bullied or see bullying take place;

- ensure that the adults do something when they are told – children must be able to rely on a sympathetic and helpful response if they do tell. In this way they learn that speaking out will make things better while keeping quiet will make things worse;

- monitor the trouble spots, like the playground, constantly – if lack of staff is a problem (where isn't it?), then enlist parent helpers;

- use stories, activities, art, etc. to reinforce the anti-bullying messages (see suggestions at the end of the chapter for ideas);

- put up a photograph of each child and write something good about the child under the photo – try just a few words like: 'A Good Friend' or 'Helps Others' or 'Kind Person' or 'Good to Pets'. Change the words once a week and ask children to help think of good things to say about each other;

- give stickers or rewards of some sort each day to a child who has been nice (sometimes it is difficult to 'catch' a problem child being nice, but it is worth the effort to reinforce good behaviour) – children will vie to be good if they get recognition, but do make sure that every child gets recognised;

- organise a 'Kindness Week' and have the children draw posters – give prizes for the best posters and ribbons or certificates for children being kind to others. Involve parents, if possible.

Set up student helpers

The idea of using students to help others is as old as teaching itself. I used this method years ago when I had a classroom of 34 five-year-old children and a few older children were making it their business to bully the younger ones. These ideas work better if there is a nursery attached to a primary school so there is a pool of older children available. Try the following:

- Assign an older 'helper' to act as an adviser, protector and mentor to each new child. Usually older or bigger children pick on younger or smaller ones *who are alone*. This eliminated that problem and the older children took pride in helping 'their' charges.

- Set up student 'counsellors' who are chosen anonymously by the children and teachers as 'other children you would most likely seek out to talk to about a problem'. This is particularly good for children who don't have close friends. It may help to foster friendships. The 'counsellors' talk to the bullied children and go with them to tell the teachers, so it is still the responsibility of the adult to sort out the problems. Children sometimes find it easier to talk initially to other children than to adults.

Help the bully

Sometimes it is possible to help a bully by recognising that she or he, too, is a victim – perhaps unloved or mistreated at home, or covering for a feeling of personal inadequacy by dominating others. In these cases, treating the underlying cause may also eradicate the bullying. For example, a child doing badly may be encouraged to work hard and excel at something – drawing, gymnastics, plasticine modelling, skipping rope, putting together puzzles, racing – and may in the process gain enough approval to stop bullying.

The younger the child the better chance we have of changing their behaviour. Reforming older chronic bullies is not easy. (Significantly, when schools organise meetings to discuss the problem of bullying, it is usually the parents of the victim who turn up.)

When working with a young child who is bullying, try to:

- remain calm;
- find out the facts;

- talk to the child to find out if she or he is upset or has been bullied and is lashing out as a reaction;
- find out if the child realises that she or he is bullying and hurting someone else – sometimes young children don't know how their actions affect others;
- talk with the parents of the victim, if possible, to set things right and to avoid the bullying carrying on;
- set up a behaviour chart using stars or stickers – give a reward for every five or ten stars but make sure that the time between the good behaviour and the reward is not too great, especially for very young children. For example, some children may need help every hour to behave while others can go for a whole day.

If the parents of a bully ask for advice from teachers, suggest that they try:

- working with you to figure out the best way to help their child;
- talking to their child and explain that, whatever problems there may be, bullying is not the way to solve them;
- working out a 'behaviour plan' to reward good behaviour;
- arranging a daily or weekly report from the school to them and vice versa;
- setting up a star chart on the refrigerator and giving a star for each good report from school, followed by some sort of reward after so many stars;
- seeking counselling or professional help if the child does not respond after a reasonable time. The child may have problems which need to be sorted out before he or she can stop bullying.

Help the victims

Some bullies, especially young ones who receive help, can be sorted out. Often, however, we have to work around bullies by teaching children how to cope with threats and how to avoid attracting them in the first place. Some children seem more prone to bullying than others. This may result from factors beyond their control: the colour of their skin, for example, or some striking physical feature – e.g. being above or below average height – that sets them apart from the others. Or it may be that, if they are repeatedly bullied, children start acting like victims. If this happens, children can be helped, both at school and at home. Try helping them to:

- walk tall and straight in a confident way, rather than hunched over, looking scared and uncertain;
- practise looking in the mirror and saying 'No' or 'Leave me alone' in a clear voice, looking into their own eyes as they say it. A firm rebuff will often deter a bully who is looking for signs of weakness;

- roleplay – something that has been used with great success with young children both in schools and at home. Act out the threatening situation and practise responding calmly but firmly. This type of imaginative play can also help defuse some of the anger that builds up inside children who are persistently bullied;
- ignore the bullying and pretend not to be upset – turn and walk quickly away and tell a grown-up;
- use humour – it is more difficult to bully a child who refuses to take the bullying seriously. This is especially useful with verbal bullying;
- stay with groups of children, if possible;
- respond to taunts saying the same thing over and over – this is called the broken record approach. For example, for a taunt such as 'You've got glasses', tell the child to respond with 'Thank you' *and* just keep saying it over and over – 'Thank you, thank you.' It is a silly response and it becomes boring for the bully after a while.

In order for children to feel confident using some of these ideas, practise with them and see if they can come up with other ideas.

Obviously the ability of the child to try these things depends upon the age and maturity of the child. Adult supervision and intervention with young children is vital.

Nursery teachers can also try to give children confidence by:

- assuring them that the bullying is not their fault;
- telling the child that you like him or her (bullied children feel unlovable);
- helping them to stop any bad habits which might be contributing to their being bullied (such as picking their nose or wiping disgusting things on their sleeves or grabbing toys from other children).

If a child continues to be bullied, it may be that counselling would help. Like the bully, the chronic victim and their families may need some professional guidance to prevent the child from becoming a life-long victim.

End the conspiracy of silence

The one thing that emerges time and time again in all surveys is that bullying is one of the most difficult social problems children have to deal with – and it's probably been made harder by the outmoded notion that everyone should grin and bear it and that the best way to deal with any problem is a stiff upper lip. But this tacit approval of bullying is one inheritance we needn't pass on to the next generation . . . they need not suffer in silence.

Anti-bullying activities for young children

RIP-RIP

Give each child a large cut-out figure of a child, on A3 paper (or smaller if you can't manage the larger size).

Explain that the 'child' is a whole, happy person who is going to school one morning feeling good. But during the day other children make comments or do things which make the child feel bad. Ask the children to make a little rip in their cut-out figure every time they think the figure is hurt by something in the story you are going to read out.

RIP-RIP STORY

I can't wait to get to school. I know it's going to be fun. Oh, look, here come some other kids.

Hello, my name is Jane. What's yours?

What are they saying to me? They said I was ugly and they wouldn't speak to me.   **(Rip-Rip)**

Here come some other children. Maybe they'll be friendlier. What are they doing? Of, they're looking away and pretending not to hear the mean children calling me names. I wish they would do something. I feel so lonely.   **(Rip-Rip)**

I guess I'll just play by myself today.   **(Rip-Rip)**

On the playground some of the children wait until no one is looking and then they trip me over. One of them says not to tell or I'll be in trouble. I don't tell.   **(Rip-Rip)**

No one will sit by me at lunch. The mean children have told them not to talk to me or eat with me.   **(Rip-Rip)**

When my mummy comes to collect me, she asks me if school was fun today. What should I tell her?

You can make up your own story or add or subtract from this one. The children's figures will be in shreds by now. Discuss with them how it feels to be picked on like this and how they could have helped the cut-out child. Make a list of their suggestions and post it up in the class. Remind them how comments and actions can affect people and encourage them to make kind comments to each other.

THAT'S MY POTATO!

Give each child a potato and ask them to look at it carefully to see things like green marks, spots, its shape, 'eyes', etc. Try to ensure that the potatoes are not completely uniform! They should give their potato a name and make up a story about it:

- What does it do for fun?
- What kinds of food does it like and dislike?
- How old is it?
- Does it have brothers and sisters?
- And so on.

Have the children tell their Potato Story to each other in small groups, or to you if you have enough time and not too many children. Then put all the potatoes in a bag, jumble them and put them on a table for the children to come and find their potato. (If the children are likely to disagree, you will have to put a dot or some mark on them to avoid arguments.)

Explain that it is the small differences that make people individual but they are still all people, just as the potatoes may each be different but they are all still potatoes. Once you take the time to look at someone and really get to know them, you can see that that person is not the same as everyone else and that differences are no reason to bully anyone. After all, just because their potato may have three 'eyes' and someone else's potato may have six 'eyes', does that mean that their potato should be singled out for bad treatment?

DRAWINGS

Ask the children to draw a picture of a playground where everyone is happy and no one is being bullied. Then ask for a picture of a playground where children are being bullied. Use the pictures to have a discussion about bullying.

5

■　■　■

The playground

VALERIE BESAG

Friends

Friends, Pals, Mates, Companions
Someone to help you
Someone to tell you things
Where would we be without friends?

Someone to boost your confidence
Someone to give you inspiration
Someone to lend you things
Someone to have fun with
Friends, Pals, Mates, Companions.

Nicholas English (age 10 years)

Bullying among schoolchildren is hard to identify, even within a supervised classroom setting. The name-calling, abusive remarks, pushes, thumps and snatching of equipment can all occur behind the teacher's back. In the bustle of a large playground it becomes extremely hard to distinguish behaviour causing distress from the general rough and tumble. Commonly in playground disputes, the aggressors, on being accused of bullying, claim to have 'only been playing'. Games, however, by definition are enjoyed by all participants. If any one child is not taking pleasure in the activity it cannot be defined as a game.

Bullying is a covert activity often causing severe stress and fear, yet leaving little visible evidence and rarely anyone willing to act as witness. Extreme vigilance is therefore required when supervising children at play.

There is, perhaps, a place for some degree of teasing, challenging and critical comment in the normal interactions of childhood play. These behaviours are used by peers to shape up the behaviour of individuals to the standard common to the group. This process continues through life whether in the form of gentle cues from friends or more direct criticism from elsewhere. Even as adults we remain watchful of our behaviour in order to maintain social acceptance but, in the case of children, it is essential to identify those repeatedly singled out for negative comment and at risk of becoming the group scapegoat.

In considering playground behaviour, it is of relevance to note the difference between the play of boys and girls as this appears to relate to the gender difference in bullying behaviour.

Boys are considered to be more physical and boisterous in their play (Maccoby and Jacklin, 1980). Correspondingly, bullying among boys is characterised by overt physical and verbal abuse (Roland, 1988). Boys appear to form larger and looser groups than girls whether as an organised team or an information gang playing a chasing game (Omark *et al.*, 1975). It appears to be the activity, rather than the relationship, that is the focus of the group.

Girls, in contrast, gather in twos or threes, with the third most likely on the periphery (Douvan and Adelson, 1966). In the case of girls there is a stronger emphasis on the quality of the relationship in that more conversation, exchange of opinions and the modelling of attitudes, presentation and behaviour of each other takes place. Due to this bonding, jealousy, possessiveness and loyalty are often in evidence and the relationship can be constantly under review. These dyads of young girls have been compared to lovers due to the intensity of the relationship, the need for frequent contact by telephone or by the exchange of notes, and physical contact such as holding hands (Lever, 1976). Rumour, malicious gossip and social ostracism are the preferred modes of bullying among girls which perhaps reflect the importance and vulnerability of these close relationships.

One aspect of bullying common to both boys and girls, and reported by both to be the most distressing, is name-calling. Young people of all ages appear to be imaginative and astute in identifying the Achilles' heel of their target, and in choosing an apt and humorous name, qualities which ensure the durability of these abusive names.

Our names are personal to us and used to distinguish us from others. Allport (1954) refers to them as 'labels of primary potency', a term still relevant today. Abusive names are often dehumanising such as 'Cow', 'Pig', 'Bitch'. Without a name we have no identity and it is significant that it is replaced by a number in situations such as prisons, or even the armed forces, where there is an intention to impose group, rather than individual, identity, discipline and control.

The distress caused by abusive names can be underestimated by adults supervising a busy playground, yet children report them causing more distress than physical assault. Name-calling appears to be used in the initial stages of bullying to test out the response of those suspected of being vulnerable. Good supervision at this stage could prevent an escalation to crisis. Adults need to be aware that the power of a threat or insult lies not in what is said but how it is said, the manner in which it is delivered and received. It is a two-way process. Hearing about an abusive incident from a third party could diminish the impact and the episode wrongly be dismissed as trivial.

From the profiles of those at risk of becoming involved in a bullying situation (Besag, 1995: 18 and 19), it can be seen that victims tend to fall into the category of passive 'watchers' who remain on the sidelines of playground fun, whereas bullies tend to be the 'doers', confident and fully involved in all activities (Besag, 1992).

One group of children, mainly boys, who frequently fall foul of playground bullies, is characterised by the 'clumsy' child, now referred to as Developmental Dyspraxia (Besag, 1995: 50, 51; see also Besag, 1992: 42–6 for a case study). These children experience coordination problems. As boys are more robust and physically active in their play, the problems these children have with running, catching and balancing skills, for example, make them more noticeable among boys and their rejection more common. In addition, these children may display mannerisms which give rise to taunts (Besag, 1995: 177). If confident and well supported by adults, these children can overcome many of their difficulties and find success with specific activities. One such is swimming as the water supports the body so that attention can be concentrated on the arm and leg movements. Opportunities for these children to gain recognition and prestige in any way should be sought as feelings of rejection and fear can exaggerate their coordination problems.

Pupils often appear to use teachers as role models so that the dismissive attitude of a teacher towards a boy who is poor at sport and playground games can encourage the rejection and bullying of the boy by the group.

Most bullying appears to start with the spontaneous testing out of those suspected of being vulnerable for the entertainment of the individual or the group. This can quickly escalate to a distressing level if the opportunity occurs. There are times and places throughout the school day when the quality of supervision can be poor due to no one teacher being nominated as responsible for oversight of the area. Examples of this are changing rooms, toilets, corridors, bus queues and lunch queues. Young people congregate in such places in their free time and the less robust could be at risk.

Good supervision over play breaks is not only necessary for the safety and well-being of all pupils, but it is in the best interests of the school as a whole, as disputes arising in the playground are often carried over into school causing later disruption in class (Blatchford and Sharp, 1994).

Attention needs to be given not only to the quantity of supervision, but also to the quality. The style of supervision, firm and friendly or authoritarian and rigorous, may reflect the ethos of the school. If there is a mismatch the supervision could enhance or detract from the work done elsewhere throughout the school day (Blatchford and Sharp, 1994).

Good supervision at play breaks demands more than the casual oversight of a couple of adults wandering around the playground. One boy in his first year at secondary school suddenly refused to attend without explanation. Only when an older boy was asked to shadow him did it come to light that, on entering the cloakroom to get his coat, he would be locked in by other pupils. His only option was to play out in the winter weather without a coat. Staff had been conscientiously patrolling the playground unaware of the distress of this young boy (Besag, 1992: 86).

One method of identifying weaknesses in a supervision system is by a member of staff tracking pupils and noting problems. One school adopting this method found that pupils allowed in school five minutes before the bell, when staff left the staffroom, were congregating on the stairs, outside registration rooms and in various nooks and crannies around the building. The joking and jostling in these unattended groups caused many pupils to enter class in either a truculent or excitable mood. In another school a teacher doing a similar exercise discovered that, for some considerable time, non-white pupils had been forbidden by others from using the stairs and were forced to wait for the arrival of a teacher for protection. No one had alerted staff to this situation (Riley, 1988).

Staff absences can also cause problems if not identified until playtime has begun for it is then too late to reallocate the duty. The tracking exercise also found unsupervised yet at times crowded corridors to be prime locations for disputes and fights. The crush also gave cover for attacks to be made on vulnerable pupils.

The school tackled these problems as a team committed to upgrading the quality of supervision (Besag, 1992: 56). Teachers are now in class at least five minutes before pupils enter the building. The corridors are supervised on a rota basis by teachers informally chatting to pupils or among themselves. The outside play areas are observed from second-storey classroom windows so that the bird's eye view supports the supervision of staff in the playground. Staff absences are routinely dealt with on the duty rota at the same time that lesson cover is arranged. Older pupils are allowed to remain inside in designated areas to chat among themselves, or with staff, to prevent overcrowding in the play areas. Most do not want to play boisterous games during the later years at school, nor do they want to stand around in the cold.

Some schools are able to offer a variety of activities for pupils of all ages to help make best use of the play breaks. Such activities as art and craft work, the library, computers, gymnastics, football, videos and comics can be arranged with volunteer adult support. These are especially valuable for 'wet' break times. Once there is recognition of the value of good leisure experiences, and the danger of poorly supervised playtimes is highlighted, it may be that voluntary help will become more readily available.

Games groups organised by older pupils have been found to be very useful in helping pupils overcome their feelings of vulnerability and in helping them develop a range of social skills (Besag, 1995: 186; 1992: 56 and 57).

Those supervising children during the longest break, the lunch hour, are often untrained and poorly paid. Many schools now support training schemes for these supervisors so that, instead of concentrating on the negative role of stopping trouble, they are able to help pupils maximise the valuable time during play breaks when they are free from the restrictions of curriculum demands. For the quality of supervision our children need, it may be that we must consider professional quality training and an appropriate salary for those working with pupils during these key periods in the school day. An overview of training schemes can be found in Blatchford and Sharp (1994).

It is not simply a matter of providing more staff and more equipment. Key skills for supervisors have been identified by the Sheffield Bullying Project (Smith and Sharp, 1994) as:

- the ability to keep calm and not rise to provocation;
- a willingness to listen carefully to all sides of an argument;
- a refusal to be sidetracked;
- care in avoiding sarcasm and personal criticism;
- labelling the behaviour as unwanted and not the child;
- the use of a hierarchy of sanctions well known to all adults and children;
- willingness to implement sanctions rather than relying on calling upon a teacher.

Schools introducing schemes where extra play equipment is taken into the playground find that they can lead to even more quarrels and upsets. With thought simple strategies can be employed to avoid this, e.g. only the pupils in the class of the teacher on duty that day are allowed to use the equipment and are responsible for its safe return.

One aspect of training for both supervisors and teachers which is often overlooked is the difficulty in defining what is rough and tumble play and what is aggression and bullying. It is not always easy to decide and adults may intervene unnecessarily. Premature intervention by adults may inhibit the natural learning process whereby young people develop their skills of mediation, resolution, negotiation and argument. Over-involvement and direction by adults may thwart the emerging skills of decision-taking, imaginative play and creativity.

Schools can play a major role in supporting good playground behaviour by encouraging friendship skills. The ability to initiate and maintain friendships is a skill which some children appear to assimilate without help, whereas others require well-planned support. As we are social animals, the ability to uphold relationships is essential to our continued well-being and success. Research indicates that those children unable to resolve relationship difficulties in childhood are at higher risk than others of continuing to have similar problems throughout the adult years (Cowen *et al.*, 1973; Olweus, 1987). The value of friendship skills cannot, therefore, be underestimated.

Children use friendships for companionship and emotional support. In the safe relationship they also learn to challenge, debate, concede and accept strengths and weaknesses in themselves and others. Friends offer guidelines to acceptable behaviour and attitudes, vicarious experiences and a wealth of knowledge about the, as yet, unfamiliar world. The isolated child misses out not only in companionship, but is also denied a valuable learning medium.

Having friends and being socially successful is more important to many young people than academic success. The rewards are more immediate and rejection can lead to shame and embarrassment. Parents too can experience these negative feelings if they sense that their child is unpopular. This may contribute to the reluctance of many parents to approach school if a bullying problem is detected.

Those identified as popular by their peers appear to possess clearly defined qualities. This information can be used to design programmes for those in difficulties for the school day and contains a wealth of formal and informal opportunities for social interactions (Jersild, 1966; Ginsberg *et al.*, 1986; Dygdon, Conger and Keane, 1987; Boulton and Smith, 1994).

The qualities highly prized by the majority of children are as follows: the ability to be supportive and complimentary, to show an interest in others and to display an obvious desire for friendship. Independence and maturity, mediation and leadership skills are valued, and the ability to generate ideas for games and activities is attractive to young people of all ages (Lagerspetz *et al.*, 1982).

From research in the field of sociolinguistics, we are able to identify the features of language and posture in the approach behaviour of children which influence the chance of a child being accepted or rejected by the group. We are becoming increasingly aware that there are many pupils in our schools with some hidden communication problem. These pupils are especially at risk as they do not appreciate the nuances of verbal communication, the differences in intonation, sarcasm, innuendo. The problem may not be simply a matter of shyness or timidity. Before this type of work can be attempted, however, an isolated or rejected child may need help to develop feelings of self-worth and confidence as many are unwilling to approach others due to fear of further rejection. (For details of this type of work see Besag, 1995: 143–7.)

The current curriculum work in school lends itself to small groups or pairs of pupils working together in a cooperative rather than a competitive mode. When choosing pairs of children, teachers should be aware of the extra dimension of relationship building and use the opportunity to initiate suitable friendships.

There are many opportunities for this type of work even within the curriculum material. A topic such as 'names' could encompass historical, mythological, geographical, art and craft material (Besag, 1992). The emotional intent and effect on the recipient of affectionate and abusive names can be explored. This type of work can effectively reduce the amount of aggression and name-calling in groups, and contribute to more rewarding playtime experiences.

Volunteering older pupils can be responsible for easing new entrants through the difficult transition period by chatting in small groups about such issues as bullying which many pupils feel wary about discussing with adults. Vulnerable pupils can be paired with slightly older or more confident ones who are able to take on the role often undertaken by older siblings or neighbourhood friends. Older pupils trained in mediation skills can support both bullies and victims in resolving difficulties. There are many advantages to enlisting the support of peers to help disputants reach an acceptable resolution, e.g. peer counselling, mediation, mentoring systems (Besag, 1992: 123–6).

Parents of isolated or rejected children could be guided by teachers to those of children experiencing similar problems or those with confident children willing to befriend a child less fortunate. Many parents may be anxious for their child to make friends but feel unable to find a way forward. Workshops held in school, supported by literature, could alert parents to the valuable role they can play in helping their own child, and others, to become socially skilled and confident in a variety of settings (Besag, 1992: 126).

One distressing case of bullying was stopped when a young girl, witnessing the repeated attacks on a classmate in the playground and being too afraid to alert the school staff, reported the incidents to her parents. The parents contacted the school and the young victim's parents. Once the bullying was exposed and the bullies taken to task, it stopped and did not recur (Besag, 1992: 42–5).

In summary, an awareness of the long-term effects of bullying on both the victim and bully should encourage adults, in whatever capacity, to address themselves to the problem of the physical and emotional distress currently occurring daily in our playgrounds so that we offer our children the quality of protection we enjoy ourselves as adults (Olweus, 1993).

Not only do we need to be aware of the safety and well-being of our children during non-teaching hours, but there is a growing recognition of the opportunity available for young people to develop socially, and to learn with and from each other, away from the restriction of rigorous curriculum demands. Current job adverts more often than not stress the need for 'good interpersonal and communication skills'. Where better can young people learn and develop these essential life skills? The playground needs to be viewed as a learning forum, an opportunity to be maximised where the energy, enthusiasm and good nature of young people relaxed and at play can be used to enhance social opportunities for all.

References

Allport, G. W. (1954) *The Nature of Prejudice*, New York, Addison-Wesley.

Besag, V. E. (1992) *We don't have Bullies Here!* (manual), 3 Jesmond Dene Terrace, Jesmond, Newcastle upon Tyne NE2 2ET.

Besag, V. E. (1995) *Bullies and Victims in Schools*, Milton Keynes, Open University Press.

Blatchford, P. and Sharp, S. (1994) *Understanding and Changing Playground Behaviour*, London, Routledge.

Boulton, M. J. and Smith, P. K. (1994) *British Journal of Developmental Psychology*, Vol. 12, pp. 315–29.

Cowen, E. L., Pederson, A., Babigian, H., Izzo, L. D. and Trost, M. A. (1973) 'Long-term follow-up of early detected vulnerable children', *Journal of Consulting and Clinical Psychology*, No. 41, pp. 438–46.

Douvan, E. and Adelson, J. (1966) *The Adolescent Experience*, Chichester, John Wiley.

Dygdon, J. A., Conger, A. J. and Keane, S. P. (1987) 'Children's perceptions of the behavioural correlates of social acceptance, rejection and neglect in their peers', *Journal of Clinical Child Psychology*, Vol. 16, pp. 2–8.

Ginsberg, D., Gottman, J. and Parker, J. (1986) 'The importance of friendship', in J. M. Gottman and J. G. Parker (eds), *Conversations of Friends*, Cambridge, Cambridge University Press.

Jersild, A. T. (1966) *Child Psychology*, 5th edn, London, Staples Press.

Jersild, A. T. and Markey, F. V. (1935) 'Conflicts between pre-school children', *Child Development Monograph*, Vol. 21.

Lagerspetz, K. M. I., Bjorgvist, K. B., Berts, M. and King, E. (1982) 'Group aggression among children in three schools', *Scandinavian Journal of Psychology*, Vol. 23, pp. 45–52.

Lever, J. (1976) 'Sex differences in the games children play', *Social Problems*, No. 23, pp. 478–87.

Maccoby, E. E. and Jacklin, C. N. (1980) 'Sex differences in aggression: a rejoinder and a reprise', *Child Development*, No. 51, pp. 964–80.

McKinley, I. and Gordon, N. (1980) *Helping Clumsy Children*, Edinburgh, Churchill Livingstone.

Olweus, D. (1979) 'Stability of aggressive reaction patterns in males: a review', *Psychological Bulletin*, Vol. 86, No. 4, pp. 852–75.

Olweus, D. (1980) 'Familial and temperamental determinants of aggressive behaviour in adolescent boys: a causal analysis', *Developmental Psychology*, Vol. 16, pp. 644–60.

Olweus, D. (1987) 'Bully/victim problems among school-children in Scandinavia', in J. P. Myklebust and R. Ommundsen (eds), *Psykolog-profesjonen mot ar 2000*, Oslo, Universitetsforlaget.

Olweus, D. (1993) *Bullying in Schools: What We Know and What We Can Do*, Oxford, Blackwell.

Omark, D. R., Omark, M. and Edelman, M. S. (1975) 'Formation of dominance hierarchies in young children', in T. R. Williams (ed.), *Action and Perception in Psychological Anthropology*, The Hague, Mouton.

Riley, D. (1988) 'Bullying: a study of victim and victimisers within one inner-city school', in-service BEd, Inquiry Report, Crewe and Alsager College of Higher Education.

Roland, E. (1988) *Report of the European Teachers Seminar on Bullying in Schools*, Strasbourg, Council for Cultural Cooperation.

Sharp, S. and Smith, P. K. (1994) *Tackling Bullying in Your School*, London, Routledge.

Smith, P. K. and Sharp, S. (1994) *School Bullying*, London, Routledge.

6

■ ■ ■

Anti-bullying exercises to use with students

MICHELE ELLIOTT

Beleaguered teachers with too much to do and too little time to do it in may welcome the following ideas which have been successfully used with students. With a couple of exceptions, the exercises are not labelled for particular ages as most can be adapted for students of different ages and abilities.

1. Collage

Collages are a non-threatening way for students to express their feelings about bullying.

You will need a variety of magazines (lots) with pictures to cut out, paper to paste pictures on, glue, scissors.

Ask the students to work on a 'bullying' theme to make collages. They go through the magazines and cut or tear out pictures which reflect the theme. Some suggestion for themes are:

- When I am bullied I feel . . .
- When I see someone being bullied . . .
- People who bully are . . .
- Victims are . . .
- What I would like to do to people who bully . . .
- How people who bully feel . . .
- How victims feel . . .
- What adults do about bullying . . .
- Bullying is . . .

- Ways to stop bullying ...
- The way I see myself ...
- The way others see me ...
- The way I wish I was ...
- The way parents / teachers / students see me ...

Display the collages if appropriate, or ask the students to discuss them in small groups. This exercise does not depend upon artistic talent and students of all ages seem to enjoy the hands-on approach of making collages (Elliott and Kilpatrick, 1994).

2. Making friends

Although we ask students to become friends, we seldom help them to think about how to go about it.

Bullying is sometimes the result of misguided attempts of children or young people trying to become part of a group or trying to approach someone to become a friend.

Ask the students to discuss ways to make friends. Have them work in small groups and come up with a list of ten ways to make a friend. Then ask them to report to the larger group and write the suggestions on the board, avoiding duplication.

These suggestions were compiled by a group of 13-year-olds:

- Showing an interest in what people do
- Being complimentary without going overboard
- Having a pleasant expression on your face
- Laughing at people's jokes
- Being kind
- Asking to join in
- Offering to help
- Inviting people to do something
- Going to places where other students are
- Being welcoming to new students
- Bringing something interesting to do
- Being willing to share
- Being humorous / telling jokes
- Being fair

- Organising games or activities
- Thinking of new ideas

Using the same method, ask the students to think about ways *not* to make friends. One group thought of the following:

- Being bossy
- Telling others how to play
- Telling others they are doing things wrong
- Talking about yourself all the time
- Being mean
- Talking about other students behind their backs
- Being negative and sarcastic
- Being too intense or serious all the time
- Bragging
- Moaning all the time
- Being a bully
- Claiming credit for something you didn't do
- Lying or cheating

Ask the students to draw up a Friendship Charter and post it in the school where it can be seen and discussed.

Follow-up exercises

- Ask the students to roleplay someone trying to make friends the wrong way, then carry out another roleplay showing the right way.
- Ask the students to conduct a survey asking students and staff for their ideas on making friends. Chart the results and discuss.
- Write a paper about an imaginary new student trying to make friends in your school. What obstacles might he or she encounter? What things would help? Include suggestions which the school might use to change for the better.

3. Story/play

There are several texts about bullying listed in the back of this book. The teacher can either choose one to read or ask children to read a story or prepare a short play about bullying. Some teachers have asked older children to read to younger children or to put on a play for young children.

4. Letter

Use an English class to ask the students to write a letter to a pen pal (real or imaginary) or a new friend describing what they like to do, what kind of a person they are and what they hope to do when they leave school. Ask them to talk about their life in school and to bring in the theme of bullying from either a victim or bully viewpoint. For example, they can write about a typical day in school and include a bullying situation.

5. Body outline

This exercise is for younger children. Ask the children to lie down on a large piece of paper (rolls of heavy lining paper from a DIY shop are perfect for this and quite cheap) and trace an outline of their bodies. Ask the children to cut out their outline and colour it in as they wish. Get a pad of Post-It notes and write something good about each child and attach the note to the outline, perhaps on the hand. Change the message as often as possible – the children will be delighted.

6. Nicknames

Ask the students what nickname they would like to be called if they had a choice. Often hurtful nicknames are given to children and young people and then used to bully them. Help each student find a positive nickname for him/herself. This might be a good opportunity to use words from other languages, such as Solecito (Spanish for little sun), Shaina (Yiddish for beautiful), Leoncito (Spanish for little lion). Ask the students for other suggestions. Come up with a list and let the students decide on their own names, but don't let anyone pick a negative nickname.

7. Student of the week

This exercise works very well with younger children. Each week put up the picture of one student. Ask each of the other students to say one good thing about the student and make a list of five statements to put under the picture. If you want to speed up the exercise, have a Student of the Day. Try to have all the pictures and comments up on Parents' Evening and ask the parents to add a comment. (If all the parents can't come, try to get a good comment either in writing or over the telephone and add it to the child's list.)

8. Poem

Ask the students to write a poem about bullying. Display the poems and choose some to be read at assembly. Alternatively have a contest in which judges from outside the school choose the winners and give book tokens (donated by the local bookshop?) as prizes.

9. Perfect school

This is fun and can lead to noisy discussions. Ask the students to design a school that is perfect for bullies. They should think about the buildings, the playground and the attitude of the students and staff towards bullying. Alternatively they can design a perfect school in which there is no bullying.

10. Positive/negative

Ask the students to draw a line down the centre of a piece of paper and write Positive at the top on one side and Negative on the other. Ask them to write in three positive things about themselves in the first column and three negative things in the second. The ground rule is that none of the traits can be physical but should be things that have been developed by the student and therefore could be changed. For example:

Positive	Negative
Honest	Bad tempered
Fast runner	Doesn't do homework
Likes pets	Untidy

Ask the students if they could work on changing one negative trait into a positive one over the next week or month.

This exercise is best done individually and not with other students unless a trusting relationship has been built up; otherwise the 'negatives' could be used to bully.

11. Class newspaper

Ask each student to contribute an article, drawing, puzzle or poem about bullying to a class newsletter. Have the students put the newsletter together and photocopy it for parents, students and staff.

12. Millionaire

Tell the students that they have each inherited £1 000 000 of which they must use 90 per cent to eradicate bullying. After they have stopped all bullying, they can then use the remaining 10 per cent of the money for personal use to make their own lives happier. How would they use the money? The students can either work individually and write about what they would do or work in small groups and report back to the class what they would do as a group.

13. Puppet play

This exercise is for younger children. Using socks decorated by the children (buttons for eyes, felt mouths, wool for hair and whiskers) or paper cut-outs of characters, ask the children to make up a puppet play about a child who is being bullied and how sad the child feels. Ask them to think of a positive way to end the play so that the child who is bullying gets help and so does the victim – a happy ending!

14. Mural

Ask the students to cooperate on drawing and decorating a class mural depicting on one panel a playground where bullying is happening and on another panel a playground where everyone is having a good time and where there is no bullying. Discuss your own playground and think of ways which could make it more like the 'No bullying' panel.

15. Make someone feel good

Ask the students to agree to each do or say at least one thing a day to make someone else feel good. Have a rule that it has to be a different person each day that they make feel good. You may want to make this a month-long project and ask each student to do or say something to each member of the class or group. Ask each student to keep a journal or record of what they do and discuss it with them.

16. Wish list

This exercise is best done on an individual basis and discussed with the teacher or a trusted friend.

Ask students to write down on one side of a sheet of paper five words which describe them. On the other side of the paper write down five words which they wished described them.

Ask them to take one of the words on their Wish List and describe what it means to be like that. For example, if they said they wished they were 'happy', what does it mean to them to be happy?

People who seem to be happy:

- Smile
- Have friends
- Do well in school
- Have money
- Come from nice families
- Feel good about themselves

Then ask the students to look at the list they have just made to see which things it might be possible for them to work on to become happy. It might not be possible to have money (or necessarily even be true that you need it to be happy) or to come from a nice family, but it might be possible to work on smiling, having friends, doing well in school and feeling good about themselves.

Ask the students to make it a goal to work on attaining at least one of the ideals on their Wish List. Help them work out an action plan to achieve their goal: for example, if the goal is to 'be popular', then the student needs to think about how they can make friends and adopt welcoming and friendly behaviour (*see* Exercise 2 above). Their action plan might start something like this:

- Try to smile at people whenever possible.
- Be kind to other people and helpful.
- Invite someone home.
- Be ready to listen to others.

For 'Doing well in school', the action plan might look like this:

- Choose one subject to work on to start with.
- Ask the teacher for extra help.
- Set aside more time to work on that subject.
- Study with someone who might be able to help you understand it better.
- Don't get discouraged if it takes some time to get better in the subject.
- Tell yourself that you will improve and believe that you can do it.
- Ignore anyone who attempts to discourage you, even a well meaning parent who says, 'I never did very well in that either.'
- Reward yourself for getting better.

This exercise helps people to develop self-esteem if they follow it through and actually are able to change the goal from a wish to a reality (Elliott and Kilpatrick, 1994). Although it does take lots of help and encouragement, it is worth it to achieve the goal. The students can do this exercise with parents and other adults, if they are supportive.

17. Bully gang

Ask the students to write a story about a child or young person who suddenly finds that they are being pulled into a bully gang and being pressured to start bullying a person they have been friends with in the past. Ask them to write about what the character might be thinking and feeling and how he or she resolves the problem. Use these stories as a springboard to discuss how hard it is to resist peer pressure and how many people who bully others might not really want to but are frightened or led into this type of behaviour and how they can get help to stop.

Follow-up exercise: Victim's viewpoint

After the students have completed the exercise above, ask them to write the same story from the viewpoint of the victim. He or she will be confused, frightened and worried, especially when one of his or her friends joins in the gang bullying. Again follow this with discussion about how the victims of bullying may feel and how they can get help.

18. Bulletin board

Using the media, ask students to look for references to bullying, including racist attacks or attacks on gay or lesbian people or incidents of suicide or suicide attempts attributed to bullying in the press over a month. Use these stories to create a bulletin board and to discuss the issue of bullying and ideas about stopping it.

19. Mystery person

Give each student the name of another student and tell them to keep the name of their student a secret. Ask them to telephone each other or talk away from school to students to find out 'different' facts about their Mystery Person – not just biographical details but names of pets, kinds of food they like, secret ambitions, etc. Have the students write about their Mystery Person without giving their name, then read aloud their writing to see if the class can guess who the person is. Start with general information like:

- My Mystery Person loves chocolate ice cream and Chinese food (not mixed together). My Mystery Person secretly wants to become a famous rock star and dye his/her hair blue.
- My Mystery Person likes to go swimming in the holidays. S/he nearly got run over by a car when s/he was three years old.
- My Mystery Person likes to draw, make plasticine models and take things apart to see how they work.
- My Mystery Person is known to smile a lot.
- My Mystery Person has two brothers, a cat, a dog and a gerbil. S/he likes the pets, but sometimes can't stand the brothers.
- My Mystery Person has brown hair and brown eyes and is 5 feet 6 inches tall. Who is s/he?

At various points before the end of the reading, ask the students to raise their hands if they think they know who the Mystery Person is – the comments being read out should all be positive (you may wish to check the stories) and gradually get specific so that the identity of the Mystery Person becomes apparent. This is a good way to focus positively on a student, making them the centre of attention in a nice way and revealing new information about him/her which might be interesting.

20. Bully letter

Ask the students to write a letter to an imaginary bully to try to explain why he or she should try to change and give some suggestions on how to change.

Follow-up exercise: Dear bullied person letter

Ask the students to write to an imaginary victim of bullying telling the victim how they will personally help him or her to stop being a victim and giving advice about how the victim might get some help.

Some of these exercises could be adapted for assemblies or plays. Schools which have successfully combated bullying find that the more time they devote to keeping bullying on the agenda, the fewer incidents of bullying are reported. So the time spent on exercises like these actually save time in the end.

Reference
Elliott, M. and Kilpatrick, J. (1994) *How to Stop Bullying: A Kidscape Training Guide*, Kidscape. (See address under Help Organisations at the end of the book.)

7

■　■　■

Bully 'courts'

MICHELE ELLIOTT

'Why were you bullying Jennifer?' asked Mark in a solemn tone. He peered across the bench at 10-year-old Marina.

'I wasn't', replied Marina, indignantly.

'Tell us what happened, then', chimed in Lucy.

'Well, I was just playin' and Jennifer came up and looked at me. You know, just her dumb look. I said "Who you lookin' at?" She said no one, but I knew she was lookin' at me. I told her to shove off, but she didn't move. I was there first. I only told her to shove off, nothin' more. She's such a wimp to come and tell.'

'Did you touch her at all?'

'No!'

'You sure?'

'Well . . . maybe I accidentally brushed against her, but I didn't hit her or nothin'.'

'Some of the kids say that you pushed her against the wall.'

'Who said that?'

'The kids who say they saw what happened on the playground.'

For the next 15 minutes, the bully, her victim and the witnesses individually told the teacher and the four children on the bench what happened.

The teacher and four children, who comprised the bully 'court', then retired to discuss the case. Was Marina being a bully? Did the witnesses tell the truth? Did Jennifer cause what happened? What sentences could the court impose if Marina was guilty of bullying? Why did she bully her classmates? She had been accused of bullying before. Did she have problems? Could anyone on the court help her? What about the contract they had all signed agreeing that they would not bully (see Chapter 19).

The court decided that Marina did bully Jennifer. In fact, Jennifer had a bruise from landing on the playground after being pushed against the wall. Now it remained to decide what solutions or punishments they would recommend. The debate was intense.

'I think that she should be suspended for two weeks,' said Tony.

'She's been a problem ever since she came to this school.'

'I don't agree,' argued Shofig. 'Suspending her won't prove anything – she'll still be a bully when she comes back.'

'But at least she won't be able to give anyone a hard time for two weeks,' replied Tony.

The teacher, Mrs Clark, intervened. 'We can only recommend suspension to the Headteacher. The court has no power to suspend her.'

'I know,' said Tony, 'but I still think we should recommend it.'

'It would be better to make her do something around school during playtime,' contributed Susan. 'Don't let her on the playground for two weeks, but make her work instead.'

'Yea, like clean the loos,' said Lucy. The children giggled.

'Stop, this is serious,' said Tony reproachfully. Suggestions came more quickly.

'Let's forbid her to go on the school journey next week. That would make her think.'

'No playtime for a month.'

'Too long – not fair.'

'How about the "long and tedious" penalty?' said Shofig.

'What's that?' asked Lucy.

'You know, tearing up ten pieces of paper, throwing them into the air and then picking them all up again.'

'That's dumb,' said Lucy.

'Of course it's dumb – most punishments are dumb.'

'Like writing lines,' said Tony.

The discussion went on fast and furious for another ten minutes. Mrs Clark pointed out that they had to come to a conclusion.

They finally decided that Marina should:

- apologise to Jennifer; then
- stay away from Jennifer and not speak to or even 'look' at her for two weeks;
- write a story about bullying from a *victim*'s point of view;
- not be allowed on the playground for a week; and
- at the end of the week, be assigned to play in a particular place for another week; and
- if she was reported for bullying again and found 'guilty', the court would recommend to the Headteacher that she be suspended.

Jennifer and Marina were called in separately and told of the decision. Marina, who had the option of appealing to the Headteacher, accepted the court's ruling instead. She knew that the Headteacher would have suspended her, so she felt it better to take her punishment from the court.

This bully court was held in a London inner-city primary school. The students, teachers and parents had all agreed to try the bully courts because the problem of bullying was getting worse. The courts were set up with the help of Kidscape, which had pioneered the idea with some 30 pilot schools, both primary and secondary.

The original idea came from a student who was fed up with the petty verbal bullying going on in her school. The teachers and parents were enthusiastic if the courts could be set up in a sensitive and effective way.

After deciding on a whole-school philosophy about bullying (*see* Chapter 19), the students elected two representatives and the teachers nominated two more. One of the teachers agreed to be the adviser and the 'court' was set up.

The idea spread and Kidscape monitored eight schools out of the 30 which took part in a pilot scheme. The students were surveyed to determine the extent of the problem. Over 70 per cent of the students said that they had been bullied at some time. Thirty-five per cent of the bullying happened either at school or travelling to school. At the end of the three-month trial period, 6 per cent of the children said that they had been bullied, a dramatic drop in reported cases. It had appeared that the courts had been a major factor in reducing bullying, so why not introduce them everywhere?

That could be a disaster. The bully courts will only work in schools which have a strong anti-bullying policy which is supported by parents, teachers, staff and children. The court system has only the authority that is given to it by the people. The danger is that it will otherwise become a place of revenge for one group against another. Without the school policy, the bully courts become simply a way of bullying the bullies. The court is the final link in the chain of setting up a complete school anti-bullying strategy involving everyone.

It takes time to forge the chain, from building the self-esteem of children to dealing with themes of safety and caring for one another, ensuring that the relationship between staff and pupils is one of trust and then gradually moving on to roleplaying ways to cope and to roleplaying the court itself.

A crucial test of a school's readiness for bully courts is when children have grasped the principle that there are no bystanders in bullying. You have to foster in children a sense of community and responsibility so they know that if an incident comes to light in which they didn't take part but just walked by, then they are culpable. They are just as guilty as if they had taken part in it. Even if they don't like the child being bullied, they can't walk by.

When that point is reached, putting children in charge of justice through a bully court is feasible. Ask the parents to a meeting, show them a mock court and ask if they approve. If they do, work out the best way forward in your school.

Kidscape suggests the following guidelines.

1 Agree guidelines for behaviour with students.

2 Sign individual contracts with each student re the guidelines.

3 Post the guidelines on bulletin boards throughout the school.

4 Call a school assembly and have students present the guidelines; include all staff, including playground supervisors.

5 As part of the guidelines, set up an arbitration court too.

6 The court could comprise of four students, two elected by the student body and two appointed (as an honour) by the teachers.

7 One teacher would sit on the court (which could be called an ('honour court').

8 The term of office depends upon the agreement of the students – one school term would be suggested.

9 Unless there was an emergency, the court would meet once a week at a set time.

10 The court would be responsible for most infractions, unless they were serious enough to involve the police (i.e. assault) or there was a family problem which made it inappropriate.

11 Solutions and/or penalties would be binding on all parties, with the right of appeal.

12 The verdict of the court would be written down and filed, with copies going to all concerned parties.

13 School governors and parents would receive information about the court and be invited to a meeting to see a mock case and to discuss the issues.

14 The effectiveness of the court would be evaluated by students, parents and teachers.

Suggestions for students

Bully courts have also been useful in coming up with suggestions for students on how to deal with bullies. The following are some of the suggestions for the victims generated by the students and teachers involved.

1 Laugh at or ignore comments or teasing. Remember that these people are ignorant. They want your scared reaction and humour or silence might throw them off. You have to keep it up for a while until they get bored.

2 You can tell them to 'Bug off, elephant breath' or something to that effect. But you must say it angrily and walk away immediately. Practise in the mirror.

3 If it is a group bothering you, look the weakest one of the group in the eye and say 'This isn't funny' and then walk away.

4 You can sign up for self-defence courses which will give you more confidence. These lessons don't necessarily mean you 'fight back', but they can help your confidence.

5 Stay with a crowd – bullies usually pick on kids alone.

6 Ask one of the gang members when they are alone why they find it necessary to gang up on one person.

7 It might help to ring up one of the bullies and ask how they would like it if this was happening to them. This will only work if you have some sort of relationship with that person.

8 Seek the advice of your parents and if they have any ideas, give them a try. You need their advice and support.

9 Do not stop if they confront you. Keep on walking. Get someone to witness what they are doing so that a teacher intervenes without you telling on them.

10 Stop thinking like a victim – you do not deserve this. Walk tall, pretend you are confident even if you are not. Look at the bullies and smile as if they are not frightening you to death, even if you do not feel this way inside. Keep

walking away and ignoring them if nothing else. They will get bored eventually.

11 Claire Rayner's book has good advice and you can get it from the local library. It may help. It is called *Growing Pains and How to Avoid Them.*

12 Keep a diary of all the events, time and place and what is said. Have your parents contact the head teacher or school parent governors (ask the secretary for the names) and tell them what is happening. It is not right that bullying be allowed to go on, nor is it right that the bullies should be allowed to get away with it.

13 Make sure that your case comes before the bully court, so that all can work on the problem together.

The bully courts may not be the right answer for every school. If the groundwork of cooperation has not been laid, they will fail. One headteacher saw the 'courts' as just another form of bullying.

Patricia Godfrey, a primary teacher of over 20 years' experience, disagrees. 'Children see bullying from a different level – they're at eye-level height with others. Their insight can be fresher; they can offer more genuine ideas than adults' (Knuppe, 1990).

Soon after the publicity in the newspapers about the courts, Kidscape received a letter from Robert Laslett, who had set up a children's court for bullies in 1961 at a school for maladjusted children. The court continued to meet twice a week until 1985. He noted that the idea was as old as Homer Lane and his New Commonwealth and that David Wills had a court at Barns in 1940. Robert Laslett confirmed Kidscape's findings about the courts.

> *The success of the court was really due to the relationships between the staff and the children at the school – in a way the court exemplified these relationships. The children knew that we were concerned about bullying and they also knew that they could be quite open about their feelings and behaviour.*
>
> (Laslett, 1975)

If not properly monitored, any system is open to abuse, including the bully courts. Properly used, the courts (we prefer the name councils or arbitration panels, but children like calling them courts) have proven to be an effective way of getting students involved in solving their own problems in a positive and constructive manner. (*See* also Chapter 11 on Scottish councils.)

Drama

Bully 'courts' can also be used as a drama exercise. If the children are secondary school age, ask them to come up with their own scene and characters. If the children are younger, the teacher may have to set the scene. It is possible to use an incident of bullying which has occurred in the past as the basis of the drama, as long as the children involved are no longer in the school. The *Sticks and Stones* video, listed in the Resources section at the back of this book, portrays a fictional bully incident and a 'court' which meets to discuss what to do. It serves as an example of how to use bully 'courts' as an effective drama exercise with students.

References

Knuppe, J. (1990) 'Pupils put bullies in the dock', *The Sunday Times*, 6 May.

Laslett, R. (1975) 'A children's Court for Bullies', *Special Education*, Vol. 9, No. 1, pp. 9–11.

8

■ ■ ■

Promoting, permitting and preventing bullying

WENDY STAINTON ROGERS

This chapter is about how teachers can help to reduce bullying both by the *way* they teach, and by *what* they teach. In terms of approaches to teaching, although it may seem apparently obvious, it may be helpful to consider teaching approaches along a spectrum with, at one extreme, approaches which actively *promote* bullying and at the other ones which specifically seek to *prevent* bullying. And in between we can consider bullying-*permissive* approaches of varying degrees of complicity, in the degree to which they provide the conditions under which bullying can flourish.

Bullying-promoting approaches to teaching

Celia Kitzinger, in an analysis she conducted on experiences of humiliation, described a number of examples of teachers who humiliated their pupils. A strand which runs through most of the accounts is the apparent 'triviality' of the event, and yet the enormous pain engendered, sometimes remembered vividly for 40 or 50 years. For example, one man in his sixties, describing what happened to him when he was nine, spoke about getting help from a cousin with maths, his worst subject, in order to prepare for a test at school. With her sympathy, patience and skill, his confidence was restored. However, this did not last long:

> The black day came, I tried hard on the ten sums presented and knew I had not done excellently, but reasonably well. A few days later our results were read out from the teacher's dias. Mr B—'s declaration ran something like this: 'Reynolds – seven out of ten. If you had done as I expected you might have got five out of ten; it is obvious that you have cheated, so I'm giving you three out of ten.' That remained my recorded mark. It was a terrible, humiliating, bitter experience.

(Kitzinger, 1988: 1–2)

Whenever a teacher deliberately humiliates a pupil, then the teacher is, quite simply, engaging in bullying. It really does not matter to the pupil whether the intention is merely to exert control or to gain personal gratification. The core of humiliation Kitzinger describes as being made to feel powerless, of 'having our noses rubbed in our own powerlessness, being forced to accept that we are without power' (Kitzinger, 1988: 11). Bullying is about the misuse of power.

It would be pleasant to assume that this kind of teacher-bullying was something that only happened in the past. Unfortunately most secondary school pupils, at least, will tell you that in their school there are one or two teachers who regularly use intimidation, sarcasm, belittling or harassment towards pupils, and that most teachers, on occasion, will resort to this kind of behaviour (Lawson, 1994).

At the risk of moralising then (and if it makes it any better, I will plead guilty for my time as a schoolteacher) the most obvious – but crucial – point is that tackling bullying first of all requires teachers themselves to stop bullying. Young people are highly sensitive to hypocrisy, and will soon tumble the school which pays lip-service to bullying as a problem, but is unwilling to challenge the behaviour of the staff.

However, I would argue that as well as *being* bullying, such behaviour also *promotes* bullying. It does this by conveying a clear message that such behaviour is legitimate – it is all right, even desirable, to exploit your superior power to get your own way. Teachers who themselves bully are saying, in their actions, 'Powerful people are those who get their own way by using their power' or, possibly more insidiously, 'It's all right to gain satisfaction or the approval of others by making another feel humiliated.' And whether they do this by wielding individual power, or whether it occurs via an ethos in the whole school of collective intimidation, pupils are being explicitly and directly shown a role model of oppression.

However, even where explicit bullying itself is not involved, similar messages may be conveyed by behaviour which implies that some people are 'fair game', e.g. teaching which promotes racist and sexist beliefs. Such forms of prejudice promote bullying, because the message here is that certain people can be treated as less than human or are legitimate targets for ridicule. Often such acts are presented as 'just a lark' in order to cover up their intent. This reminds me of a Turkish saying that, 'When the cat wants to eat her kittens, she calls them mice.' In other words, one way to pretend you are not mistreating others is to redefine what you are doing – as a joke, as something not to be taken seriously.

For example, such a motivated delusion allows some male teachers to make suggestive comments to young women pupils, because what they are doing is not 'bullying' but 'just a bit of fun'. Such treatment, in whatever form it comes, conveys the subtle message that if the 'victim' objects, it is because she or he does not have a sense of humour. Jaqui Halson, in a study of gender relations in schools, stresses just how common this sexual harassment is in schools:

Some of the more common forms of sexual harassment are often trivialized or dismissed as 'inoffensive' or 'friendly'; 'just teasing' or 'just larking around'.

(Halson, 1989: 131–2)

Yet Halson suggests that sexual harassment between teachers and pupils is common:

It is ordinary, everyday behaviour. It conforms to what is widely considered 'normal' in mixed-sex interactions. Although it is clearly inappropriate given the relationship here – that of teacher and student – it is commonplace masculine behaviour, behaviour which makes those on the receiving end – women and girls – feel uncomfortable and threatened.

(Halson, 1989: 133)

Similar treatment may be meted out to the child who is overweight, or poor at sports, or otherwise different. On the surface this may seem a long way from bullying. In truth the message is more subtle, but much the same as with overt racism or sexism: 'This person's discomfort is really rather a joke,' and, 'It's OK to get pleasure out of another person's uneasiness.' And again, although it may be obvious, even mildly sexist or racist jokes or innocuous comments about a child's physical appearance may not only directly humiliate the child, but may also 'set up' the child as the bully's victim.

Bullying-permissive teaching

Schools and classrooms which rely on status differentials, where hierarchical divisions of power are evident and where strict and impenetrable barriers are imposed between staff and pupils offer the conditions under which bullying can flourish. They do this in two main ways. First, the official sanctioning of status and power as mechanisms for control creates an ethos within which the *misuse* of power can thrive. Second, such structures make it very difficult for pupils to seek help if they are being victimised, or for them to negotiate for conditions which make them less vulnerable.

We are slowly learning, as parents, that the best defence we can offer our children against being sexually abused is to listen to their worries, and for them to feel they can come to us for protection when they need it. Much the same message is true for the school that truly wants to tackle bullying. It will need to make sure that all children have somebody they can trust, to whom they will turn in times of trouble, in the knowledge that this person will listen to their fears, take them seriously, and do something about them. But such conditions cannot comfortably coexist within a system where there is, for example, mutual mistrust between teachers and pupils, or where the pupil who turns for help is treated like a 'sneak' or a 'cissy'. A school where a request for help is treated like an admission of weakness will be a place where the bully will prosper.

Bullying-preventive teaching

The contrast comes when we consider bullying-*preventive* teaching. I would suggest this is of two kinds. The first is, straightforwardly, an approach to teaching which is alert to and aware of the conditions which make some pupils vulnerable, and avoids endorsing these. This is about treating all pupils with a level of respect, and avoiding (whatever the temptation) making jokes at the expense of the weakest. It is about not contributing to a pupil's vulnerability, about not setting up victims. It is also about acting as a good role model, as somebody who does not misuse the power they have.

More proactively bullying-preventive teaching is about publicly acknowledging that bullying is not acceptable, putting it specifically on the agenda at your school and in your class, and creating opportunities which will help staff and pupils to develop strategies to counteract bullying. Overall what is needed is to change the way that pupils behave towards each other. To do this the pupils themselves must *want* to change. And they need strategies – they must *know* how to change.

Wanting to change comes down to 'changing hearts and minds' – to alter what people do, you need to get them to alter the way they see the world. To reduce bullying we need to make such actions 'unthinkable'. Unfortunately, the processes which underpin changing minds are not at all easy to influence – if they were, advertisers would not spend the massive sums they do. Getting somebody to change their perception or opinion takes a lot more than simply telling them to.

Wanting to change

Pupils need to be convinced that change is necessary, and that they have something to gain themselves out of making changes. To do this they need to develop greater empathy with those subjected to bullying. A good place to start is to get the class to describe incidents when they felt helpless and frightened. They can work, for example, in pairs, together writing a list of the feelings they had, which then gets shared with the wider group. Younger children may do this with few inhibitions. Older pupils may well find it easier to work from a short 'story' about somebody their own age, than talk directly about themselves. This is particularly useful for exposing the hurtfulness of apparently innocuous teasing or being the butt of jokes. Another approach is roleplay, though this needs careful handling. For example, pupils can work in pairs to play out a scene of a tease that turns nasty, and then talk about what they felt.

Knowing how to change

An approach that has worked well in adult training is an exercise based on getting people to construct a blueprint for a *Bully's Paradise*. It works like this.

The class divides into seven groups, each of which examines a particular aspect of the school: physical features (like buildings, surrounding roads, furniture); time (such as timetabling, pressures, flexibility); communication; rules; people; resources; and knowledge and expertise. Their task is to design the features of the school, so that bullying is easy to do, hard to discover, difficult to stamp out – a bully's paradise (*see* Chapter 17).

They will need at least twenty minutes to draw up their blueprint, and should then report back to the class as a whole. The final result should be a description of those features of school which encourage and permit bullying, from the presence of unsupervised areas to the difficulty of finding somebody sympathetic to turn to. Usually this whole process is quite amusing – people often take wry pleasure in devising something really dreadful – and especially where it is all so close to home! It tends to get more serious once attention is directed upon the potential for unhappiness and harm that is uncovered in their own school.

This is the point at which to begin working with the class to see how the 'nightmare' qualities can be tackled, with the class drawing up a manifesto of what needs to change to make the school somewhere where bullying is made as unlikely as possible – somewhere that, when bullying happens, it can be rapidly detected and challenged.

It is important for pupils to have the opportunity to do this, since they are the experts about where and how bullying goes on. Even those explicitly engaged in it themselves may find it hard to resist the nightmare 'game', which may offer insights otherwise extremely elusive. But it is also an excellent activity for staff, for parents and governors. Indeed, although the idea is simple, it has proved highly effective in helping schools to devise anti-bullying strategies by getting pupils, teachers and parents to work together.

References

Halson, J. (1989) 'The sexual harassment of young women', in L. Holly (ed.), *Girls and Sexuality: Teachers and Learning*, Milton Keynes, Open University Press.

Kitzinger, C. (1988) *Humiliation*, paper presented to the British Psychological Society London Conference, December.

Lawson, S. (1994) *Helping Children Cope with Bullying*, London, Sheldon Press.

9

■ ■ ■

What can be done about the bully?

JOHN PEARCE

Introduction

Aggression comes in many different forms and bullying is one of them. Our attitude to bullying is important because it sets the standard for the general level of aggression that is deemed to be acceptable. So when we say to the victim of bullying, 'You will have to get used to it – bullying is just part of everyday life,' we make a statement accepting that degree of aggression and violence. Many of the issues that relate to bullies also apply to vandalism, hooliganism and other forms of violence and aggression in society. Until we are prepared to deal with bullying wherever it occurs, there seems little chance that other forms of aggressive and destructive behaviour will reduce in frequency.

Definitions of bullying vary, but there are three essential elements that are always present:

- the deliberate use of aggression;
- an unequal power relationship between the bully and victim;
- the causing of physical pain and/or emotional distress.

The aggression of the bully can take many different forms, ranging from teasing at the mild end of physical violence or emotional abuse at its most extreme. The overlap between bullying and teasing is an important one to recognise because teasing is usually considered to be quite acceptable. But if the teasing involves intimidation and results in distress, it clearly falls within the definition of bullying.

It is the intentional use of aggression that makes bullying on the one hand so appalling and yet on the other hand it means that the aggression can, at least potentially, be controlled. In the same way that bullying is started on purpose, it can also be stopped deliberately – if the bully so wishes. It is this element of control over the aggressive behaviour that makes it possible to be optimistic about being able to reduce the frequency and severity of bullying.

In order to deal effectively with the bully it is helpful to have some background information about the frequency, methods and outcome of bullying and aggressive behaviour. This chapter will consider these aspects first and then go on to look at what makes a bully and what can be done about the bully.

How often does bullying occur?

The research on bullying has produced results that show a wide range in how often it occurs. Much of this variability is due to differences in the way bullying is defined and how the data is collected. Some researchers, such as Olweus (1987) in Scandinavia, have used a definition that requires bullying to be repeated, which therefore excludes the single episode, no matter how severe. For many years Professor Dan Olweus at the University of Bergen has been a leader in the research on bullying within schools. He has mainly used questionnaires completed by pupils to identify bullying behaviour. The use of peer report has much to recommend it because the children are directly involved and they can give first-hand information. There is no evidence that children give false answers.

Using reports from children, teachers and parents Olweus (1989) found that about 11 per cent of primary school children experienced significant bullying. By secondary school age the number of victims had been reduced by half. On the other hand, the number of children identified as bullies stayed fairly constant at around 7 per cent at both primary and secondary age. An overall figure of 15 per cent of Scandinavian children involved in bullying as victims or bullies is rather lower than some of the UK findings. For example, Elliott (1994) found that almost 40 per cent of children had experienced bullying and Stephenson and Smith (1988) noted that bullying in some primary schools was found to involve up to 50 per cent of children, but some children – usually in much smaller schools – reported no bullying at all.

Bullying is carried out in many different ways. When it occurs in groups, it has been referred to as 'mobbing' (Pikas, 1975). But more usually bullying occurs with a single victim being the target. Bullying can be either direct or indirect. Direct bullying consists of physical aggression, hurtful words or unpleasant faces and gestures. Boys engage in direct bullying about four times more frequently than girls. Indirect bullying involves ignoring, isolating or denying wishes and is used more frequently by girls (Olweus, 1993).

An important subgroup are both bullies and the victims of other bullies. In a nationwide survey of schoolchildren in Norway, Olweus (1989) found that about 20 per cent of the bullies fell into this category. These children who bully and who are themselves bullied are generally regarded as more disturbed than the typical bully. They will be referred to again later.

Looking at the problem of more generalised aggression, up to 30 per cent of children aged 8–12 years were found to be significantly aggressive (Pfeffer *et al.*, 1987) and in the classic study of children of a similar age on the Isle of Wight, 1 per cent were observed to show seriously aggressive behaviour (Rutter *et al.*, 1970). It is reasonable to conclude that at any one time at least one in seven schoolchildren are either bullies or victims, but during a whole-school career an even larger number of children will have been affected by bullying. The finding that the frequency of bullying reduces by half in secondary school does not mean that children stop bullying as they grow older; in fact it seems that the number of bullies remains much the same, but the victims are fewer and the episodes of bullying are less frequent (Olweus, 1989).

Does bullying matter?

If bullying is so common, why should anyone bother about it? What is the evidence that it is harmful? Could there be a connection between the level of aggression we accept in our children and later acts of violence, such as football hooliganism and domestic violence? The answer is almost certainly 'yes', but so many different factors have an influence that it is difficult to disentangle them.

There is good evidence that aggressive behaviour in children over 8 years old has a strong tendency to continue. In the important 30 year follow-up the sociologist Lee Robins (1978) found that children with aggressive and antisocial behaviour were likely to continue to behave in this way with more than one in four still showing significant aggression control problems. Very similar findings have been reported in a 22 year follow-up by Eron *et al.* (1987) and a review of 16 shorter longitudinal studies of aggressive children followed up over various periods from 2–18 years, also concluded that about one in four grow up into aggressive adults (Olweus, 1984).

The following adult problems have been shown to be significantly associated with aggressive behaviour during childhood – especially for older children:

- aggressive behaviour;
- criminal convictions;
- alcohol abuse;
- child care problems;
- employment problems;
- marital breakdown;
- psychiatric disorder.

The very poor outlook for some 25 per cent of aggressive children seems to be similar for males and females. However, it is probably not a direct relationship and is more likely to be due to an accumulation of negative life experiences. Although the prognosis for aggression in childhood is gloomy, it is important to remember that a significant number of aggressive children manage to gain some control over their antisocial behaviour and do reasonably well.

What happens to children who bully is less well researched than the fate of children with generalised aggressive behaviour. However, in a 12 year follow-up of 12-year-old bullies, Olweus (1989) has shown that they were twice as likely to have a criminal conviction by 24 years old than the general population. And multiple offending was four times more frequent in the bullies.

Unfortunately even less is known about the long-term effects of bullying on the victims. The short-term distress is obvious enough, but what happens later on is less clear. There are reports from adults who have been subjected to physical abuse as children that there are serious long-term effects (Abramson et al., 1987), but it is not clear how much of this is due to the direct experience of violence and how much due to a more general neglect of their emotional needs.

Olweus (1978) suggests that victims – he calls them 'whipping boys' – tend to be unpopular, generally anxious and to have low self-esteem. How many of the victim's characteristics were there before the bullying and how many are caused by it is unclear, but a three year follow-up showed that there was little change in the victims and they remained as unpopular as ever. The social isolation and anxiety of victims is bound to have an adverse effect on the development of self-image and self-esteem which have been shown to be so important in protecting children from negative life experiences (Rutter, 1987).

Being bullied is a potentially damaging experience for the victim and there may be long-term consequences for vulnerable children. There is some evidence that merely observing another child being bullied can be emotionally damaging (Olweus, 1978). The outlook for the bully is particularly poor with a significant number continuing to behave aggressively, causing a heavy cost to society in terms of finance, emotional distress and physical damage over many years.

The typical bully

It is helpful to make a distinction between three main types of bully because each one requires a rather different approach in the way they are managed.

The aggressive bully

Most bullies are in this group. They are generally aggressive and are prepared to direct their aggression against teachers, parents and other adults as well as other children and they see little wrong in their aggression and bullying. Aggressive bullies are often involved in other antisocial behaviour and they are *not* anxious, insecure or friendless. The following characteristics are typical of the aggressive bully:

- aggressive to any person, no matter what position of authority;
- poor impulse control;
- violence seen as positive quality;
- wishing to dominate;
- physically and emotionally strong;
- insensitive to the feelings of others;
- good self-esteem.

The anxious bully

About 20 per cent of bullies fall into this category. They are generally more disturbed than any of the other types of bully or victim and they share many of the characteristics of the victim at the same time as being a bully, such as:

- anxious *and* aggressive;
- low self-esteem;
- insecure and friendless;
- pick on 'unsuitable' victims (e.g. more powerful than they are);
- provoke attacks by other bullies;
- emotionally unstable.

The passive bully

The majority of bullying involves more people than just the bully and the victim. The bullies often gather a small group around them and then select a single victim who is isolated from any protective relationships. The bully's followers get involved partly to protect themselves and partly to have the status of belonging to the group. These bullying gangs sometimes operate in a rather similar way to the Mafia and engage in extortion and protection rackets. The followers become involved in bullying in a passive way and have the following characteristics:

- easily dominated;
- passive and easily led;
- not particularly aggressive;
- have empathy for others' feelings;
- feel guilty after bullying.

How bullies are made

So far we have looked at how frequent and how serious bullying is. And having identified the three main types of bullying we now need to consider the various factors that encourage children to be aggressive and to bully. This in turn will help us to know what to do about this destructive form of behaviour. It is now clear that there are a wide range of different factors that interact with each other to produce aggression in children. In order to simplify the very complex issues the main causative factors will be grouped under three headings: those that arise within the child, those in the family and those that come from society and the outside world.

The child's contribution

Being male seems to predispose to aggressive behaviour, but is this innate or due to cultural expectations? A detailed review by Maccoby and Jacklin (1974) concluded that both human and animal males show more aggression than females. Another study that looked at children from six separate cultures found that the sex differences persisted across cultures (Whiting and Edwards, 1973). It is reasonable to assume that constitutional factors (i.e. 'how you are made') play an important part in aggressive behaviour.

The male sex 'Y' chromosome may play a direct part in the development of aggression, or may work indirectly through the production of the hormone testosterone. These effects are brought about through the complex interactions of many different factors rather than by a single cause. David Shaffer *et al.* (1980) examined the various constitutional influences and noted the following research findings:

- individuals with an extra Y chromosome tend to show increased aggression;
- criminal males are more likely to have additional Y chromosomal material;
- XYY individuals are more likely to have abnormal brain function as measured by the electro-encephalograph (EEG);
- some studies show that exposure to high levels of female hormones are associated with a decrease in aggression in children;
- some studies show an increase of aggression associated with high levels of testosterone in both boys and men;
- other studies don't show this, but none show that testosterone decreases aggression;
- certain parts of the brain, particularly the hypothalamus and the mid-brain, can cause or inhibit aggression, although this may depend on previous experience of aggression and the social context.

It is well recognised that boys are more overactive than girls and this increased activity is, in turn, linked to the later development of aggression and antisocial behaviour (Richman *et al.*, 1982).

A child's temperament has been shown to have an influence on behaviour. Important research in America by Thomas and Chess (1977) reported on nine temperamental characteristics that were noted shortly after birth and then followed up into later childhood. The following characteristics were found to be associated with an increased frequency of difficult behaviour, including aggression, tempers and irritability:

- irregular, unpredictable eating and sleeping habits;
- strong, mostly negative moods;
- slow to adapt to new situations.

Very similar findings were reported by Graham *et al.* (1973) in the UK. Using the above characteristics, they identified a temperamental adversity index that was able to predict those children who were likely to have problems a year later. A high score gave a threefold increase in the risk of difficult or aggressive behaviour at home and an eightfold risk of problems at school. Children who show the above characteristics from birth onwards are often said to have the 'Difficult Child Syndrome'. Such children are reported to push, hit and fight more in nursery school (Billman and McDevitt, 1980).

Outside influences

The children who are eventually excluded from school share some of the characteristics of bullies in that they are usually boys who are physically and verbally aggressive (Nicol *et al.*, 1985). But they also have some of the characteristics of the victim in that they are likely to have been rejected by the other children and to have had a poor school attendance. Excluded girls are just as aggressive as the boys and the majority seem to fall into the category of the 'anxious bully', adding to the evidence that this is a more disturbed group. Unfortunately, once excluded, very few of these aggressive children return to normal schooling (Galloway *et al.*, 1982).

The school itself may influence the development of aggressive behaviour (Besag, 1995). Several studies show that even if school-intake factors are controlled for, there remain consistent findings that bullying and aggression occurs more frequently in schools with:

- low staff morale;
- high teacher turnover;
- unclear standards of behaviour;
- inconsistant methods of discipline;
- poor organisation;

- inadequate supervision;
- lack of awareness of children as individuals.

Large schools, large classes and the type of punishment were not directly linked with aggressive behaviour in children.

Influence of TV and films

There is increasing evidence that watching aggressive acts in real life or on TV lowers the threshold for aggressive acts in children and that this effect is more marked in children who already tend to react aggressively (Friedrich and Stein, 1973). A review by Henningham *et al.* (1982) concluded that the introduction of TV to the United States has led to an increase in crime rates. Similar findings have been reported in the Lebanon where the effect of real-life and film aggression as well as cartoons on children attending a primary school was studied by Day and Ghandour (1984). They found that:

- boys showed more aggression than girls;
- filmed violence increases aggression in boys but not girls;
- real-life violence increases aggression in both boys and girls;
- Lebanese boys are more aggressive in their play than American boys;
- the effect of aggression in cartoons was as powerful as human aggression on film.

There is evidence that some children are more vulnerable to the effects of TV than others. The 1982 US Public Health Report on the effects of TV concluded that:

- children with low ability and restricted social life watch more TV;
- heavy viewing was associated with high anxiety, maladjustment, insecurity and a feeling of being rejected (i.e. the anxious bully);
- heavy viewing and aggression were strongly linked in younger children;
- bright children tended to fall behind with their work.

In spite of all the accumulated evidence, the adverse effects of TV remain difficult to quantify because there are so many variables. However, there is general agreement that certain children are particularly susceptible to becoming more aggressive as a result of watching violence on films, even if this is in cartoon form.

The influence of the family

Family influences are frequently blamed for the bad behaviour of children, but as has been noted above, there is plenty of evidence to suspect factors outside the control of the family. So what part does the family play? A review of the research on aggressive and antisocial behaviour in children by Wolff (1985) concluded that the following family factors were associated with childhood aggression:

- absence of the father;
- loss of a parent through divorce rather than through death;
- a depressed mother;
- an irritable parent;
- marital discord;
- socioeconomic disadvantage;
- large family size.

Some of these factors could cause childhood aggression, but they could also be the result of having an aggressive child. For example, having an aggressive and difficult child would be enough to make any parent irritable, but on the other hand it is easy to see how an irritable and hostile parent could make a child feel aggressive. What usually happens is that a vicious circle develops between the child and the parent, each making the other more aggressive. Patterson (1982) has described aggressive behaviours in children and parents which lead on to a predictable sequence of events called 'the coercive system' as follows.

1 Aggressive children make it difficult for their parents to use the more subtle forms of management of deviant behaviour and to encourage good behaviour.

2 The aggressive child may produce an aggressive response from the parent, which then serves as a model or example for the child to follow. Or the parent may give in 'for a quiet life', in which case the child will learn that it pays to be aggressive.

3 The level of aggression in the family rises and anarchy follows, leading to a further breakdown of caring and helping behaviours in family interactions.

4 As a result, the parents tend to become miserable and irritable. They lose their confidence and self-esteem and their children have similar feelings of frustation.

5 Family members disengage from each other, the parents become disunited and the control of aggressive behaviour breaks down, resulting in still further violence.

Olweus (1984) has suggested that there are family factors that predispose children to become bullies. In particular, the style of relationships and attitude to aggression seem to be most important – as outlined below:

1 a negative emotional attitude from the primary caretaker, characterised by lack of warmth and lack of involvement;

2 a tolerant or even permissive attitude to aggression, with no clear limits for aggressive behaviour;

3 a power assertion approach to child rearing, where physical punishment and violent emotional outbursts are the usual control methods.

The links between the characteristics of the individual child, the family and the social setting in which the aggressive behaviour occurs are increasingly seen as important (Goldstein and Keller, 1987). Therefore what happens in the home and at school must always be taken into account when trying to work out why a child is aggressive.

What can be done about the bully?

It may seem that a lot of background has been covered before considering how to deal with the bully. However, unless there is a very good understanding of the underlying issues it will be difficult to manage aggression successfully. This section will look only at the strategies for dealing with the individual bully rather than more general approaches such as the bully courts and non-aggression contracts between the school, the parents and the pupil. The more general approaches that schools can use to deal with bullying are dealt with in other chapters.

There are some principles of aggression management that need to be identified before starting out to deal with the bully:

- bullying in any form is unacceptable;
- early intervention is important;
- individuals must take responsibility for their own actions;
- parents must take responsibility for their own children;
- failure to deal with the bully will only encourage further aggression.

Prevention of bullying is obviously the first goal to aim for, but if this fails, the motivation for the aggression needs to be considered before taking action against the bully. At the same time, the victim will need protection and given help to become more assertive and less of a target for bullying (*see* Chapter 11). Finally the bully must always be expected to make reparation for any damage and distress that has been caused.

Prevention of bullying

Most of the preventative actions against bullying should be started at home before a child even enters school. Parents have the important task of preparing their children to fit into the social world outside the family. By the time that children start at school they should have been taught to have some control over their aggressive impulses and to appreciate that other people have needs too. Children vary a great deal in how easily they learn to be socially competent, but however slow they may be, the process is the same. Parents can help to socialise their children in the following ways:

- setting an example of good relationships;
- having good aggression control themselves;
- making it clear that violent aggression is unacceptable;
- stopping any show of unacceptable aggression immediately;
- identifying and naming the effects of aggression;
- describing how the victim of aggression feels;
- teaching caring and empathic relationships.

Unfortunately there has been a tendency to assume that any repression of aggression is bad and that children should be allowed or even encouraged to show their feelings openly. In fact most young children are only too ready to let everyone know how they feel! Children can best learn self-control by being given external control first, which is then internalised to become incorporated as part of themselves. As children grow older the amount of external control and supervision that they need decreases, but if it is phased out too quickly or not provided in the first place, the result is likely to be an uncontrolled and disobedient child. The balance between external and internal control is a delicate one that has to be continuously readjusted to the needs of each child at each stage of development – a process that is more an art than a science.

Children who are constitutionally predisposed to aggressive behaviour as a result of their genetic, hormonal or temperamental make-up will require special attention to prevent the development of aggression and bullying. However, the approach is no different than that for ordinary children. There is no magic solution or missing extra ingredient that is necessary. In practice all that these difficult children require is 'super parenting' – in other words, the best possible child care, which would include:

- teaching responsibility for self and others;
- teaching respect for self and others;
- teaching caring and gentleness;
- teaching appropriate assertiveness and aggression;
- providing firm, clear and consistent standards of behaviour;
- maintaining a predictable, regular routine for everyday life;
- channelling all show of aggression by distraction and early intervention;
- supervising situations where aggression is likely;
- avoiding exposure to violence in the home, at school or on video/film/TV;
- never allowing unacceptable aggression to produce beneficial results for children – it must always have a 'cost' that has to be paid in reparation.

Note that the first four items on the list involve teaching. This is an important point that underlines the necessity for active prevention of bullying. It is no good expecting children to naturally grow out of their aggression without adult intervention. The active training of children is so significant in the prevention of unacceptable aggression and bullying that each of the above items will be dealt with with an outline of some practical approaches that can be made.

Teaching responsibility for self and others

There is only one way of learning responsibility and that is by being given it. But if children are given too much responsibility before they are ready, this can lead to excessive anxiety or even failure to cope. The responsibility has to be increased gradually step by step and adjusted to the individual child's special requirements. This can only be done with a good understanding of the unique needs of each child and with continuing supervision. The supervision is necessary to identify any problems early on and protect children from failure, which in the context of taking responsibility can be particularly damaging or even dangerous.

These points may be obvious, but the implications are frequently missed. To teach a child responsibility not only demands a detailed knowledge of that particular child but also takes time. This is made even more difficult when children have to be dealt with as a group or where the adults have other commitments or priorities. However, if concerned adults do manage to take time out to consider the needs of an individual child and to provide one-to-one attention when required, the payoff for all concerned is great.

Teaching respect

Self-respect and respect for others are intimately bound up together. They complement each other, the one being the mirror image of the other. So a child who lacks self-respect cannot be expected to have respect for others. It is not difficult to find children who have little self-respect – in other words, a poor self-image. Children who feel bad about themselves will not only find pleasure in behaving badly but will also have minimal respect for themselves or for others – unless they too are also bad in some way. Teaching respect can, therefore, be achieved by improving children's self-image and by showing them respect. The setting of a good example by adults is one of the best ways of teaching children about these highly complex issues that are extremely difficult to explain in words. Just saying 'Do it this way' is not sufficient – most children also need an example to follow.

Teaching caring and gentleness

Some children seem to be naturally caring, but most are not and have to be patiently taught. As has already been highlighted, an adult's good example is one of the best ways of helping children to learn how to be caring – children who feel cared for will also care for others. In addition to this, it is usually necessary to specifically teach children how to be kind and gentle. This may mean taking a child by the hand and demonstrating in minute detail exactly what is required, in much the same way that a child might be taught to write a word – 'This is how you do it. Now you do it.'

Teaching appropriate assertiveness and aggression

There is nothing wrong with aggression that is properly directed and adequately regulated. For example, many sports require the use of controlled aggression which can serve as good learning experiences for practising the management of anger and aggression. Some of the martial arts are particularly good at aggression control. There are very clear rules about how and when aggression can be used and very close supervision is given to make sure that the strict code of conduct is followed.

Children also learn about aggression control through play, both in imagination and in play-fighting games with other children. Once again, close supervision, and if necessary active intervention, is required if the level of aggression gets out of hand. It is not unusual for children to play very aggressive imaginary games with bombs, blood and bodies everywhere and it is easy to be perplexed by how such seemingly innocent children could be so aggressive. Imaginary play and rough and tumble games are a helpful way for children to learn how to gain control over strong emotions. However, excessively aggressive play of any kind should be actively discouraged and the energy directed more constructively. This limited setting for aggressive display in the safe situation of play and imagination is by far the best way of teaching children about aggression control.

Setting rules and routines for everyday life

To some extent the display of unacceptable aggression or bullying can be seen as a failure of discipline – where the child has either not learned the rules of reasonable behaviour or has deliberately broken them. It is worth remembering that the word 'discipline' comes from the Latin *disciplina* meaning to teach. The importance of teaching the management of aggressive impulses has already been stressed and clear, consistent discipline is a necessary precondition if children are to have a chance of learning right from wrong.

It obviously helps if there is consistency between the standards set at home and those set at school, but this is not absolutely essential because children are quite good at knowing what is acceptable behaviour in different situations. For example, children soon learn to behave very differently with those teachers who are strict compared with other teachers who are easy-going in the standards of acceptable behaviour that they set.

Rules usually need to be repeated over and over again until they become an automatic part of everyday life. This is the advantage of making aggression control so much part of the regular daily routine that bullying would be unthinkable in the same way as it would be to go to bed with shoes on or to eat sitting on the table! The incorporation of rules of social relationships into the routines of daily life is a very effective way of achieving required standards of discipline. Once this has been achieved it will only occasionally be necessary to repeat the rules or to have to use discipline, and bullying would be much less likely to occur.

Supervising and channelling aggression

The crucial importance of closely supervising children to prevent bullying has already been stressed. The necessary level of supervision that each child requires will vary, but it is not difficult to tell whether or not the level has been judged correctly – if bullying occurs it can be reasonably assumed that there is insufficient supervision. Although this may sound an impractical and superficial approach, most bullying takes place when normal supervision is at its lowest. Good supervision is not only very effective, but it allows any bullying to be dealt with immediately before too much damage is done.

One of the advantages of channelling aggression into sports, as suggested above, is that sporting activities usually have a high level of supervision. The rules of behaviour in all sports are clear and have to be applied consistently under close supervision. Sport and competitive games have the potential to provide an excellent basis for channelling and managing aggression.

Avoiding the promotion of aggression

All the hard work outlined above may be to little effect if at the same time bullying and other unacceptably aggressive behaviour is being encouraged either by example or by being rewarded. The adverse effect on vulnerable children of observing violence and aggression either in reality or fictional is now so well established (*see* page 77) that it would be incongruous to allow children to be exposed to this and then to complain that they are aggressive bullies.

If aggressive behaviour is seen to bring rewards, it is, of course, likely to continue. The reward of bullying may be something that is less obvious than the immediate excitement of having power over another person, such as achieving high status within a group or gaining a perverse personal satisfaction by passing on to someone else the aggression received from another bully. All possible rewards that could be had from bullying must be considered and avoided as far as possible.

Most of us would find the above programme for the prevention of aggression difficult to keep to and some less adequate parents could not be expected to follow it through at all. In such cases extra help from relatives or other family supporters, playground leaders or teachers will be needed with these parental tasks. This additional help can be very effective and make all the difference to a child.

Dealing with the bully caught in the act

Bullies who are caught in the act can be very difficult to deal with because they will easily turn their aggression onto whoever tries to intervene, often with very little concern for who it is. Here are some guidelines to take into consideration when planning to stop bullying at the time that it is happening.

- It is usually best to remove the victim from the scene as quickly as possible rather than challenge the bully. This resolves the problem without the risk of escalating the violence.
- Telling a bully that he or she will be dealt with later without specifying how or when can be very effective. The bully is likely to worry about what may happen and will have a chance to reflect on what's been done wrong.
- There is no point in being aggressive with a bully. Aggression only breeds more aggression so the problem will probably become worse.
- Any physical intervention will almost certainly lead to someone getting hurt, unless the bully is very young. And if the bully is a teenager, some form of damage is predictable. Very rarely it may be necessary to get physically involved to protect a victim in which case it is best to obtain as much additional help as possible.

After the bullying

Every time bullying takes place it marks a failure, a failure that could potentially have been prevented. There are several different aspects to the failure which affect the bully, the victim and the observers:

- the bully has failed to learn that bullying is unacceptable;
- there has been a failure to teach the bully aggression control;
- the victim has failed to be assertive enough and failed to be protected;
- there has been a failure in adult supervision.

The above points highlight the fact that responsibility for a bullying episode should not be focused on the bully alone. Parents, teachers, other adults and the victims all have a part to play, so that just focusing on the bully is unlikely to be effective on its own.

All the issues highlighted in the section on the prevention of bullying need to be reviewed following an episode of bullying, as well as a further consideration of the factors that predispose to bullying. Have all the points been thought through? Has everything been done to change those aspects that can be altered to make bullying less likely – probably not!

Although it should be made clear to bullies that they are responsible for their own actions, it is important that the adults responsible for the supervision and teaching of aggression control should also take some responsibility. The parents and teachers must therefore cooperate to improve the supervision and training to try and prevent a repetition of the bullying. Adults are good at making excuses and it is important not to be thrown by these. Preconceived ideas need to be challenged and excuses such as, 'I can't do anything about it – I have tried everything' or 'It is nothing to do with me – you deal with it' should not be accepted.

The fact that adults are taking bullying seriously can have a powerful effect on children, especially if they see adults coming together and acting in unity against the bully. Action also needs to be seen to be taken to protect the victim. The serious discussion of a bullying episode (involving everyone concerned) is an important step to take whether at home or at school. The bully court is a helpful and structured way of doing this, but may not suit all situations (*see* Chapter 7). The seriousness with which adults take the bullying can be enhanced by exaggerating the formality of the occasion and of the discussion, even if it occurs within the informality of a family home.

The three different types of bullies may require rather different management, although the basic principles are the same and have already been covered.

The aggressive bully

The approach that has been outlined above is particularly relevant to the aggressive bully. The more aggression the bully shows the more applicable it is. A very aggressive child will require special management and extremely close supervision if the aggression is to be brought under control. It may help to ask for outside help at an early stage and to be prepared to put a great deal of effort into getting things right – and most important of all, to stick at it. As a rough guide, if every intervention is being carried through correctly it should be possible to achieve an improvement in six weeks and a satisfactory state of affairs in six months. However, it must be recognised that other children also have needs and there are natural constraints to what can be done within the context of everyday life.

The anxious bully

This small but important group of bullies need special consideration over and above the general management described above. The so-called 'anxious' bully can be recognised by the fact that they are victims as much as they are bullies. These are the bullies who are cowards at heart and usually have a strong feeling of failure. The combination of low self-esteem and provocative aggression is an indication of a disturbed child. The motivation for the bullying is likely to be due to abnormal psychopathology rather than the pure excitement derived from aggressive display and having power over others. The motivations are complex and may include:

- anger against someone other than the victim (who makes an easier target);
- low self-esteem that is improved by having power over another person;
- poor self-image that is confirmed by bad behaviour – the bully is reassured that the self-image fits with reality;
- a desperate need for success even if only to be a successful bully;
- a desire to be noticed and to have attention – whatever the cost.

Clearly the motivation of the anxious bully is both unusual and indicative of some abnormality of personal functioning. Unless this deficit is attended to it will be very difficult to stop further bullying because the motivation is pathological. Expert professional help may well be required.

The passive bully

Children who become involved in bullying by being led into it or by wishing to seem one of the gang are generally easy to deal with. The desire for self-protection and the easy option is usually the driving force behind the bullying rather than a purely aggressive motive. In the case of an easily-led, passive bully it is usually particularly effective to increase the child's feelings of guilt and so exaggerate the possible costs of bullying that bullying no longer seems the easy option.

It is very easy for children to join in group bullying because the responsibility is dissipated between them and it is easy to shift the blame to someone else. To hold each group member fully responsible for what has happened may seem unreasonable, but it deals with the undermining effect of shared responsibility and increases personal accountability to the point where children will think twice before joining a bully gang again.

Making amends

Punishment in the normal sense of extracting a penalty for bullying can be effective. Bullying should never be allowed to pay, but all too often punishment involves the use of anger, aggression and humiliation – precisely what is not wanted. Aggressive punishment is more likely to be ineffective and may even encourage further bullying. By far the most effective punishment is to insist that the bully makes amends for the distress that has been caused. Exactly how this is best done will depend on the circumstances. However, it is important to try and achieve a balance between the distress caused and the reparation by the bully. There are a number of different ways that a bully might make amends to a victim, for example:

- a public apology;
- a private apology, face to face;
- an apology in writing;
- a gift or a special favour for the victim.

Care has to be taken that any contact between the bully and the victim is with the victim's agreement and is closely supervised to make sure that it is successfully completed. This type of reparation by the bully is not an easy option. It can be surprisingly effective and gets to the heart of the matter by showing that bullying is unacceptable, that it has a cost and should not be repeated.

Conclusion

The optimistic message of this chapter is that although bullying is a serious matter with a poor prognosis, there is a lot that can be done to stop it provided that bullying is taken seriously and there is agreed and concerted action involving parents, teachers and children.

References

Abramson, L. Y., Seligman, M. E. P. and Teasdale, J. D. (1987) 'Learned helplessness in humans: critique and reformulation', *Journal of Abnormal Psychology*, Vol. 87, pp. 49–74.

Besag, V. E. (1995) *Bullies and Victims in Schools: a guide to understanding and management*. Milton Keynes, Open University Press.

Billman, J. and McDevitt, S. C. (1980) 'Convergence of parent and observer ratings of temperament with observations of peer interaction in nursery schools', *Child Development*, Vol. 51, pp. 395–400.

Day, R. C. and Ghandour, M. (1984) 'The effect of television-mediated aggression and real-life aggression on the behaviour of Lebanese children', *Journal of Experimental Child Psychology*, Vol. 38, pp. 7–18.

Elliott, E. (1994) *The Kidscape Kit*. Kidscape, 152 Buckingham Palace Road, London SW1W 9TR.

Eron, L. D., Huesmann, R., Dubow, E., Romanoff, R. and Yarmel P. W. (1987) 'Aggression and its correllates over 22 years', in D. H. Crowell, I. M. Evans and C. P. O'Connell (eds), *Childhood Aggression and Violence*, Plenum Publications.

Friedrich, L. K. and Stein, A. H. (1973) 'Aggressive and prosocial television programs and the natural behaviour of preschool children', *Monographs in Social Research and Child Development*, Vol. 38, No. 151.

Galloway, D. M., Ball, T., Blomfield, D. and Boyd, R. (1982) *Schools and Disruptive Pupils*, London, Longman.

Goldstein, A. P. and Keller, H. (1987) *Aggressive Behaviour: Assessment and Intervention*, Oxford, Pergamon Press.

Graham, P., Rutter, M. and George, S. (1973) 'Temperamental characteristics as predictors of behaviour problems in children', *American Journal of Orthopsychiatry*, Vol. 43, pp. 328–39.

Henningam, K. D., Del Rosario, M. L., Heath, L., Cook, T. D., Wharton, J. D. and Calder, B. J. (1982) 'Impact of the introduction of television on crime in the United States: Empirical findings and theoretical implications', *Journal of Personal Social Psychology*, Vol. 42, pp. 461–77.

Maccoby, E. E. and Jacklin, C. N. (1974) *The Psychology of Sex Differences*, California, Stanford University Press.

Nicol, A. R., Willcox, C. and Hibbert, K. (1985) 'What sort of children are suspended from school and what can we do for them?' in A. R. Nicol (ed.), *Longitudinal Studies in Child Psychology and Psychiatry*, Chichester, Wiley.

Olweus, D. (1978) *Aggression in Schools: Bullies and Whipping Boys*, Washington, DC, Hemisphere.

Olweus, D. (1979) 'Stability of aggressive reaction patterns in males: a review, *Psychological Bulletin*, Vol. 86, pp. 862–75.

Olweus, D. (1984) 'Aggressors and their victims: bullying at school', in N. Frude and H. Gault (eds), *Disruptive Behaviour in Schools*, New York, Wiley.

Olweus, D. (1987) 'Bully/victim problems among school children in Scandinavia', in J. P. Myklebust and R. Ommundsen (eds), *Psykologprofesjonen mot ar 2000*, Oslo, Universitetsforlaget.

Olweus, D. (1989) 'Bully/victim problems among school children: basic facts and effects of a school based intervention program', in K. Rubin and D. Pepler (eds), *The Development and Treatment of Childhood Aggression*, Hillsdale, NJ, Erlbaum.

Olweus, D. (1993) *Bullying at School: What We Know and What We Can Do*, Oxford, Blackwell.

Patterson, G. R. (1982) *Coersive Family Process*, Oregon, Castalia Publishing.

Pfeffer, C. R., Zuckerman, S., Plutchik, R. and Mizruchi, M. S. (1987) 'Assaultive behaviour in normal school children', *Child Psychiatry and Human Development*, Vol. 17, pp. 166–76.

Pikas, A. (1975) 'Treatment of mobbing in school: principles for and the results of the work of an anti mobbing group', *Scandinavian Journal of Educational Research*, Vol. 19, pp. 1–12.

Richman, N., Stevenson, J. and Graham, P. (1982) *Preschool to School: a behavioural study*, London, Academic Press.

Robins, L. N. (1978) 'Sturdy childhood predictors of adult antisocial behaviour: replication from longitudinal studies', *Psychological Medicine*, Vol. 8, pp. 611–22.

Rutter, M. (1987) 'Psychosocial resilience and protective mechanisms', *American Journal of Orthopsychiatry*, Vol. 57, pp. 317–31.

Rutter, M., Tizard, J. and Whitmore, K. (eds) (1970) *Education, Health and Behaviour*, London, Longmans.

Shaffer, D., Meyer-Bahlburg, H. F. L. and Stokman, C. L. J. (1980) 'The development of aggression', in M. Rutter (ed.), *Scientific Foundations of Developmental Psychiatry*, London, Heinemann.

Stephenson, P. and Smith, D. (1988) 'Bullying in the junior school', in D. Tattum and D. Lane (eds), *Bullying in Schools*, Stoke-on-Trent, Trentham Books.

Thomas, A. and Chess, S. (1977) *Temperament and Development*, New York, Brunner/Mazel.

Whiting, B. and Edwards, C. P. (1973) 'A cross cultural analysis of sex differences in the behaviour of children aged three through eleven', *Journal of Social Psychology*, Vol. 91, pp. 171–88.

Wolff, S. (1985) 'Non-delinquent disturbance of conduct', in M. Rutter and L. Hersov (eds), *Child and Adolescent Psychiatry: Modern Approaches*, Oxford, Blackwell Scientific.

10

■ ■ ■

Bullying pays!
A survey of young offenders

JANE KILPATRICK

Introduction

Kidscape, the children's safety charity, carried out a survey of young offenders in March and April 1994. The results indicate that unchecked school bullying tends to promote a climate of violence and aggression which can encourage crime.

Kidscape questioned 79 young offenders in two institutions, HMYOI Onley (Rugby) and HMYOI Glen Parva (Leicester), about their experiences of school bullying. Young offenders were asked whether bullying happened often in their school, whether they were involved in bullying, whether they thought unchecked school bullying led to a decrease in respect for authority, and what they thought schools should do to tackle bullying effectively.

One hundred per cent of the 79 young offenders we surveyed had been involved in bullying in some way. The majority (85 per cent) were themselves bullies or were involved as gang members or bystanders, either encouraging the bullying or joining in from the sidelines.

Fifteen per cent of the young offenders started out as victims of bullying – but some of these victims went on to become bullies themselves (7 per cent). Some of these victims (5 per cent) committed offences to emulate the bullies.

Kidscape found that 92 per cent of the young offenders had engaged in bullying behaviour and went on to commit offences; 5 per cent committed crimes under the influence of bullies; 3 per cent of the total group of young offenders were and remain victims of bullying. It would seem from the survey that there is a direct correlation between unchecked bullying behaviour and juvenile crime.

Ninety-eight per cent of the young offenders thought that unchecked bullying did make pupils less respectful of authority and 95 per cent of those who admitted to being bullies at school said that getting away with bullying for so long had made them more likely to commit offences.

Only three inmates out of the total surveyed said that bullying happened rarely in their schools. All the other inmates indicated that bullying was a frequent and inescapable fact of school life. One inmate said that the 'pecking order in schools prepared you for real life'.

All the young offenders wanted bullying stopped in schools. The majority thought that the bully's parents should be involved and that more counselling should be available for bullies. Several favoured excluding persistent bullies together.

All those questioned, even victims of bullying, were against reporting bullying incidents to staff or naming particular bullies. 'Grassing' was seen as a far more heinous offence than even the most violent of bullying attacks.

The survey

Seventy-nine young offenders aged from 16 to 21 responded to Kidscape's initial questionnaire. The majority of respondents had attended schools in or near Rugby and Leicester. For ease of analysis and reference, Kidscape categorised respondents according to their answers as either 'bullies', 'victims' or 'witnesses' (i.e. those who had encouraged the bullying or joined in from the sidelines).

Respondents were also asked if they would be prepared to participate in an interview relating to the questionnaire. Those who did not wish to be interviewed remained anonymous. Kidscape then interviewed 33 respondents. In these interviews inmates were asked to expand on some of their answers to the questionnaire and were encouraged to describe their involvement in school bullying.

Bullying: who is involved?

The majority of the young offenders (62 per cent) had themselves been bullies at school, while 23 per cent were involved as bystanders or witnesses and 15 per cent had been the victims of bullying.

When Kidscape asked those who had admitted bullying others at school why they had become bullies, the answers were similar: 'to be number one in my year'; 'it made me feel big in front of my friends'; 'I did it to show off'; 'I wanted to show the girls who was best'. These were typical responses. One inmate said that he was a 'nobody' at home but that at school he was 'top dog and it was great'.

Generally the bullies belonged to a gang. Only six inmates said they had bullied on their own and one of these was unusual in that he fought other bullies when their victims asked him for help. Two of the bullies said they had joined their gang because if they hadn't they would have become gang victims. However, the majority of bullies were either gang leaders or had joined a gang because their friends belonged. 'I wanted to be with my mates' was a frequent reason. Gangs often had a 'hard image' and belonging conferred high group status on members: 'It was really cool to belong to this tough gang.'

Most of the victims said that they felt they had been bullied because of their small size or because they were quiet. The bullies admitted that they targeted weaknesses and what they perceived as differences. One victim said he had been picked on because of rumours that he was gay.

Only eight of the bullies had begun bullying in primary school; the rest had started bullying at 12 or 13. Most of the victims had only been bullied in secondary school, although a few had been bullied for the whole of their school careers. Witnesses confirmed that, although bullying only happened occasionally in their primary schools, it was very common in their secondary schools.

What sort of bullying?

The bullying ranged from name-calling and persistent taunting through theft, kicking, punching and beating to assault with weapons. Threats were usually backed up by violence. Obtaining money or possessions like Walkmans or getting homework done were often motives for bullying. Weapons involved in bullying incidents included a decorating tack-gun modified to fire darts and wooden clubs.

Violent and aggressive bullying was the rule. The bullies were very matter-of-fact about using violence to get what they wanted. One bully talked about giving a victim 'a couple of whacks' and another said, 'If they didn't pay up, I'd give them a good hiding and threaten to kill them next time.' Not surprisingly, he found this worked. The bullies had no compunction about using violence. For them it was merely an effective way of getting what they wanted. In fact, one bully told us that he never thought of the intimidation practised by his gang as bullying; for him it was nothing more than 'a bit of a laugh'.

Climate of violence

As the interviews progressed it became apparent that the violent bullying which seems to have been endemic in the majority of schools the young offenders had attended reflected the violence present in their lives outside school. Many said that fighting often took place around the estates and streets where they lived and these fights often involved different gangs. Two of the bullies were very specific about their involvement in these gang fights. One said he was always surprised when he saw other pupils giving in completed homework. He said he never had time for homework as he was out all evening fighting with rival street gangs.

When Kidscape asked one inmate why he had become a bully, he answered succinctly, 'Rough school, bad area.' He did not think he'd had a choice; as far as he was concerned, bullying and violence were an integral part of life inside and outside school. A victim said that when he'd told his mother he was being bullied, she had clouted him and told him that life was tough and he'd better learn to fight back if he was going to get on. Another victim said he had seen both his brothers beaten by his father when they had said they were being bullied so he hadn't dared tell when he was also bullied. His father expected all his sons to fight their way out of trouble. Another inmate told Kidscape that he had had to rescue his younger brother on several occasions from bullies and that he despised him because he couldn't stand up for himself.

It seems that the only way to win approval in a culture like this where violence is the norm is by being more violent than others. This is a fact recognised by all those Kidscape questioned. You could only be 'number one' if you were prepared to fight and use violence. Small, quiet or studious boys were held in contempt and a tough, 'hard' image was the ultimate goal. The endemic bullying these young offenders described in their schools reflects these beliefs. One inmate said, 'Violence is what bullies understand.' In fact, everyone at these schools understood violence: it was the touchstone of their lives.

A number of inmates commented that, if victims had had the requisite physical strength, they would have been bullies. 'Everybody wants to be top', and it was accepted that the only way to be 'top' was to fight your way there. At the same time, a few witnesses recognised the hollowness of the successful bully's position. 'Bullies don't have friends,' one said. Nevertheless, being part of the top gang was important to many. One inmate said that he hadn't particularly enjoyed the bullying but he had gone along with the gang as they were his 'mates'. Belonging to the gang was essential for him.

Adult responses to school bullying

Two-thirds of the victims said that they had never told anyone about the bullying. They gave several reasons for their silence: 'I was too scared to tell'; 'If you tell, it will come back on you'; 'I just tried to keep my head down'; 'I was afraid it would get worse if I told'. The most common reason cited by the victims and witnesses for not telling anyone about the bullying was 'I'm not a grass'. Some of the witnesses explained that the bullies were their friends and they didn't 'grass' on mates.

This survey revealed very clearly that the taboo against 'grassing', 'sneaking' or 'ratting' is very strong. Victims would rather suffer continued bullying than face the opprobrium of being branded a 'grass'. It is apparent that if schools are to take effective action against bullying the taboo against 'grassing' has to be broken. This means that the victims and bystanders who tell about bullying have to be protected from revenge attacks by bullies. The names of those who do pluck up the courage to tell should be kept secret so that the bully never learns who has reported him. Effective anti-bullying policies encourage pupils to report all incidents of bullying and the onus is on the adults to ensure that those who tell about bullying are safe.

Only a third of the victims said that they had ever told anyone about the bullying. Only one victim said that the adult he told had stopped the bullying. In all other cases, telling did not lead to effective action against the bullies. The actions taken by school staff usually consisted of no more than a general injunction not to do it again, although some imposed detentions. None of the bullies thought that this sort of punishment was effective. One bully said that he'd quite enjoyed detentions as they gave him 'a bit of peace'.

As a final resort, some schools excluded the bully but the exclusion was rarely permanent and, on the bully's return, the problems started up again. One bully said that he'd been excluded and sent to a special boarding school but that, on returning to his old school, no one, not even the staff, believed he could have changed and he said they all 'expected' him to go back to bullying. Another bully said that once he'd started bullying, everyone labelled him as a bully and that's how he was treated. One bully who took dinner money from other pupils said that even after he stopped threatening people or intimidating them, they'd still come and give him their money. By then his reputation as a bully was enough to frighten other students. It seems that after a while bullies get trapped in their role by other people's expectations and it is hard for them to change their behaviour without considerable support.

What respondents would do about school bullying

All the bullies said that punishment didn't work and wasn't the answer to bullying. Perhaps this was only to be expected! However, 52 per cent of witnesses thought that punishment should be used. Witnesses also favoured excluding the bully. One bully said that he hated being excluded as he 'enjoyed school'. Some suggested that bullies should be sent to special schools where they would get a taste of their own medicine and one victim thought that 'quiet' pupils should be separated into different classes from 'noisy or rough' pupils.

The bullies all said that they thought counselling would have helped. One bully said he stopped bullying when he was 15 because a teacher he respected had taken the trouble to talk to him about his problems. Most of the young offenders thought that involving the bully's parents was important. One bully told us his mum had known about the bullying but she was 'soft' and hadn't wanted to tell his father. This bully said that if his dad had known what was going on he would have given him 'a right kicking'. Inmates thought that parents could punish bullies more effectively than school staff because they could stop privileges and 'ground' bullies. All the victims said that if they had children they wouldn't want them to suffer as they had done. They said they would certainly try to stop the bullying if their children told them they were victims.

There were two cases where schools had stopped bullying by threatening the bully with police action if he persisted.

Many of the bullies said that they hadn't realised the effect of bullying on a victim until they themselves were bullied in prison. One bully said that he had known that his victims suffered but he had 'blanked it out'.

In cases where victims had tried to stand up to the bullies they were usually forced into a fight. One bully said that if people stood up to him they had to be prepared to back it up with force. He said he respected them for taking a stand. One victim eventually turned on his tormentors and knifed one of the bullies. The gang 'avenged' this by beating the victim so badly he had to be hospitalised. In another case a victim waited until he grew bigger than those who had bullied him and then began to bully them in his turn. He said he then got into trouble for fighting.

Does unchecked school bullying lead to crime?

As effective action to check the bullying was not taken by school staff, it flourished and bullies concluded that bullying pays. In their experience, using intimidation, violence and blackmail to get what you wanted were successful strategies. They were told at school that bullying was wrong but, as nothing was ever done to stop their bullying behaviour, they had never had to face the consequences of their actions. As far as they were concerned, bullying paid off and they were good at it.

Given this background, the progression from school bullying to crime was apparently inevitable. As one witness said, 'If they think they can get away with it, 'course they'll go nicking things.' Bullies who were never brought to task for their behaviour in school thought that they would continue to get away with theft, intimidation and violence outside school. They had got used to their power over weaker individuals and expected such 'easy pickings' would continue. They had not learned that they were accountable for their actions and they did not expect retribution.

The inmates Kidscape questioned had usually been convicted of stealing cars (taking a vehicle without the owner's consent or 'twocking') or burglary. It appeared that twocking was generally the first criminal act committed by most of the inmates and some then 'progressed' to burglary. Some also had convictions for GBH. One bully told about a raid on a shop he and a friend had committed. Kidscape asked if they had used weapons. 'Not really,' he replied. 'I just had a baseball bat and my mate had an iron bar.' He seem surprised that anyone could take exception to this – after all, they hadn't used knives or guns and they had been using bats and bars for years at school. Another bully had sprayed CS gas at a security guard. He said the guard 'was this great big bloke. I thought he'd laugh if I punched him.'

A couple of inmates said that they had been bullied into twocking – they were told that they would be beaten up if they did not go along with the gang. One victim said he had started to take drugs to boost his confidence and then had become a thief to pay for the habit. Some commented on the fact that the bullies had built up a 'hard image' for themselves and that, once they had all left school, they could no longer intimidate their peers so easily. Crime was one way of maintaining their 'hard image'.

Kidscape asked all the young offenders whether they knew what had happened to the bullies in their schools. In every case where the inmate knew what had happened to the bullies once they had left school they said that the bullies were now in prison for a variety of offences. A few inmates told us that some of the bullies they knew had committed offences but hadn't been caught. In one case where the inmate had been one of a gang of eight bullies, he told us that the whole gang was now in prison and his own three-and-a-half year sentence was the shortest any of them had received.

Several of those Kidscape interviewed understood that what they had done had damaged their chances of finding jobs and making succesful lives for themselves. A victim who had been convicted of twocking said he had done it to be 'like them' (i.e. the bullies) but he hadn't expected to end up in prison. Some of the bullies Kidscape interviewed said that they regretted the fact that they had wasted their schooldays and had left without qualifications. One bully of 20, who was serving his second sentence, said he had a wife and a baby and he wished he could get a job and settle down but no one wanted him with his record. Another said, 'It was stupid what I did – fighting and twocking, all that. I don't know what will happen when I get out or what I'll do.'

Conclusion

The results of this survey indicate that unchecked school bullying encourages bullies to believe that bullying gets them what they want and that, no matter how aggressive their behaviour, they can get away with it.

Although this Kidscape survey was qualitative rather than quantatitive, its findings are supported by other researchers. Professor Dan Olweus in his 30-year follow-up studies in Norway found that approximately 60 per cent of boys who were characterised as bullies in grades 6–9 (11– to 14-year-olds) had at least one conviction by the age of 24. As many as 35–40 per cent of these former bullies had three or more convictions by this age, compared to only 10 per cent of the control group who had not been involved in bullying in grades 6–9 (Olweus, 1993).

If we ignore bullying in schools or if we tackle it half-heartedly, we are storing up trouble for the future. Bullies must learn as soon as they begin to bully others that such behaviour will not be tolerated and that sanctions will be imposed if they persist. The sooner bullies learn that their actions have consequences the better it will be for them, for their victims and for society.

Many of the young offenders who took part in the Kidscape survey were intelligent and articulate. They were honest about their experiences and several of them had given considerable thought to the problem of bullying. However, they were all learning in prison a lesson they should have learned at school: society will not tolerate violent and criminal behaviour and will punish those who break its laws.

Reference

Olweus, D. (1993) *Bullying at School: What We Know and What We Can Do*, Oxford, Blackwell.

11

■ ■ ■

Helping victims

ANDREW MELLOR

Bullying cannot be cured just by treating the victims. They are not suffering from a disease but are involved in complex social situations, each of which is unique and requires individual action. Parents, teachers, friends and bystanders all play a part in the confrontation between bully and victim so they must also be included in any coping strategy.

Lone parents or teachers have little chance of successfully helping victims unless a school has a clear, well developed anti-bullying policy. Many do not – despite the publicity given to this issue in the last few years. In such cases the first step must be to create a climate of concern: teachers and head teachers must understand the feeling of helplessness experienced by victims.

> *I think I felt that I was the only person that had ever been bullied and if I told anybody they would think I was stupid and a wimp.*

(11-year-old girl)

Victims need to be reassured that they are not alone and that it could happen to anyone; all it takes is to be in the wrong place at the wrong time. Such an assertion may contradict the popular wisdom of the playground:

> *I would say that bullying usually happens to people who are different (e.g. colour, religion or some disability). People who are shy or have a weak character are usually the ones who are bullied.*

(15-year-old girl)

If this is believed by victims they may feel, however erroneously, that they are to blame for what has happened. The endless repetition of the bully's taunts can cause such distress that rational thought becomes impossible. Victims believe that they are being bullied because they are fat, bespectacled, shy or just different and that no one, least of all an adult, can help. It only takes one bad experience to confirm this belief:

> *When a friend told the teacher I was being bullied he said I was old enough to deal with it myself.*

(14-year-old girl)

Lest we be too censorious of this girl's teacher it is well to remember that, until recently, virtually no guidance was available to schools on how to deal with bullying. Official recognition of the problem had been limited. The Pack Report on *Truancy and Indiscipline in Scottish Schools* (1977) merely listed bullying as a form of indiscipline, without further comment. In 1989 the Elton Report on discipline in schools in England and Wales devoted three paragraphs to the subject. While three English paragraphs may be better than one or two Scottish words, this was not much progress in 12 years.

Elton recommended that head teachers and staff should:

- be alert to signs of racial harassment and bullying;
- deal firmly with all such behaviour; and
- take action on clear rules which are backed by appropriate sanctions and systems to protect and support victims.

All perfectly valid points, but teachers may have difficulty in implementing these recommendations because victims and others are afraid to talk. The section on bullying concluded with a unique and vacuous recommendation that 'pupils should tell staff about serious cases of bullying and racial harassment of which they are aware'. The other recommendations in the Report were aimed at adults such as teachers, parents and educational administrators. It is difficult to believe that any children would read this weighty tome, so it seems that this recommendation was included without much thought as to how it was to be implemented. A firm and clear discipline policy will never succeed in tackling bullying unless strategies are adopted which encourage victims to seek adult help. The taboo against telling that exists in British society ensures that children will go through agonies before seeking help. It is not only the threat of physical retaliation that deters them but also the endlessly repeated playground taunts:

> *Tell-tale tit, your mammy cannae knit.*
> *Your daddy cannae go to bed without a dummy-tit.*
>
> (Scottisb playground rhyme)

School must create an atmosphere in which telling is always encouraged and teachers must create situations in which it is possible. But this still leaves the victim with the responsibility of judging if an incident should be reported or shrugged off. Would the complaint be treated seriously and wisely?

> *I honestly don't know if I would tell someone if I was being bullied. I would feel I was being silly about the whole thing. I'd be too frightened in case I'd be laughed at.*
>
> (15-year-old girl)

Most older children will have learned through experience to assess the gravity of bullying and identify those incidents which are likely to be taken seriously – and which are the best adults to approach. However, younger children do not have this experience to draw on. Anything that is happening to them at the time is serious, and for all they know, permanent. Teachers of such children run the risk of being overwhelmed by trivia so it is perhaps understandable that they may sometimes seem less than welcoming.

Inspiration from Scandinavia

Fortunately, help and guidance on dealing with victims started to become available in the late 1980s, in the form of a number of books and the creation of specialised agencies like Kidscape and ChildLine. This awakening of interest was largely a result of the European Teachers' Seminar on Bullying in Schools held in Stavanger, Norway, in 1987. Many of the delegates, inspired or influenced by the Scandinavian example, later became involved in promoting research into anti-bullying strategies in their own countries.

When the Norwegians began to be concerned about bullying in the early 1970s they did not have a word of their own to describe the phenomenon so they borrowed the English word 'mobbing' from the work of Konrad Lorenz. Throughout the 1970s and 1980s there was extensive research and a government-funded campaign against bullying. This was in marked contrast to the situation in the UK where there was a paucity of large-scale research and only limited expressions of concern. A sign of some official recognition, albeit small, came when I was awarded a grant by the Scottish Office Education Department to investigate bullying in ten Scottish secondary schools. The 942 pupils who completed questionnaires in February and March 1989 represented a cross-section of the Scottish secondary school population stretching from the inner city to the agricultural periphery of the country. The project set out to do two main things – to identify variations in the incidence of bullying and to investigate and describe successful coping strategies. The children's responses provided the assurance that being a victim of school bullying is a common experience. However, their candid comments also revealed the anguish of victims, and how adults often underestimate the scale of the problem.

How many victims?

Half of the 942 pupils said that they had been bullied at least once or twice during their school careers. Forty-four per cent admitted they had bullied someone else. Less than a third said that they had never been involved either as bully or victim. These figures seem all the more remarkable when it is realised that a narrow definition was borrowed from Norwegian researchers: 'Bullying is long-standing violence, mental or physical, conducted by an individual or a group against an individual who is not able to defend himself or herself in that actual situation.' One-off incidents and fights between equals were specifically excluded.

Many of the victims wrote about what had happened to them years before, but some revealed a current torment:

> I am scared stiff all the time and my schoolwork is being affected. I am also scared to go out. I want to stand up to the girl who is bullying me because she is making my life a misery, but I can't.

(14-year-old girl)

The pupils were asked how often they had been bullied since Christmas. This was chosen as an occasion which all could remember well and provided an accurate measure of their experiences over the previous six to ten weeks. Six per cent of the children said that they had been bullied 'sometimes or more often' in this short time, which was identical to the proportion of victims found in the very large Norwegian government-sponsored survey carried out by Dan Olweus in 1983.

Caution must be used in making general assumptions from these findings because of the small size of the sample, but interesting trends were noticed which may be of use to teachers, parents and others who are trying to help victims.

Although boys and girls were equally likely to be victims during their school career as a whole, there were fewer girls than boys among recent victims.

As children grow up they are less likely to become victims, presumably developing protective or avoidance strategies of their own. But older girls seem to do this better than older boys, who sometimes feel that they have no one to turn to:

> I have been picked on. People think I am nothing and say anything they want to me. Every day I feel rejected. It's not that people use violence much but I feel as if I am treated as a dustbin. I do want to come forward about this but as I am leaving in a few months I don't see any reason to do so. Nor have I the courage.

(16-year-old boy)

Although the proportion of 15–16-year-old boys who were victims of bullying was relatively small (4 per cent) their sense of alienation and failure could be severe:

> Sometimes you feel like dying because you can't face up to it.

(15-year-old boy)

Twelve per cent of 15–16-year-old boys claimed that they had recently bullied others. For them there seems to be less shame in admitting to being a bully than in being a victim. Virtually all the girls who commented thought that the answer to bullying lay in the adoption of a collective remedy:

> People that are being bullied feel as if they are alone in that problem and most people, if not everybody, are against them. They need to be shown that they are not alone and unless they tell somebody, nothing can be done.

(15-year-old girl)

Boys tended to suggest that victims should stand up for themselves. Quite a few said that they had taken up weightlifting or the martial arts – but with varying success:

I get bullied quite a lot. I try not to let it happen but I just can't find the courage to fight back. I do press-ups and weights to give me more muscle so I can fight back and have a chance of winning. I don't like fighting anyway. I think it's a mug's game.

(15-year-old boy)

Society expects its young men to be aggressive but, paradoxically, punishes those who fight and alienates those who reject violence. No wonder adolescents are sometimes mixed up. Sue Askew and Carol Ross have described the social pressures which force many boys to choose, what is for them, an inappropriate method of defence:

Toughness and aggression are approved of in boys – the argument goes as follows: boys are encouraged to be tough and stick up for themselves. This is not usually meant as an open encouragement for them to be violent, but more of a message that violence is all right if not taken to extremes . . . and can, in many circumstances, be a way of improving social status with other boys.

(From *Boys Don't Cry*, 1988)

An older boy who is not aggressive and who is bullied by others may lose so much status that life becomes unbearable. Seeking help could be perceived as a further sign of weakness. Perhaps as a result of this only 38 per cent of male victims had told someone else that they were being bullied, in contrast to 61 per cent of girl victims. Given the success of older girls in avoiding bullying and their readiness to seek help, it is clear that schools must develop a telling ethos. Nobody, of whatever age or whatever sex, must ever feel that there is any shame in speaking openly about fears or concerns.

There are many potential benefits in store if this ideal can be achieved. Children may talk about other problems they are experiencing at school or at home; most will be fairly minor but others could be of the utmost gravity. Encouraging children to talk about being bullied by other children will make it easier for them to talk about being victimised or abused by adults. But this will only happen if schools are successful in creating an atmosphere of openness – and that will be difficult unless there is a national climate of concern about bullying and aggression.

Just flavour of the month?

Between 1990 and 1995 it seemed that a national climate of concern had been created. Central government funded a number of research and development activities. In England and Wales, the DFE/Sheffield University anti-bullying project provided the focus for this activity. North of the border, the Scottish

Office sponsored the production and distribution of training and support packs for teachers, and advice leaflets for pupils, parents and school boards. It also funded my appointment as the Scottish Anti-bullying Development Officer, with the remit of providing support to schools and local authorities which were developing their own policies.

This flurry of activity is now over, which might appear to make the senior education official who opined to me that bullying was 'just flavour of the month' seem prophetic. On the contrary, I believe that real progress has been made – training materials and advice are available to local authorities, schools and concerned individuals; we know a lot more than we did about the complexities of the relationship problems which can underlie a seemingly 'simple' case of bullying; a number of strategies have been evaluated and continue to be developed; but, most importantly, there is now a much greater chance of the victims of bullying having their pleas heard and their predicament acknowledged.

An anti-bullying policy for schools

Many schools have now developed anti-bullying policies – and, considering the amount of help and advice which is available, there is no excuse for those which have not. Bullying happens in every school in the country, although research suggests that some have more than others.

There were very significant differences in the level of bullying in the ten schools studied in my 1989 survey. The number of recent victims varied from 2 to 15 per cent. Attempts to explain this in terms of social class, family background, deprivation or privilege were not very convincing but it was clear that some schools were far more successful in containing the problem than others. Three schools had less than 3 per cent of recent victims, but they were very different; one was in a rural area, the other two were in inner-city areas of multiple deprivation. These schools had little in common – other than that pupils and teachers seemed to treat each other with concern and respect.

Observing schools which are tackling bullying effectively leads me to believe that whatever the moral, religious or disciplinary standards of a school, there are three prerequisites for the creation of a successful anti-bullying policy.

- **Honesty**. Teachers and parents must be prepared to acknowledge that a problem might exist. There is no difficulty about this in Norwegian schools – but they do not have a parents' charter which obliges schools to compete for the available pupils. Head teachers have a right to expect support from parents and the community when they admit that a problem exists and take positive steps to address it.

- **Openness**. The creation of an open atmosphere is a major challenge to schools.
- **Involvement**. If parents, teachers and pupils are involved in formulating an anti-bullying policy they will have a vested interest in making sure it succeeds.

Just how these ideals are to be achieved will vary from school to school. To be effective any policy must recognise the history and traditions of the school; it must build on existing strengths and repair recognised weaknesses. Table 11.1 shows how this could be achieved.

Table 11.1: Developing a school strategy against bullying

Stage	Groups involved
1 Recognition	Teachers and parents
2 Investigation	Teachers and pupils, possibly with outside help
3 Consultation	Teachers, parents, pupils, ancillary staff
4 Implementation	As above
5 Evaluation and modification	Teachers using existing consultation procedures

Stage 1: Recognition

Some school boards, which were established in Scotland in 1989, have helped this process. Elected parent and teacher members have the power to require head teachers to make reports on matters of concern. In the past, individual parents who have complained about bullying have felt isolated. They were often told that their children's problems were exceptional incidents, or they were told that there was nothing that the school could do. Now there is a forum in which the issue can be discussed but whether or not this happens depends upon the personal interests of the handful of parents and teachers who are elected to the boards. It also depends upon the ability of members to persuade head teachers to treat the matter seriously. A report showing that there was little or no bullying could easily be concocted by a head teacher who was determined to sweep things under the carpet.

Those schools which have no board, or where the business of the board becomes bogged down in minutiae, will have to rely on groups of forceful parents, or possibly concerned teachers, to initiate change. Whoever performs this function will have the task of trying to create an atmosphere of common concern about bullying. There must be clear agreement that aggressive behaviour will not be tolerated and that all concerned – pupils, parents, teachers and ancillary staff – will work together to eliminate it.

It is possible that the schools which have already developed policies are those where head teachers and staff are most progressive and receptive to the notion that education is about more than just academic endeavour. If this is true, then campaigners for change in the remaining schools will have a particularly difficult task. A very powerful argument they can use is that schools in all parts of the UK are now officially encouraged to develop anti-bullying policies.

Stage 2: Investigation

Teachers are in the best position to carry out this process but they could come from a number of different departments. In most schools guidance teachers will be the obvious choice. They have the opportunity to carry out surveys as part of a programme of social education. In other schools it could be teachers of Religious Education, Social Subjects or English who do the work. The result of the surveys will allow an assessment of the size of the problem and should also indicate any aspect which needs special attention, such as particular age groups or places where bullying is common. Sometimes, such a survey will reveal other, related problems which require policies on matters such as child protection, anti-racism or equal opportunities to be examined and modified.

Stage 3: Consultation

A successful strategy to defeat bullying needs the cooperation of teachers, parents, pupils and anyone else involved with a school. Human nature is such that this will be more easily achieved if all these groups are involved in the development process. Schools with a consensus style of management will be best able to do this. Authoritarian head teachers may feel threatened by this suggestion. Thus the degree of involvement will vary widely. In Norway special meetings about bullying are held, to which parents, pupils and teachers are invited. Pupils sit with their parents rather than as a group and all are invited to contribute to this discussion. A video is usually shown first to create the right climate and the parents may be given the result of a school survey on bullying.

An alternative to an open meeting specifically about bullying is to raise the topic at a meeting of the school board or parent–teacher association. The disadvantage of this is that it could exclude children from the discussion. No policy against bullying can be successful without their active cooperation.

Lest the idea of pupils having a say in the formulation of school rules is considered too revolutionary, let us recall what the Pack Committee said in 1977:

> ... we think that there could be some advantage in rules being the product of joint consultation between headteacher, staff, parents (e.g. parent/teacher association) and pupils (e.g. internal school council).

Only a small minority of Scottish secondary schools have school councils. It is difficult to know how many of those that do exist are functioning well. The

Elton Report suggests that school councils are a way of encouraging the active participation of pupils in shaping and reviewing the school's behaviour policy in order to foster a sense of collective commitment to it. But Elton also discourages the creation of token councils.

If it becomes clear to pupils that staff are taking no notice of their views the council is likely to become a liability rather than an asset.

R.F. Mackenzie introduced councils to Scottish state education in the 1960s with limited success.

This experiment in self-government could hardly be called successful. The council have had considerable success in recovering stolen money and property ... but in other ways the council have been less successful. I had hoped that by now they would be arranging their own meetings, preparing the agenda, discussing quietly, and carrying out their own decisions, but it doesn't work like that so far.

(*State School*, 1970)

To see how a school council operates, a visit was made to Kilquhanity School at the invitation of the Principal, John Aitkenhead. With his wife Morag, he founded the school in 1940. Although inspired by A.S. Neill's Summerhill, Kilquhanity soon developed a distinctive character of its own. Unlike Summerhill, lessons are compulsory – and so is the weekly council meeting. Staff and pupils are summoned to the purpose-built circular building at 1.55 p.m. every Thursday. By two o'clock everyone is in place and the meeting begins on time.

This particular meeting turned out to be especially interesting. It was chaired, extremely ably and efficiently, by a teenage girl. The secretary was also a pupil. No one spoke until invited to do so by the chair.

Like all committees there was some routine business to begin with, but this was dealt with promptly and calmly. The agenda seemed to be dominated by domestic arrangements – broken plates, noisy dormitories and the like. But the pupils are allowed to raise any matter that is concerning them, so the latter part of the meeting is unpredictable.

On this occasion an 11-year-old boy complained that some older boys had been teasing him. Two admitted it and said they were sorry – but with little conviction. There seemed a danger that the matter would be glossed over but some of the other children (mostly older girls) described how the boys constantly teased the younger one about his hair and clothes.

Even though the staff had to wait their turn to speak, they were able to play a very significant part, pointing out that it is not good enough just to apologise without meaning it. Morag Aitkenhead became angry at some of the older boys who seemed to think that a fuss was being made about nothing.

We must recognise that it took a lot of bravery for ... to say that he was being teased and no one should ridicule him for this. This is one of the most central things to this school – everyone must feel this is a good place for them and that they are happy in it.

What was a comparatively minor case of bullying was dealt with at some length. John Aitkenhead asked the bullies to consider why they had behaved as they had. Other pupils expressed dissatisfaction with their explanations. Eventually the bullies were prompted to make a more fulsome apology and a promise to stop the teasing. Although outnumbered by pupils, the teachers had been able to show their dislike of aggressive behaviour but it was a pupil who eventually suggested that bullying could become a regular agenda item, just like laundry and breakages.

It is doubtful if such a forum could operate so successfully in a state secondary school. Kilquhanity only has about sixty pupils and the council, as it operates today, is the end result of fifty years of research and development. One could not help being impressed by the way that even young and less articulate children were able to express their viewpoint and play a part in decision-making.

The next point that was raised showed that the meetings did not always go smoothly. Some older pupils challenged John Aitkenhead to explain a decision he had made with regard to a member of staff. John declined to do so because:

Adult decisions are not always well understood by kids. This is a matter concerning professional ethics – I don't mind being asked but I don't think I should answer.

In the ensuing discussion the pupils accused John of being a dictator and of pretending that the school was a democracy when it was not. Morag explained that she saw the school as being like a family and sometimes parents had to take tough decisions which they could not explain but which were, nevertheless, in their children's best interests. John conceded that the school was not a true democracy but was a good training for democracy.

The children had been able to express their dissent in a forceful way and they had been courteously listened to. But they had explored, and reached, the limits of the power of the school's council. Consulting pupils does not mean that teachers have to lose all their authority. Giving pupils a voice does not destroy a school's hierarchy, but it does make it more accountable.

Not every school will want, or be able, to form a pupils' council but it is surely necessary to have some mechanism for consultation. The sheer size of most secondary schools means that it is not practicable to have a council composed of all pupils and teachers. An alternative is to have an elected body, with each year group choosing one or two representatives. But this has the disadvantage that the representatives may become distanced from their electorate especially if their efforts seem to produce little effect. Schools which totally reject the idea of pupil councils could utilise the guidance system to measure opinion, teachers holding discussions within tutor groups and reporting back to management. Under this system pupils would have no direct voice and would not be responsible for the agenda, so it would be fairly easy to introduce such a system and might be more acceptable in a traditional, authoritarian school.

Stages 4 and 5: Implementation, evaluation and modification

These stages, together with the previous one, form an interlinked and continuing process. Whatever policy a school adopts, regular consultation must take place. Without this there is a danger that the bullying policy will become just another booklet filed away until the next visit from the school inspectors.

It is likely that a school will discover various bullying flashpoints during the consultation process. Perhaps it is common on school buses or in the playground. Maybe it happens at certain times of the day, for example during the morning interval. Playgrounds are often unsupervised and victims may have literally nowhere to hide. Sometimes bullying involves only a small group of children while others are only vulnerable at particular times, perhaps during a family crisis or after transfer from another school.

In all these cases supervision arrangements will have to be carefully reviewed. It is not enough to tell children that they will be safe if they spend their break and lunch times in sight of the staffroom windows. This merely adds to the victim's sense of isolation and may increase their attractiveness as a target for the bullies. Supervision must be carried out by an adult who has been trained to spot signs of bullying and to provide appropriate support for victims.

Of course children cannot be supervised all the time – to do so would restrict their freedom to develop as individuals – but they can be protected in situations where bullying is known to be common. Pupils themselves can help to provide this protection but they will need the assurance that the sanctions to be imposed against bullies are sufficiently strong to deter them from seeking retribution against a helpful bystander.

Counselling should be provided for victims who have been seriously affected by their experiences. This could come from a guidance teacher, educational psychologist or simply a trained adult with whom the pupil can identify. But children will only seek such assistance if bullying has been raised as a topic during normal classwork. This can happen in Social Education, English, Drama or RE – it does not really matter where providing it is dealt with seriously and it is unequivocally condemned.

Since 1990 a number of new anti-bullying strategies have started to be developed and introduced. These include the shared concern method, the no-blame approach and various types of peer support or counselling. All of these have their merits and can be made to work within the framework of an agreed whole-school anti-bullying policy. But none of them will work effectively over a long period unless they are subjected to regular evaluation and modification.

A cause for concern

If helping the victims of bullying is so difficult, if it requires schools to make a fundamental re-evaluation of policy, why bother? Such thoughts probably explain why bullying has been largely ignored for so long. That, and the fact that it was difficult for teachers to provide a non-violent role model for pupils when the normal method of punishment for serious offences was the cane or the tawse. But now that shadow is lifted there is the opportunity for teachers to work with parents and pupils to minimise bullying.

Children who are bullied are unable to concentrate on their schoolwork. A few are physically hurt, many are psychologically damaged. The lesson that they learn may toughen them up but it may equally well make them believe that adults just don't care about children. If that is not sufficient reason for doing something about school bullying then consider the poignant plea with which one 12-year-old girl concluded her questionnaire:

> *People just go against me in everything I say and laugh at me. In science I said something and everyone laughed except my best friend Linda who helps me out when they make a fool of me. They call me K9 Keenan. That hurts me very much. I get very upset. I tried to tell my Mum but she told me to tell a teacher – but I just can't. Please help me.*

Scottish schools – a note

Although Scottish schools have many similarities to those in England and Wales there are important differences. Children transfer from primary to secondary schools a year later, at the age of 12. Most schools are run by local councils under the overall direction of the Scottish Office Education and Industry Department. In 1989 school boards were introduced. They have some similarities to boards of governors in England and Wales but with fewer responsibilities. A system of promoted posts in Guidance was introduced in 1974. This means that all secondary schools have a number of teachers who are responsible for the pastoral care of pupils and are experienced in interviewing and counselling.

References

Askew, S. and Ross, C. (1988) *Boys Don't Cry*, Milton Keynes, Open University Press.

Besag, V. E. (1989) *Bullies and Victims in Schools*, Milton Keynes, Open University Press.

Department of Education and Science (1989) *Discipline in Schools – Report of the Elton Committee*, London, HMSO.

Johnstone, M., Munn, P. and Edwards, L. (1992) *Action Against Bullying: A Support Pack for Schools*, Scottish Council for Research in Education.

Mackenzie, R. F. (1970) *State School*, Harmondsworth, Penguin.

Mellor, A. (1990) *Bullying in Scottish Secondary Schools*, Scottish Council for Research in Education.

Mellor, A. (1993) *Bullying and How to Fight it: A Guide for Families*, Scottish Council for Research in Education.

Mellor, A. (1995) *Which Way Now? A Progress Report on Action against Bullying in Scottish Schools*, Scottish Council for Research in Education.

O'Moore, A. M. (1988) *Bullying in Schools – Report on European Teachers' Seminar*, Strasbourg, Council for Cultural Cooperation.

Roland, E. and Munthe, E. (eds) (1989) *Bullying – An International Perspective*, London, David Fulton.

Scottish Council For Research in Education (1993) *Supporting Schools Against Bullying*, SCRE.

Scottish Education Department (1977) *Truancy and Indiscipline in Schools in Scotland – The Pack Report*, SED.

Smith, P. K. and Sharp, S. (1994) *School Bullying – Insights and Perspectives*, London, Routledge.

Tattum, D.P. and Lane, D. A. (eds) (1989) *Bullying in Schools*, Stoke-on-Trent, Trentham Books.

12

■ ■ ■

Parents and teachers working together

VALERIE BESAG

It is every child's democratic right to attend school in safety. As education is one of the very few compulsory activities we impose on our children it behoves all adults, in whatever capacity, to ensure that this is possible. Parents and teachers, being the most closely involved, have the most valuable role to play.

There are many advantages in parents and teachers working in partnership (Besag, 1992, 1995). One of the most obvious is that in this way the two halves of the child's life can be put together, so eliminating the risk of a tiny, but essential piece of information being overlooked. Parents can offer valuable insights and information, not only concerning the child, but also on family matters which may be causing distress (Elliott, 1996). In addition, there are often more opportunities to offer rewards in the home environment than in school, so that by teachers and parents working together, behaviour in school, for example, could be successfully reinforced and rewarded at home.

Parents are often extremely anxious to have a bully situation speedily resolved and so will offer the highest level of commitment. Their level of distress can often be reduced by inviting them to become actively involved in any plan as feelings of helplessness may be increasing their concern (Besag, 1992: 54).

It may be easier for a bullied child to confide in a teacher than in parents who are often bewildered by the child's reluctance to discuss the matter and refusal of their offers of help. The situation, in such cases, remains shrouded in mystery, and parents rely heavily on teachers to support the child and communicate with them appropriately.

There are several reasons why children are often reluctant to confide in their parents (Lewis, 1988). Frightened victims often fear reprisals from the bullies, or even classmates, if reporting an attack is viewed as 'telling tales'. If the bullying is severe or prolonged they may not wish to worry their parents, especially if they feel that parents are unable to effectively change a situation in school. Children are sometimes wary of admitting that expensive items or money have been given to bullies. Bullied children feel rejected and unpopular and may feel ashamed to talk about this to their parents for, although it is widely accepted that many parents are eager for the academic success of their children, we are perhaps less aware that parents can be equally sensitive to the social success and popularity of their offspring.

In the case of adolescents it may be that with a growing and necessary sense of independence, victims feel that they should be able to cope alone without turning to their parents for help. Often, at this stage, the links between young people and their parents become loosened – less time being spent in the company of parents – or even strained, as social norms are flaunted or challenged. The pathways of family communication are often subtle and can easily fall into disuse. There are, then, many reasons why children may prefer to disclose the bullying to a trusted teacher, who is less closely emotionally involved than their parents (Myers, 1992).

Given that many bullied children find it difficult to approach their parents for help, the optimum situation must be that all parents are alerted to the possibility of bullying occurring and are made aware of the warning signs (Elliott, 1994b; Besag, 1995: 132). They should be encouraged to approach the school should they suspect anything untoward.

The quality of the initial contact made between home and school, should bullying be suspected, is of the utmost importance. It is essential that clear signals be given that the problem is being taken seriously (by all parties), and a resolution is to be sought with the utmost urgency. Once all are alerted to the problem the most appropriate course of action will probably be for the school to set up an informal meeting for all those concerned so that all viewpoints are represented. It may be feasible to invite the parents of both victim(s) and bully(ies), but this would serve no useful purpose if their views are known to differ radically and there is obviously no common ground from which to work (Besag, 1992). Staff present at the meeting need to be aware of the severe tension and distress many parents experience on realising that their child is being bullied or bullying others.

The first thing to consider is whether or not bullying is the root problem. It may be that the child is using this claim to avoid school for some other reason. A general fear of separation from the parents, or of leaving the home, may well go unnoticed – other situations being easier to avoid – but be highlighted when the child has to leave home for school (Green, 1984; Besag, 1995: 159).

Before this initial meeting it may be useful for parents to be advised of some of the points to be raised so that they have time to reflect, observe and discuss with each other in private beforehand (Besag, 1995: 158). Having guidelines to focus their thoughts could result in them coming better prepared and with valuable information. The meeting should be of a problem-solving format with the outcome being a positive line of action for all to follow, so allowing little room for an over-emotional response from any party.

The role of the school, meanwhile, will have been to collate all school-based information, possibly even contacting schools previously attended by the pupils involved. Every way possible should be used to collect information as direct questioning of the bullies or bullied may result in sparse or inaccurate accounts. Sensitive observation, by staff or reliable pupils, can result in startling revelations. Training all pupils to alert staff to others in trouble is not 'telling tales' but taking responsible action (*see* Chapter 1).

Asking well-chosen pupils to observe and report may be thought of as controversial, but may be necessary for the well-being and safety of all. There are many ways in which the peer group or older pupils can support vulnerable pupils. Such programmes include mediation, peer counselling and mentoring systems (Besag, 1992: 123, 124). Staff often have access to valuable information by hearing pupils chatter among themselves. Once alerted to the suspicion of a child being bullied, useful insights could be gleaned from overhearing these conversations. In collecting information more directly from staff, attention needs to be drawn to such things as:

- quality of peer interactions;
- evidence of rejection by peers;
- submissive behaviour;
- isolation and vulnerability.

The value in gathering and collating information in this indirect manner cannot be underestimated as bullying is a covert activity, hidden in that curriculum organised by the pupils themselves which may be more pertinent than that organised by the school (Besag, 1986). Adults do not witness bullying, but the peer group does. Boys in particular may actively seek out an audience to gain kudos (Ekman, 1977, quoted in Olweus, 1978). An emphasis on a community ethos, where all have a responsibility for the welfare of all, and the development of good and trusted lines of communication between pupils and staff could lead to pupils being more forthcoming in protecting the vulnerable. On questioning pupils recently in a secondary school, I found that they were able to identify those among them who had been bullied repeatedly since their first years in school.

Parents need to be aware that the collection and collation of information takes time, especially when at least 70 teachers work in all but the smallest secondary school. Often parents expect the situation to be resolved on the spot, although they are aware that any other system of justice can be slow. Once clearly identified, bullying often stops immediately, having thrived previously on secrecy, but the stage of identification may take time. This being so, it is imperative that parents contact the school immediately if they suspect bullying is taking place, even if their own child is not directly involved. We know now that children merely witnessing bullying can be very distressed and anxious (*see* Chapter 1; Measor and Woods, 1984), and in the case of the victim, a speedy resolution is essential as the situation can easily escalate and the confidence of the victim be rapidly reduced (Lewis, 1988).

Parents should encourage their children to approach those teachers they feel most comfortable with first, rather than a designated teacher such as the year tutor. It is important that some responsible adult is alerted to the situation, rather than that a child be left feeling helpless and guilty due to a reluctance to approach a less familiar teacher.

It is to everyone's advantage that some form of written record be kept of the meeting, who is to be the key person, the proposed course of action and the date set for a review meeting. The latter is essential to ensure that the situation has been resolved satisfactorily, as parents may be hesitant to contact school a second time if the bullying is continuing – yet the school may assume that all is well. The situation will need monitoring for some time, especially to reassure the bullied child who may have lost confidence in the level of adult protection. If the parents of the bully(ies) were not at the meeting they should be advised by letter of any proposed action concerning their child. All parents should be made aware if their child has been involved in any bullying either as bully or victim.

If parents approach a school but receive a negative response, they are able to turn for support to other bodies such as school governors, doctors, nurses, psychologists and advisers who all work to support children in school. All can be contacted directly by parents through the education department of the local authority. The administrators in this sector of any local authority are also able to offer guidance and support to parents. Depending on the age of the child (over 9 years of age), and the severity of attack it may be appropriate for parents to contact the local police. In one case I worked with, alongside parents, young people who had left school frequently hung around the gate of the secondary school they had previously attended, taunting and bullying pupils on their way home. At the request of the head teacher, the local police informally approached these young people and supervised the area. This resolved the situation speedily and, contrary to the fears of parents, the bullying did not re-emerge elsewhere.

All the above suggestions concern the liaison work of parents and teachers once a bullying problem has been identified. The optimum approach, however, is the type of preventative work carried out in Norway where Professor Dan Olweus (Olweus, 1978) brought bullying in schools to the attention of the public.

In recent years there has been a well-established preventative programme of work carried out in schools in Norway organised by Professor Olweus, involving booklets, discussion groups, videos and workshops for pupils, parents and teachers. It is important that parents, as well as teachers, have the opportunity to receive this type of training for they have more contact hours with their children than professionals, but receive little advice or support (Olweus, 1993b).

In the UK, pioneering work on prevention has been done by Michele Elliott with the Kidscape programmes in schools. These are taught by teachers in the curriculum of the school and involve discussions, roleplays and parent meetings (Elliott, 1994a). An excellent book on all aspects of parenting is *501 Ways To Be a Good Parent* by Michele Elliott (1996).

One aspect of the problem of bullying which could be dealt with in such workshops for parents is the effect it can have on a child, so that the parents are able to respond appropriately to, what can be, difficult behaviour. A bullied child can become irritable, volatile and fearful (Lewis, 1988). In the words of one victim, he used his young sister as his 'personal punchbag'. Parents may be the butt of feelings of pent-up rage and frustration. The sudden lack of confidence many victims experience may bewilder their parents (Olweus, 1993a). It is not uncommon, for example, for a bullied child to avoid any contact with others, to the extent of crossing the road on the approach of even an unknown peer group or waiting for a bus several yards away from a queue. This avoidance of others, and perhaps their rejection, leaves many bullied children isolated in school. If they are not included in the network of informal chatter, and so miss the constant reminders and cues passing among the peer group, this could result in them being in the wrong place at the wrong time, with wrong equipment or materials. Parents and teachers need to be particularly patient and supportive at this time (Besag, 1992: 41–4; Myers, 1992).

The parents of a child being bullied may approach the school for advice on how to support the child at home during this difficult period (Besag, 1992: 126). They need to be advised to remain calm and confident in front of the child, and to resist persistent questioning which may add to the stress. The child must be assured that the bullying will be stopped, and to understand that this taunting is something that many people encounter in some form or other at some time. The child needs to feel confident that he or she is going to be helped to develop coping skills in case he or she should encounter it again, as well as to manage the current trauma. It may be helpful to discuss name-calling (Besag, 1992: 52). This is often the most distressing aspect for young to cope with (Elliott, 1993; Besag, 1995) and yet the damaging effect is underestimated by adults. Ways of coping with this 'testing out' – by keeping calm, laughing if off, ignoring it – can help the child shrug off a potentially distressing situation (Besag, 1995: 131). It is always helpful to talk to other parents who have had similar experiences, not only to share ideas and solutions, but to reassure the bullied child that this is something that can happen to anyone, and has not occurred because of a particular defect in the victim. The best outcome would be for the bullied children to reach a solution for themselves, with the support of concerned adults, so that they feel confident in their own ability to cope. It must be stressed that research shows that victims left to struggle with the problem alone are unlikely to extricate themselves from the bullying, which can continue for years (Cowen *et al.*, 1973; Cole, 1977; Stephenson and Smith, 1988). With adult support, victims can gain in confidence and self-esteem if they find that a resolution is within their own grasp. It is important that the victims be encouraged, in a sensitive manner, to examine any behaviour, attitude or response of their own, which could be initiating or exacerbating the bullying. It is essential, however, that this work is approached in a practical manner, where victims identify for themselves how they could best work towards resolving the problem, for, if approached in a prescriptive way, they could feel that they have 'deserved' the bullying and they have been solely at fault (Besag, 1992: 125, 126).

One of the ways in which liaison work between home and school can be most effective is in restoring the self-esteem and confidence of victims (Lewis, 1988). Positive comments and praise help to do this but, in addition, mastering a skill leads to a sense of achievement, so giving tangible proof of self-worth. Encouraging young people to take up something such as swimming or chess, for example, gets them out of the house and in the company of others, whereas they may prefer to sit in a bedroom turning more and more to solitary occupations. On examination of the profiles of those children at high risk of becoming involved in bullying (Besag, 1995: 17, 18; 1992: 29, 30) it can be seen that potential victims are often 'watchers' rather then 'doers' and so could need a lot of encouragement to join in groups and make new friends, even before the experience of being bullied. It is, however, easier for a shy and hesitant person to join a skill-based group where adults are present, for example a dance class or tennis club, as adults are more tolerant and in a skill-based group there is less emphasis on social skills. This is one way in which those who have been bullied, and so become wary, can be eased back into functioning happily within a group. Later moves can be made towards similar skill-based groups attended by peers but under adult supervision, for example a badminton club in after-school hours, and, lastly, to less supervised and purely social peer groups, e.g. a youth club or disco. Details of such programmes of work for both bullies and victims can be found in Besag (1995: 143–9; 1992: 126).

It is unfortunate that many clubs organised by schools demand good coordination skills, e.g. football, table tennis, etc. Many young people who are bullied, especially boys, do not have these skills, e.g. football, table tennis, etc. (*see* 'profiles' in Besag, 1995: 17, 18). Once aware of the value of such experiences for those who are socially vulnerable, schools and parents could work in liaison to offer these opportunities to pupils so that they can interact within the peer groups without fear of ridicule and rejection. The long-term value of such work is that even in adult life, those who are naturally shy may find a bank of skills such as chess or photography can help them join groups in unfamiliar situations, so enabling them to make friends and develop confidence in social situations. The sparse research indicates that those who are socially vulnerable in childhood are at high risk of remaining so in later years if left to cope alone and unsupported (Lewis, 1988; Olweus, 1993a).

The style of work attempted between concerned teachers and the parents of a child bullying others largely depends on the attitude and reaction of the parents. If the parents admit that this behaviour is unacceptable, the prognosis for change will be more favourable. Many parents, finding themselves in this situation, feel under considerable stress and experience feelings of shame, guilt and confusion. A child, however, may be bullying others for a variety of reasons independent of parental guidance, for example jealousy of a sibling, over-boisterous play or a confusion between leadership and dominance (Elliott, 1994b). Children being bullied themselves may bully others due to frustration. In cases such as the above, if parents and school have a common approach, the situation can be resolved speedily.

There are, however, those parents who ignore repeated reports and warnings from the school that the bullying behaviour of their children will not be tolerated. Such parents may consider that aggressive behaviour is an acceptable means of settling disputes or expressing frustration. Having taught their children to 'stick up for themselves' they feel others should behave in a similar way. Children from such families are modelling behaviour they have witnessed at home (Besag, 1992: 121, 122). It is not uncommon, in such families, for the father to be the disciplinarian, using a harsh and punitive style, and the mother to be lax and inconsistent, or ineffective (Besag, 1992: 30). Depending on whether or not the parents are cooperative, the school could have a valuable role to play in directing the attention of such parents to alternative styles of management, either directly in discussions or indirectly in workshops and parent meetings (Elliott, 1996). Patterson *et al.* (1973, in Besag, 1995: 164) shows the damaging effects of harsh discipline. Not only does the child learn to model the aggressive behaviour, but the relationship between child and parent can rapidly deteriorate, whereas a positive style of management can help to strengthen bonds (Elliott, 1996).

If young people are accustomed to using aggression as a means to an end, whether it be material gain, kudos or entertainment, the use of modes such as persuasion, advice or counselling may be found to be ineffective to counter such deviant behaviour at bullying.

Good supervision and a firm policy, in addition to counselling, is often necessary as there may be little enthusiasm for change on the part of the bully, although all others, victim, parents and school staff, may be urgently seeking a successful resolution. The bully has been gaining in some manner and may show no guilt or remorse, whereas all others may have found the experience destructive and distressing.

In conclusion, we are now aware that bullying is a form of abuse, child-to-child abuse, and, as such, can be a most damaging experience. In the short term it can be a traumatic experience for a child of any age to experience, whereas the long-term prognosis for both bullies and bullied is poor. Those bullying during their school years are known to go on to young adulthood at higher risk of

116

embarking on a deviant career than others (Olweus, 1973) whereas those who have been bullied, and left alone to cope, can be expected to lead a life of impoverished social experience and all that entails. We now have profiles of those at high risk of becoming involved in bullying (Besag, 1995: 17, 18), so a variety of preventative work can be embarked on by adults. As teachers and parents have the most contact hours with young people, and parents, in most cases, are the most committed to their own children, by working together on preventative programmes (Elliott, 1994a) or in liaison in an identified situation, we should eventually be able to ensure that all pupils feel that they are able to attend school in safety.

References

Besag, V. E. (1986) 'Bullies, victims and the silent majority', *Times Educational Supplement*, 5 December, pp. 22–3.

Besag, V. E. (1992) *We Don't Have Bullies Here* (manual), available from 3 Jesmond Dene Terrace, Jesmond, Newcastle upon Tyne NE2 2ET.

Besag, V. E. (1995) *Bullies and Victims in Schools*, Milton Keynes, Open University Press.

Cole, R. J. (1977) 'The bullied child in school', unpublished MSc dissertation, University of Sheffield.

Cowen, E. L., Pederson, A., Babigian, H., Izzo, L. D. and Trost, M. A. (1973) 'Long-term follow-up of early detected vulnerable children', *Journal of Consulting and Clinical Psychology*, Vol. 41, pp. 438–46.

Ekman (1977) quoted in Olweus, D. (1979) 'Stability of aggressive reaction patterns in males. A review', *Psychological Bulletin*, Vol. 86, No. 4, pp. 852–75.

Elliott, M. (1993) *Bully Leaflet*, London, Kidscape.

Elliott, M. (1994a) *Kidscape Primary Kit*, London, Kidscape.

Elliott, M. (1994b) *Keeping Safe: A Practical Guide to Talking with Children*, Hodder & Stoughton.

Elliott, M. (1996) *501 Ways To Be a Good Parent*, Hodder & Stoughton.

Green, C. (1984) *Toddler Training*, Century Hutchinson.

Lewis, D. (1988) *Helping Your Anxious Child*, London, Methuen.

Measor, I. and Woods, P. (1984) *Changing Schools: Pupil Perspectives on Transfer to a Secondary School*, Milton Keynes, Open University Press.

Myers, B. (1992) *Parenting Teenagers*, Jessica Kingsley Publishers Ltd.

Olweus, D. (1973) *Hackycklingar och oversittare: Forskning om skilmobbring*, Stockholm, Almqvist and Wikzell.

Olweus, D. (1973) *Aggression in the Schools: Bullies and Whipping Boys*, Washington DC, Hemisphere.

Olweus, D. (1993a) 'Victimisation by peers: antecedents and long-term outcomes', in N. A. Rubin and J. A. Asendorg (eds), *Social Withdrawal, Inhibition and Shyness in Childhood*, Hellidale, NJ.

Olweus, D. (1993b) *Bullying in Schools: What We Know and What We Can Do*, Oxford, Blackwell.

Patterson, G. R., Cobb, J. A. and Ray, R. S. (1973) 'A social engineering technology for retraining families of aggressive boys', in H. E. Adams, I. P. Unikel (eds), *Issues and Trends in Behaviour Therapy*, Springfield, Ill., C. C. Thomas.

Stephenson, P. and Smith, D. (1988) 'Bullying in the junior school', in D. Tattum and D. Lane (eds), *Bullying in Schools*, Stoke-on-Trent, Trentham Books.

13

. . .

Bullying: a guide to the law

CAROLYN HAMILTON

Are schools required to stop bullying?

While s.154 of the Education Act 1996 places responsibility on head teachers for discipline and behaviour in schools, the section does not require schools to have a written disciplinary policy. However, guidance issued by the Department for Education (DFE Circular 8/94, *Pupil Behaviour and Discipline*, paras 1–9) encourages head teachers, in consultation with their governing bodies, staff and parents, to develop 'whole-school' behaviour policies and approaches which are clearly understood by pupils, parents and the school staff. The guidance recommends that schools should also have an anti-bullying policy. Moreover, paragraph 56 of the guidance states that:

> *School Staff must act – and importantly be seen to act – firmly against bullying whenever and wherever it appears. School behaviour policies and the associated rules of conduct should, therefore, make specific reference to bullying. Governing bodies should regularly review their school's policy on bullying.*
>
> *School prospectuses and other documents issued to parents and pupils should make it clear that bullying will not be tolerated. Prospectuses should also explain arrangements through which pupils troubled by bullying can draw their concerns to the attention of staff in the confidence that these will be carefully investigated and, if substantiated, taken seriously and acted upon.*
>
> *Individual members of staff must be alert to signs of bullying and act promptly and firmly against it. Failure to report incidents may be interpreted as condoning the behaviour.*

More detailed practical guidance is contained in *Action Against Bullying: A Support Pack for Schools*. This was sent to all schools in England in July 1992. It is important to note, however, that neither the guidance contained in Circular 8/94, *Pupil Behaviour and Discipline*, nor the guidance contained in *Action Against Bullying* create legal obligations. A school is not *required* by law to have an anti-bullying policy, but the guidance strongly *recommends* that it should as a matter of good practice. If your school does not have an anti-bullying policy, you should write or speak to the head teacher and the school governors, pointing out the recommendations of the DFEE.

If schools fail to tackle bullying, then it may be necessary to make a complaint to the school.

Although the advice in this chapter is aimed at parents, teachers need to be aware of the procedures suggested to parents by the Children's Legal Centre.

Complaints

What follows is a step-by-step guide through the complaints procedure. If your child is being bullied at school, you should first make an informal complaint.

Making an informal complaint

Step 1: Talking to the class teacher

You should:

- talk calmly with your child about his/her experience;
- make a note of what your child says – particularly who was involved, how often the bullying has occurred, where it happened and what has happened;
- reassure your child that he/she has done the right thing to tell you about the bullying;
- explain to your child that should any further incidents occur he/she should report them to a teacher straightaway and tell you about it;
- make an appointment to see your child's class teacher or form tutor;
- explain to the teacher the problems your child is experiencing.

Be realistic when talking to the teacher – the school will not be willing to immediately exclude the 'bully' from the class or the school on a vague, first allegation of bullying from you. However, the teacher should investigate your allegations and take reasonable steps to protect your child from bullying.

Remember:

- When you are talking to the teacher try to be as specific as possible. The teacher may have no idea that your child is being bullied and will need dates, places, times and the names of the other children involved if action is to be taken to stop the bullying.
- You should make a note of what the teacher has said to you and the action that the teacher intends to take.
- You should stay in touch with the school after this meeting and let them know if things improve as well as if problems continue.

If you are not satisfied with the class teacher's or tutor's response, you will need to speak to the head teacher.

Step 2: Talking to the head teacher

The head teacher has day-to-day responsibility for discipline in state schools, for securing that the standard of behaviour is acceptable and otherwise regulating the conduct of pupils. This is equally true of independent (private) schools and grant-maintained schools (those schools that receive public funding but have opted out of local education authority (LEA) control). The head teacher does not, however, have a completely free hand on pupil behaviour: he or she must act in accordance with any written statement of general principles provided by the governing body. Before you go to see the head teacher it is a good idea to ask to see a copy of the school's disciplinary policy.

- You should speak to the school secretary or school office and make an appointment to see the head teacher.
- You should ask for a copy of the school's disciplinary policy, statement of general principles issued by the governing body and the anti-bullying policy, if they have one. Be familiar with these documents before you attend the meeting.
- Before you attend the meeting, you should be prepared with times, dates of the bullying incidents, the names of those who have bullied your child and an account of your conversation with the form teacher or tutor.
- At the meeting with the head teacher, try not to be antagonistic and aggressive. Try to be reasonable. Remember, the head teacher may not be aware of the bullying and the problems your child is facing.
- When talking to the head, try and stick to the point. Try not to digress to general and unrelated criticisms of the school or raise irrelevant points to your main concerns. Present the facts to the head in a reasoned way. Remember, most complaints are resolved by informal discussions between the parent(s) and the school.
- Explain to the head teacher that you are concerned that your child is suffering as a result of the bullying and ask what action will be taken.
- Ask the head teacher to keep you informed of what action has been taken and when.
- If further bullying incidents occur, you should contact the head teacher straight away.

If the head teacher does not resolve your complaint, or you feel that insufficient action has been taken to stop the bullying, you may need to take matters further by making a formal complaint.

Making a formal complaint

Step 3: Finding out about formal complaint procedures

If you do not know, find out whether your child attends an LEA-maintained school or a grant-maintained school.

- **LEA-maintained schools**. These are schools that are under the control of the LEA.

- **Grant-maintained schools**. Grant-maintained schools have opted out of LEA control. Although publicly funded, these schools are largely responsible for their own government.

There is no legal requirement for a school to have a formal written complaints policy or procedure (except in relation to complaints about the curriculum). However, many schools, as a matter of good practice, do have a written complaints procedure. Where the school does not have such a procedure, a complaint may still be made by writing to the chair of governors or, in the case of an LEA-maintained school, to the County Director of Education or the Chief Education Officer (the names of these officers should be in the school prospectus). The letter should state that you wish to make a formal complaint and that you would like to be informed of the procedures for having your complaint considered.

Where the school does have a written complaints procedure, you should ask for a copy from the school office or, in the case of an LEA-maintained school, from the County Director of Education or the Chief Education Officer.

Step 4: How to make a written complaint

Complaints procedures may differ substantially from school to school. Some require that a letter be sent to the head teacher while others require the letter to be sent to the chair of governors. In some LEA-maintained schools, complaints must be addressed to the Chief Education Officer. However, the example of a letter of complaint to the chair of governors shown in Figure 13.1 highlights what the letter should contain.

Step 5: Response of the governors

The response of the governors to a complaint will vary from school to school depending on the procedures adopted by the school. Each school has the power to set its own procedures. There are, however, some common elements in complaint procedures:

- As a matter of good practice, most complaints procedures will contain time limits in which the governors will reply to the letter initiating the complaints procedure. This usually varies between about seven and 21 days.

- Commonly, governors will appoint a subcommittee of between three and five governors to hear the complaint and determine what action should be taken.

Figure 13.1: Example of a formal letter of complaint to the chair of governors

Mr/Ms . . . .
Chair of Governors
. . . . School
. . . .
. . . .

Dear Chair

I wish to make a formal complaint. My daughter, S, has been bullied over a period of three months by X, Y and Z. The incidents complained of are as follows:

(Parent should list the bullying incidents)

I have complained to the teacher and head teacher on numerous occasions. These are listed below:

(Parent should list the occasions on which he or she has spoken to the teacher and head teacher)

My daughter is now suffering anxiety and depression and is frightened to attend school. I would like a full and thorough investigation of these bullying incidents. Please let me know what action you will be taking, both in relation to the bullying that has occurred, and to ensure that my child is not bullied in the future.

Yours faithfully

A N OTHER

- In the case of some LEA-maintained schools, the governors can request that the LEA investigate the incidents complained of and report to the subcommittee. Yet others may appoint one of the governors to investigate or ask the head teacher to present a report.

- Normally, parents will be allowed to attend and present evidence to the subcommittee, although some governing bodies make a decision on paper submissions alone.

- Usually, parents are allowed to take a friend or representative (which could be a legal representative) with them to the meeting.

- Generally, the head teacher, or another teacher who was responsible for investigating the evidence, will be invited to give a report on the incidents complained of. The parent may be allowed to question or cross-examine the head teacher and vice versa.

It is rare for children, especially those at primary schools, to be allowed to appear before the subcommittee, or to be allowed to give evidence or to present a complaint themselves.

Step 6: Complaint to local education authority

Note: This section is not applicable to grant-maintained or independent schools.

If the governing body appears to be inefficient or obstructive, it is possible to make a complaint to the Director of Education via the LEA. This can be done through the local town hall or county hall. The Director should respond to any complaint and can contact the school on a parent's behalf. It is, however, important to be aware that the LEA cannot interfere in the internal management of the school, neither can they actually instruct a school to take any specific action.

Step 7: Complaint to Secretary of State for Education

A formal complaint to the Secretary of State for Education can only be made in limited circumstances and as a last resort, since a complainant must have exhausted all other complaint procedures first.

The grounds for complaint are as follows:

- A complaint can be made against the LEA or the governing body of any county, voluntary, maintained special school or grant-maintained school who have acted unreasonably with respect to the exercise of any power or the performance of any duty imposed on them by the Education Act 1996 (Education Act 1996, s.496).
- A complaint can be made against the LEA or the governing body of any county, voluntary, maintained special school or grant-maintained school who have failed to discharge any duty imposed on them by or for the purposes of the Education Act 1996 (Education Act 1996, s.497).

If the Secretary of State is satisfied that either of the above two grounds exist, the complaint will be investigated. Parents should be warned that the above two grounds are very difficult to fulfil and few complaints have resulted in any action by the Secretary of State. You can expect to wait up to six months for a reply to your letter of complaint.

The Secretary of State has no control over independent schools.

Step 8: Local Government Ombudsman

Parents can complain to the Local Government Ombudsman. However, the Ombudsman may only investigate complaints in very limited circumstances.

- You cannot complain about the internal management of schools, for example if the school has heard your complaint but you do not agree with the decision reached.
- You cannot complain about the actions of independent schools.
- The Ombudsman can only investigate complaints about the way, or how, the LEA or school has done or failed to do something, not simply because parents disagree with the action of the LEA or school.

- The Ombudsman will not investigate something that happened over 12 months ago unless he or she thinks it is reasonable to look into the matter despite the delay.
- The Ombudsman will not investigate if the case has already been heard by a court or a tribunal. It is also unlikely that the Ombudsman would investigate if a complaint has already been made to the Secretary of State for Education.

The Ombudsman can only investigate complaints where there has been maladministration by a school under the control of the LEA or by the LEA itself. Maladministration occurs where:

- the school or LEA has taken too long to take action without good reason;
- does not follow its own rules or the law;
- breaks its promises;
- gives the wrong information; or
- does not make a decision in the correct way.

Remember:

- Before complaining to the Ombudsman, you must give the LEA the opportunity to deal with the complaint.
- You should check with the Ombudsman that your complaint is one that they can investigate.
- You must make your complaint in writing.
- You must sign the letter yourself.

If the Ombudsman decides to investigate, parents will be kept informed and a formal report will be produced which will say whether there has been maladministration by the LEA and/or school. The Ombudsman may recommend compensation be paid or some other action be taken to put matters right. Although most schools and LEAs comply with the Ombudsman's recommendations, the Ombudsman cannot force the school or the LEA to pay compensation or comply with any other recommendations.

Withdrawing children from school

The Children's Legal Centre has received numerous queries from parents who have either withdrawn, or are considering withdrawing, their bullied child from school. Under the Education Act 1996, s.7, parents have a legal duty to ensure that their child receives an efficient full-time education suitable to the child's age, ability and aptitude, whether this be at school or otherwise than at school.

Electing home education

The law allows parents to educate their child at home provided that the standard of education is satisfactory.

There are a number of organisations that can assist parents by way of materials and moral support. (*See* 'Help Organisations' pages 206–208.) Parents should be warned that if they decide to home educate, they have opted out of the state education system and should not expect any assistance in educating their child from the LEA.

It is advisable to contact the LEA before asking for your child's name to be removed from the school roll to ascertain whether the programme of home education would meet with LEA approval. This approval would avoid giving rise to a situation where parents remove a child from a school roll or register, only to discover shortly after that their programme does not meet the LEA's requirements. The LEA have an obligation to ensure that the child is receiving a suitable education. If the LEA is of the view that the home education parents are providing is unsuitable, parents could face legal action (see below).

Remember:

If you decide to withdraw your child from school and provide education at home, you must inform the school and LEA (Figure 13.2 provides an example letter) to ensure that your child ceases to be registered at his or her school. Failure to deregister the child may result in action for non-attendance at school being taken (Education Act 1996, s.444(1)).

Figure 13.2: Example of a letter at deregistration to the LEA

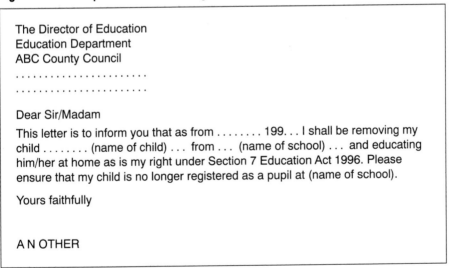

The Director of Education
Education Department
ABC County Council
. . . .
. . . .

Dear Sir/Madam

This letter is to inform you that as from . . . . 199. . . I shall be removing my child . . . . (name of child) . . . from . . . (name of school) . . . and educating him/her at home as is my right under Section 7 Education Act 1996. Please ensure that my child is no longer registered as a pupil at (name of school).

Yours faithfully

A N OTHER

Flexi-education

Some children and parents feel that their child should only return to school part-time, perhaps while they build up confidence and problems are resolved. If the school agrees, the child can attend for just part of the week, with the parents providing education at home for the rest of the week. It is up to the head teacher (and the governing body will normally delegate this power to the head teacher) to decide whether they will agree to this arrangement. The school is under no legal obligation to agree and the parent has no right to insist on this arrangement. If the school does agree, the parents have a considerable responsibility to ensure that the child keeps up with the other pupils in the class.

LEA duties to provide education otherwise than at school

Under the Education Act 1996, s.19(1), the LEA has a duty to make full- or part-time education provision for pupils who cannot attend school because of illness, exclusion or otherwise. If a parent decides not to send a child to school because of extreme physical danger, the child refuses to return to school or the child is suffering from anxiety or depression and is failing to cope, the child may be entitled to home tuition or education at a special unit such as a pupil referral unit. However, a medical or psychological assessment may well be necessary to convince the LEA that the bullied child falls within this category.

Parents should be aware that education provided under s.19(1) may not be of the same quality or quantity as that provided by schools. Recent research has indicated that LEA-funded home tuition can be as little as two hours a week and is rarely more than ten hours.

It should be emphasised that parents should not keep their child away from school unless the circumstances are serious enough to warrant such action. The Children's Legal Centre has had cases where parents have been threatened with legal action if they do not return their bullied child to school.

Although LEAs often fail to state exactly what legal action they are going to take if the child does not attend school, this could be any of the following.

School attendance order

A school attendance order may be served under the Education Act 1996, s.437, if it appears that a child is not receiving suitable education.

- **Step 1.** Before serving the order, the LEA will serve a notice on the parent in writing, requiring the parent to satisfy them within the period specified in the notice that the child is receiving suitable education.

- **Step 2.** If the parent cannot satisfy the LEA, or if, in the opinion of the LEA, it is expedient that the child should attend school, the LEA will serve a school attendance order requiring the parent to register the child at a school named in the order.

Mrs K called the Children's Legal Centre's advice line having removed her child from school. Her daughter, J, had been bullied over a period of 14 months. J was a special needs child and had a statement of special educational needs. Despite both informal discussion with the school and formal written complaints, the school had failed to deal with the bullying. Not only was Mrs K frustrated at the school's failure, she was also worried about the anxiety state of J. She decided her only course of action was to remove J from school. She hoped that this would spur the school into taking some action against the bullies. However, Mrs K was threatened by the LEA with prosecution for non-attendance of J at school. Furthermore, the LEA had also notified social services who decided that they must investigate under the Children Act 1989, s.47. Mrs K was unwilling to cooperate with the social worker. The social worker threatened Mrs K, saying that the local authority would make an application to the courts for an interim care order if J was not returned to school forthwith. When Mrs K rang the Children's Legal Centre for advice, the advice officer advised Mrs K to cooperate with the social worker in her investigations. Mrs K was also advised to obtain medical and psychological reports to support her withdrawal of J from school. In the event, medical and professional backing was obtained, and the LEA agreed to provide some home tuition for J, as is their duty under the Education Act 1996, s.19, until another school was found that was more suitable to her special needs.

- **Step 3**. Before actually serving the order, the LEA must send the parent a notice, in writing, informing them that they intend to serve a school attendance order, and specifying the school which the LEA intend to name in the order. The LEA may, if they wish, name one or more other schools which they regard as suitable alternatives. If the parent chooses one of the schools in this notice within the 15-day period given for reply, that school will be named in the school attendance order. A parent can apply to other schools not named in the notice and provided the parent can show the LEA, within 15 days, that the child has been offered a place by the school, that school can be named in the order instead. The school can be any registered school, and this would include registered independent schools (Education Act 1996, s.438(4), (5)).

- **Step 4**. If a parent fails to comply then they will be guilty of an offence unless the parent proves that the child is receiving suitable education otherwise than at school (Education Act 1996, s.443(1)). A parent will be prosecuted through the Magistrates' Court and fined. A parent cannot be imprisoned for non-attendance of their child at school.

Failure to attend school regularly

The LEA may also decide to prosecute the parents where their child is registered at school and is not attending regularly (Education Act 1996, s.444(1)). Prosecution can result in a fine. There are a number of defences for parents prosecuted for this offence: no offence is committed if the child was away from school for a religious holiday or as a result of sickness or some other unavoidable cause (Education Act 1996, s.444(3)). Parents would probably need to produce evidence to the court in the form of medical or psychological reports.

Education supervision order

The LEA, after consultation with Social Services, may also apply for an education supervision order where the child is not receiving a suitable education (Children Act 1989, s.36, and Education Act 1996, s.447(1)). An education supervision order lasts for one year. If an order is made, a supervisor will be appointed to advise, assist and befriend the child and parents. The supervisor also gives directions to the child and the parents to ensure that the child is being properly educated (Children Act 1989, Sch. 3, Part III, para. 12). Failure to comply with the supervisor's directions is a criminal offence and can result in prosecution of the parents and a fine (Children Act 1989, Sch. 3, Part III, para. 18).

Care order

Where a child persistently fails to attend school, it is not unknown for local authorities to initiate proceedings to take the child into care. The local authority will have to prove in court that the child is suffering, or likely to suffer, significant harm and that this harm, or likelihood of harm, is attributable to being beyond parental control, or that the child was not receiving the care it is reasonable to expect (Children Act 1989, s.31). If granted by the court, the effect of a care order is that the local authority gains parental responsibility for the child in addition to the parent(s), and has the power to remove the child.

Legal action

If all else fails, parents may wish to consider legal action. Before starting any form of legal action it is wise to consult a solicitor. It is worth finding out whether there are any solicitors in your area who specialise in education law by contacting your local Citizens' Advice Bureau, the Law Society or an organisation of education lawyers called ELAS. (*See* 'Help Organisations', pages 206–208.)

Criminal law

Some forms of bullying may amount to criminal behaviour. Where a child has been bullied and has been threatened, the bully may have committed the offence of 'threatening behaviour' under s.4, Public Order Act 1986. This provides that:

> A person will be guilty of threatening behaviour if he or she uses threatening, abusive or insulting words or behaviour, or distributes or displays to another person any threatening, abusive or insulting written material, sign or other 'visible representation' to:
> (i) cause another person to fear violence; or to
> (ii) provoke the immediate use of unlawful violence by another person.

If the bullied child is assaulted either physically or sexually, the bullies may have committed the criminal offence of common assault or indecent assault. Both common and indecent assault can be committed without touching the victim. However, in practice the police are unlikely to act unless physical contact has been made.

It is important to point out that children under the age of ten cannot be prosecuted for a criminal offence. This means that the police cannot charge a child under the age of ten, no matter how criminal his behaviour. Where the child is aged 10–14, special rules apply. The child can be charged with committing a criminal offence, but will only be convicted if the prosecution prove that at the time of the offence the bully knew that what he or she was doing was seriously wrong.

Remember that the police cannot charge a bully with committing a criminal offence unless they have evidence that the incident occurred. If a child has been injured, parents should take the child to a doctor to obtain medical evidence. As soon as possible, the child should write down the details of all the bullying incidents. This is important, because this piece of paper can be used in court provided it is written immediately after the event. This means that should the child be required to give evidence, this evidence can be given by simply reading from the original document, rather than giving evidence from memory.

It is advisable to contact the police where the assault is of a serious nature and where the school and LEA have consistently failed to deal with the bullying. The experience of advice workers at the Children's Legal Centre shows that sometimes just the threat of informing the police is enough to spur the school or LEA into action.

Private prosecution

Sometimes parents are frustrated when the Crown Prosecution Service (CPS) or the police decide not to prosecute the bully where there has been a physical or sexual assault. Provided there is sufficient evidence, it may be possible to bring a private prosecution against the bully. However, there may be good reasons why the CPS or police have decided not to prosecute. Parents are entitled to a reason and should ask for an explanation. There are two justifications for deciding not to prosecute under the Prosecution of Offences Act 1986, s.10: these are evidential insufficiency and against the public interest. Most cases are frustrated on the latter ground: an example would be where the bully was a special needs child.

Civil action

Judicial review

It may be possible to seek judicial review of a school's or LEA's decision to refuse to take action to deal with the bullying situation and to force the school or LEA to act.

Judicial review is a public law action that can only be taken against public bodies or private bodies that perform a public duty.

Therefore, LEAs are susceptible to judicial review, as are boards of school governors of state-funded schools, which includes LEA-maintained schools (*R v. Haberdasher Aske's Hatcham Schools, ex p. ILEA* [1989] 1 Admin LR 22) and, because they are funded by public money, is likely to include grant-maintained schools. It is unlikely that judicial review can be taken against independent schools as they are not public bodies and the relationship between those paying the fees and the school is founded upon the law of contract (*R v. Fernhill Manor School, ex p. A* [1993] 1 FLR 620). (For claims against independent schools see section below on 'breach of contract'.)

Before you make an application for judicial review, all rights of appeal against the school and LEA must have been exhausted, so parents must have followed complaints procedures first. Furthermore, parents must act promptly and applications for judicial review must be brought within three months from the date when grounds for the application arose, although this time limit can be extended where the court considers that there is good reason for doing so.

In judicial review, the court examines how a decision has been reached but cannot examine the merits of the decision. A successful application, for example, would be where the school or LEA failed to follow proper or correct procedures, did not apply the law correctly, or acted so unreasonably that no other school or LEA would have reached such a decision. Although the Children's Legal Centre knows of no such case, an action may be possible where, for example, a school or LEA disregarded guidance issued by the Department of Education which states that school staff must act and be seen to act firmly against bullying, and that governing bodies should regularly review school policy on bullying (DFE Circular N. 8/94, para. 56). A further example would be where the LEA or school had a stated policy on tackling bullying and failed to follow it.

The child can apply for judicial review, provided the court believes he or she has sufficient interest to apply. If a child has left the school and is settled at a new school, he or she is unlikely to have sufficient interest. The application is made in the name of the child, but brought on behalf of the child by a 'next friend' who is usually one of the parents. The advantage of the child making the application is that the child may pass the legal aid financial tests whereas the parent(s) may not.

A successful application is unlikely to result in the payment of damages unless it is proved in court that the LEA, school or teacher has also been negligent. However, a judicial review action, if successful, may result in forcing the school or LEA to act to stop the bullying.

Negligence

Parents, acting on behalf of the bullied child, may be able to sue the school, teacher as well as the LEA for damages as compensation for psychiatric damage or physical injuries suffered as a result of a school or teacher negligently failing to act to protect pupils from bullying. Negligence arises where duty of care is owed to the child *and* that duty of care is breached resulting in damage to another person.

The law of negligence is very complex. For a case to be successful, it would be necessary to prove the following in court:

- **That the child has been bullied.** There is no legal definition of bullying. In deciding whether bullying has occurred, the court will look at all the circumstances. It will be necessary to prove that the bullying went beyond normal social interaction between children and was of a serious nature.

- **That the teacher or school owes pupils a duty of care.** It is well settled in law that a school owes its pupils a general duty of care. It is still unclear, however, how far a school must go to protect a pupil against bullying.

- **That the bullied child had suffered harm as a result of the bullying incidents.** This could be physical injuries or psychiatric damage. Expert evidence would be needed in both cases in order to prove the damage in court. For psychiatric damage it would be necessary to prove that the person bringing the claim is suffering or suffered a recognised form of psychiatric illness. The harm must arise as a result of the bullying incidents.

- **That it was reasonable for the teacher or school to foresee that the child might suffer harm or damage as a result of the bullying incidents.**

- **That the harm suffered was as a direct result of the teacher or school negligently failing to act to protect the bullied child.** It would be necessary to show that not only did the teacher or school know what was going on, but that they failed to take reasonable steps to stop it. It is important to point out that schools are not required to guarantee absolute safety for children. They must, however, ensure that pupils receive the same level of care and supervision as a reasonably careful and prudent parent would take of his or her own children (*Beaumont* v. *Surrey County Council* [1968] 66 LGR 580). In the *Beaumont* case, the court provided further explanation of the standard expected of head teachers. The judge said that a head teacher should take 'all reasonable and proper steps to prevent any of the pupils under his care from suffering injury from inanimate objects, the actions of their fellow pupils, or from a combination of the two.'

There have been few negligence actions relating to bullying in schools. Whether or not a claim is likely to be successful will depend very much on the individual circumstances of the case.

If the school is an LEA-maintained school, any claim for damages will usually be against the LEA who, as an employer, will be vicariously liable for the acts of the teachers employed by them, provided the teachers were acting in the course of their employment at the time of the incident. If the school is an independent or grant-maintained school, the claim will be against the school governors. It is possible to make a personal claim against individual teachers. However, such a claim may not be worthwhile since individual teachers are unlikely to be covered by insurance and may not be able to afford to pay damages.

The child him or herself may sue a teacher, school or LEA for negligence. Although the application will be made in the name of the child, it will normally be brought on behalf of the child by a 'next friend' who is usually one of the parents. Most children will qualify for legal aid. Without legal aid, such actions can be extremely costly.

Trespass to the person

A civil action claiming damages for trespass of the person may be brought against a bully. For the action to be successful, it would be necessary to prove that the bully threatened the use of immediate force or that the bully hit the victim or threw something at him or her. Practical jokes such as pulling a chair away so that the bullied child falls on the floor may also be covered (for example, see *Pursell* v. *Horn* [1838] 8 Ad & E 602). It is also necessary to prove that the bully intended to cause harm. While there are no age limits, if the bully is very young, it may be difficult to prove that he or she is capable of having the necessary intent. Unlike the law of negligence, it is not necessary to prove that harm or damage was *actually* inflicted on the bullied child.

An action of this kind would normally have to be brought on behalf of the bullied child by a 'next friend'. This can be the child's parents or another responsible adult. Proceedings would be brought against the bully rather than the parents of the bully.

If successful, the court may award damages against the bully which would compensate for any injury inflicted. However, if no harm or damage was suffered by the bullied child, then the amount of damages awarded would not be high. The bully would be responsible for paying the damages, although if the bully has no money he or she may not be able to do so. It is possible to obtain an injunction to prevent the bully continuing his behaviour. It should be noted, however, that the courts are generally reluctant to grant injunctions against teenagers who are still at school. Moreover, if an injunction is granted against a bully who is under 17, there is little the court can do if the bully breaks the injunction. The bully cannot give be given a custodial sentence.

Breach of contract

Parents of children who attend independent (private) schools enter into a contract with the school on behalf of the child.

The school agrees to provide services to the child and may be sued for breach of contract if they fail to provide such services. Obligations are reciprocal. The parent may be sued for failing to pay fees etc. Such a contract is no different from the type of contract which might be entered into with any other supplier of services which are bought by a consumer.

Under a private school contract there may be an express obligation to provide a reasonably safe environment for the child. If not expressly stated, such an obligation would be implied into the contract by the courts. A school which failed to provide such an environment, for example by failing to provide adequate supervision to prevent serious bullying, may be sued for breach of contract in the civil courts if a child suffers physical or psychological harm as a result of the bullying.

In LEA, grant-maintained and other state schools the situation is different. During the last ten years there has been an attempt by the government to introduce the system of 'contracting' into services formerly provided by central government and local authorities. One of the aims of this new approach is to make the service provider more accountable to the customer, with whom there is said to be a contract. However, contracts between citizens and the providers of public services are clearly distinguishable from private contracts. One of the most distinguishing features of these artificial contracts is that they are unenforceable in the civil courts. These contracts are not based on an exchange of economic value between the citizen and the service provider. They do not, therefore, give the citizen any enforceable rights in a court of law. The citizen is not a consumer or customer in the usual sense as in the private school contract. Thus, although the provision of rights has been one of the central themes of the Citizens' Charter, no clear approach has been developed in relation to such public services for enforcing those rights.

Bullying out of school

Often the most frightening and severe bullying takes place when a child is not in school. Schools are able to take action against pupils whose bullying behaviour occurs outside the school, but it is unclear to what extent the school *must* take action to stop bullying.

Disciplinary Action

Bullying incidents on the way to and from school

Parents are often told that the school cannot deal with bullying that takes place out of school hours, for example on the way to and from school. The courts have held, however, that a teacher does have the power to discipline a pupil for misbehaviour outside school premises (*R* v. *Newport Salop JJ, ex p. Wright* [1929] 2 KB 416; *R* v. *London Borough of Newham and Another*, The Times, 15 November 1994). In the *Newham* case a boy was excluded from school for bullying behaviour towards a younger child at the school on the way home.

The law is less clear where parents expressly withdraw their consent to the school disciplining their child for incidents off the school premises. In such cases, schools may not be able to take disciplinary action.

Where bullying has occurred outside school, particularly on the way to and from school, a complaint should be made to the teacher or school according to the steps laid out earlier in this chapter.

Negligence

To make a successful claim against a school or LEA for damage to a child arising from bullying off the school premises, or outside school hours, it would be necessary to show that the school or LEA were negligent. This would require the parent or child to prove in court that the duty of care owed to pupils extended to incidents that occur outside school hours, and that the damage was foreseeable. The law is unclear whether a duty of care is owed, although examination of case law does provide some guidance.

Bullying incidents on school premises before and after school hours

It is unlikely that schools will owe a duty of care to supervise pupils who arrive on the school premises before the start of the school day, unless the school voluntarily accepts responsibility for them (*Ward* v. *Hertfordshire County Council* [1969] 114 Sol J 87).

Bullying incidents on the school bus

If the transport to and from school is provided by the LEA or school, then it is likely that there is a duty to supervise pupils (*Jacques* v. *Oxfordshire County Council* [1967] 66 LGR 440). If pupils travel to school using public transport, then while the bus company is responsible for ensuring the safety of passengers, it is unclear whether this extends to a duty to supervise pupils.

Bullying incidents on the way to and from school

It should be pointed that while the law may allow teachers or schools to discipline for incidents off the school premises, it is by no means clear that they have a duty to do so and, if there is no duty, then it is not possible to make a claim for negligence.

Criminal law

If the bullied child is assaulted either physically or sexually, the bullies may have committed a criminal offence. (*See* earlier section on 'criminal law'.)

Civil actions

Parents may be able to take other forms of civil action. (*See* earlier section on 'civil action'.)

14

■ ■ ■

A child's view –
how ChildLine UK helps

HEREWARD HARRISON

Introduction

When ChildLine ran its two special Bullying Lines in 1990 and 1994, the response from children and parents exceeded all predictions. The first bullying line, open for three months in 1990, counselled 2054 children and counsellors on the second line, open for six months in 1994, spoke to 4494 children.

After each line closed, ChildLine published a report on what children said about bullying. For the second report, *Why Me?*, we supplemented the data with questionnaires and interviews with parents, teachers and children of all ages.

Our first report, *Bullying: The Child's View*, showed that children adopt a broad and inclusive definition of bullying, including verbal bullying and excluding behaviour, as well as physical violence, extortion and intimidation. The report looked at how and why children do or do not report being bullied.

Why Me? describes how children perceive bullying and their views on how it should be tackled. A few years on in the debate on bullying, there was evidence that children now feel more able to report bullying, but it was clear that speaking up did not always end the bullying. The messages from children emerged loud and clear: children want to be involved in tackling bullying. *Why Me?* focused on practical suggestions for children, parents and teachers on strategies for effective action against bullying.

The following chapter about 'Sandra' – disguised to preserve confidentiality – is a vivid example of how bullying can ruin the life of a young person and how, with careful help, change can take place. We hope that all those children and young people who ask for help with bullying in the future will meet with a sympathetic response from school, home, friends and neighbours and that 'Sandra's' experience will be an increasingly rare occurrence.

Sandra's story

My name's Sandra. I'm 14 and in the third year at a comprehensive school in our town. I don't say much to the other girls in my form and don't have a lot of friends. I'm not what you would call a sociable person; my Mum describes me as shy and arty and she's probably right. A lot of the time I can't think why anyone would want to be friends with me. I don't have a spectacular personality, or get a lot of attention from boys, and I'm not very good at schoolwork. I've just got one friend, Sarah, who lives on my street, but she doesn't talk to me much at school. She wouldn't dare, because she's afraid of them too.

It started at the beginning of this school year when my closest friend, Jess, moved away. Jess was pretty popular at school, and because she made friends easily there were a group of us who could hang around together. I didn't always get on with the other girls as well as Jess did, but it did feel like I was part of a crowd. After a while I felt comfortable with our little group, and I told them all lots of things about me and my family which I wish now I hadn't.

When Jess left, the others started ignoring me. Then they started teasing me and calling me names, and then they started doing things much worse. At first they would snigger if I got something wrong in class and they'd take the mickey about it during break. One time I was really nervous in Geometry Class because they all kept smiling at me and giving each other knowing looks. I found out later that they'd stuck a sanitary towel to my blazer. (Later they soaked a whole package of tampons in ketchup and left them in my desk.) When the teacher asked me a question about the homework I got flustered and said something about circumcising a triangle. I'd meant to say 'circumscribing'. Ever since that they make motions with their fingers like scissors and whisper 'Snip, Snip' at me.

They decided that the reason I missed Jess so much was because I'd been in love with her. They went from calling me 'rat-face' to calling me a 'rat-faced lesbian'. While they stood in queue to buy dinner they'd sing, or rather scream:

Sandra and Jess were up in a tree
K-I-S-S-I-N-G
First comes love, then comes marriage
Then comes Little Sandra in the baby carriage.

I think that the teachers on dinner duty thought it was just a joke. Some of them probably thought we were all still good friends, and some of them might even have thought I deserved it, because the girls who were picking on me were good students, and I wasn't. One teacher bent over the table where I was sitting and said, 'It'll blow over.' It was like having someone say, 'There, there, keep your chin up. It's not that big a deal.' But it was a big deal to me.

I tried ignoring them. I thought that maybe they were looking for some kind of a reaction from me and that if they didn't get it they might get bored and stop. It didn't work; in fact, they got worse.

I feel really lonely at school now. No one talks to me, except for them, and if any of them approach me I know it's because they're setting me up for something. I spend my break times in the loo, or anywhere else where I think they won't find me. I feel very isolated, like I'm completely cut off from every other person at the school. Sometimes it's really difficult to keep from crying. I've thought about killing myself.

Recently things have got really bad. They tore up all my textbooks last week, and they ruined my uniform by covering it in make-up. My Dad will go mad if he finds out. A few days ago they waited for me outside the loo. It was time to go home, and I was hoping they'd go first.

'Snip, snip, Sandra,' they giggled as they poked me with their fingers. 'Tell us, Lesbo, how do you circumcise a triangle?'

'Speaking of lesbos, do you know that she made a pass at me in the dinner queue yesterday? She pinched my bum. Next she'll be sticking her tongue in my ear!'

'Maybe we should leave the circumcision to someone else and just give her a lesbo haircut.'

'I think we need to teach her a lesson.'

They held my hands behind my back and punched me in the stomach a couple of times. One of them slapped me across the face and called me a dirty-minded slag. I was glad that school was over and that I didn't have to go back into a class. I waited a bit and headed home.

I don't know what I can do about this anymore. I can't tell anybody at school about it. That would make it worse, because I'd be a grass then as well as a wimp. And besides, who'd believe me? My Dad would be really angry if he had any idea at all. And my Mum – well, I couldn't bother her with it. She thinks I'm doing OK at school. Worst of all is my brother, who lives with his wife a few miles from us. He used to make me feel really special, but last week it was my birthday, and he forgot.

That was the story I told a counsellor at ChildLine the first time I rang. I was surprised that I told him all those things. A lot of it was embarrassing, like admitting that the girls had stuck a sanitary towel to my clothes. He made it easy for me to tell him about what was happening at school, because he encouraged me to talk about it and sounded like he believed me. I was half expecting him to tell me to pull myself together, or to fight back or something, but he didn't say anything like that. He listened, mostly. I found that at the end of the call I had a lot to think about. He told me, for instance, that it wasn't my fault that this gang were hassling me. They weren't picking on me because I was ugly or stupid or worthless, but because it made them feel good to give someone a hard time. Maybe they didn't think much of themselves either. He also suggested that being bullied didn't *make* me ugly or stupid or worthless, but it may take some time before I can really believe that. Most of the time I still feel like people wouldn't like me. I think it will be a while before I feel like I have any confidence.

The counsellor started me thinking about other things as well, like the fact that I felt really angry with these people at school but didn't sound very angry when I talked about them. He said that I sounded really flat and hurt, almost like I was feeling that I didn't have any right to speak about it at all. When the counsellor pointed that out to me, and said that it was OK for me to feel pissed off with what was going on, I started talking faster, like there was a lot of bottled-up stuff inside that came pouring out. I realised that I was really afraid of these girls, and also that I was really afraid of letting any emotions show. In the past whenever I told anybody about how I was feeling, I always lived to regret it. They would either stop being friends with me, or they'd use my feelings against me.

I was surprised when the counsellor said that we'd been talking for nearly an hour and that maybe I should go away and think about what we'd said so far before we started looking for a solution. I wasn't expecting him to say that, but in a way I was relieved, because I felt pretty tired after telling the whole story to someone. I think as well that I actually appreciated the fact that someone was telling me that there was no easy answer to the situation I was in. Though it would have been nice to have left the phone box feeling like it was all sorted out, I knew that *I* hadn't been able to come up with any answers, and it was nice to hear that that wasn't because I was just stupid. As well as going home with a lot of things to think about, I also had a practical suggestion to work on before I phoned and spoke to a counsellor again. I was going to work on expressing my feelings. I was going to tell my brother, who's the one person I might feel safe trying it out on, that I was hurt and annoyed that he'd forgotten my birthday.

I phoned ChildLine back a few days later, having worked things out with my brother (at the same time increasing my confidence just a little bit) but having left things at school to get worse. What I didn't say in my first call was that I didn't go back to school after the incident in the toilets. It was too difficult to admit that I just couldn't cope with what had happened, especially when the counsellor had made me feel like there were some good things about me, so I just said that I could probably avoid that gang of girls for a few days while I thought about what I might do. That was a lie, because there was no way to avoid a group of people at my school, and the bullies showed no signs of leaving me alone. I bunked off for five days, and I knew that soon the school would contact my parents about it. I haven't told Mum and Dad anything. The first day I pretended I was sick and after that I spent my days walking around the town.

I'm really afraid of what my parents will do when they find out. Dad doesn't like me very much. Well, he doesn't like women much generally. When I was younger he used to beat Mum up pretty often. I remember spending a lot of time in women's refuges and staying with Mum's relations. She's gone back to him so many times now that they don't want to know any more. My Mum's sort of cut off from her family, and though Dad doesn't hit her as much as he used to, I can tell that she's still really unhappy. I used to tell Mum that things would be better if they just split up, but she'd get upset about it, and I'd always have to apologise. She feels that she can't leave him. She doesn't have any money, for one thing, and he's threatened her about leaving. He says that he'll kill himself if she tries. Mum's still afraid of him, and I can't tell her anything that will add to her worries. Back when we were all friends, I told some of the girls at school about how tough things were at home sometimes. I'm afraid that they'll tell the whole school about it and that I'll end up in care. I couldn't bear leaving Mum with him.

I think I'm in big trouble. I always thought that Dad would go mad if he found out about the girls at school, and now it looks like there's no way he won't find out. Mum will be really worried and upset. I don't want to do that to her. She's got enough to worry about without me on top of it. I could lie and say that I was just skiving for a week, but that won't make much difference as far as my Dad's concerned. Should I tell the Head why I haven't been at school? I'm not sure that I could. It isn't right to tell on people, no matter who they are. And what if the Head doesn't believe me anyway? I don't think he could do anything so horrid to them that they'd stop. They might just wait a few days and then really make sure that I didn't talk about it again. Worse still, if I get a reputation for being a grass then everyone else at school might start being horrible to me. And what if the school decide that I'm a problem student and send me to meet with the social worker? I'd die if she found out about my Mum and Dad. But maybe things can't get any worse than they are now. Would it really make a difference if instead of everyone ignoring me they joined in with the name-calling and things? Either way, I should probably try to go to a different school. But I don't know if Dad would let me.

I was glad I got to talk to the same counsellor again. I was in real need of some help this time, and it might have been hard starting the whole story over again with someone new. I found that it was even easier telling him about things this time, because I was beginning to feel like I could trust him to keep what I was saying confidential, and because I knew from last time that he wouldn't start preaching about my bunking off. He listened to me go on for a while, and he helped me sort things out in my own head. He helped me look at what I was saying. I realised that I was sounding really confused about what to do, and it seemed that was OK with him. Instead of telling me what to do, which would probably have cheesed me off a bit, he let *me* figure out what I might do. He didn't seem too annoyed that I kept whinging about how it seemed like nothing would work, or that I kept saying that nothing could make things at school change.

I found that, like the last call, this call helped me to start looking at some of what was going on in a different way. I'd never thought, for example, about how alike my situation at home and my situation at school were. Thinking about it now, my Dad does sound like a bit of a bully. In some ways I guess it's not too surprising that I haven't been able to stand up to the bullies at school. I never saw my Mother really get angry with Dad, and I've never really been able to tell him what I think about it. Mum must be scared of him in the same way that I'm scared of these girls at school. She's probably humiliated about it too, which is a lot of what I've been feeling. I could always see that what was happening at home wasn't my Mum's fault, and having it pointed out to me helped me see that I wasn't to blame for the girls at school, either. Though to be honest, I think that I've let them hassle me to some extent just by not doing anything about it.

I was surprised, and probably lucky, that things went as well as they did. I went to school the next day so that I could talk to Miss Lee, my English teacher, about bunking off. I knew that it would be hard to tell her everything that I wanted to, but maybe it was a bit easier because I'd been able to practise what I was going to say with the counsellor at ChildLine. I went into her office before school started, told her that I needed to talk about why I hadn't been to school, and admitted to her that it was difficult for me to say what I needed to. I'd never had to talk to a teacher before, so I really wasn't sure what to expect. She seemed concerned by the things I told her. I didn't tell her the names of the girls right off; I waited to see if I felt OK about doing that. In the end I decided to trust her and I told her the names. She called my parents in, though my Dad wouldn't come, and we all had to see the Head. He said he would need to wait a few days before he made any decisions so that he could meet with the other pupils' parents. In the meantime he put them all on litter duty, so that they'd have plenty to do in breaktimes besides pick on me.

The first time I saw the lot of them trudging around with the rubbish, I was afraid of what they might do to me. One of them said, 'Phew! I thought the rubbish smelled bad,' and another added, as she picked up some used napkins with the gloves she was wearing, 'Look, Lesbo, you've, uh, misplaced your towels again.'

'Come on, Lesbo, if you like girls so much surely you're not going to get squeamish at the sight of some female blood.'

They all started to giggle, though I could tell that a couple of them didn't feel as good about doing it as they had done before.

The leader encouraged the others with, 'Come on, girls, let's shower her with love,' and as she tried to fling the towels across the lawn towards me: 'It's your bridal bouquet, Rat-face, flowers for you and your girlfriend.'

The missiles didn't hit me, but fell between us on the grass. I, for once, didn't budge.

'You really do think you're clever, don't you?' I said. Then I got angry and told her that I found her pathetic. Then I walked off, and I don't think any of them noticed that I was trembling.

After the Head met with their parents a few days later, they were all suspended from school for two weeks. I was surprised that the school had decided to take it so seriously. I thought that they might get a stiff talking to if anything at all. Since none of them have been around this week it's been a lot easier for me to answer in class, and yesterday Sarah sat down to eat her dinner with me. The other kids haven't acted as horrid as I thought they might. Though some of them did start the week by giving me really filthy looks, others seem to think a bit more of me for what I did. It isn't that things are all rosy. I don't know what they'll be like when they come back, whether they'll give up altogether or just try to torture me in less obvious ways. Miss Lee said that she's going to be watching them all closely, though I think it would be too optimistic of me to think it's all over. Things at home are the same as they ever were. We don't talk about the bullying or about me not going to class that week. Mum and Dad still have lots of problems, and Dad still takes things out on us. Maybe when it's all settled down I might try talking to someone a bit more about home. I'll have to wait and see what happens when the girls get back.

15

■ ■ ■

How drama can help

FRANCIS GOBEY

Drama as a resource

There are now many more drama and video resources on bullying than there used to be. Over the past eight years many Young People's Theatre, Theatre in Education and TV companies have produced work on the theme, and bullying has emerged as a popular topic in children's programmes such as *Grange Hill*. Artists, academics, educationalists and pressure groups have together succeeded in lifting the taboo. Few schools now claim that bullying doesn't exist or that not talking about it helps it go away; more young people now take part in anti-bullying initiatives or do curriculum work in the area.

I think this is all to the good. My concern is that the best use be made of such drama and video, both as valid art and as effective tools in personal, health and social education. The stories in the bullying drama, whether of lonely victimhood, alienated aggression, group action or eventual comeuppance, make for powerful entertainment, but this can remain the level at which they are perceived – entertainment. I would hope, however, that they could also be starting points for effective, experiential learning.

Drama work which involves participating as well as spectating is sometimes shied away from by teachers who are not specialists. Remembering how drama perhaps was taught in their own schooldays, they might feel that asking a group to 'Go away and make a sketch about bullying' would probably be chaotic and perhaps actually reinforce bullying behaviour. And I think they'd be right.

But it needn't be like this. Participatory drama work offers:

- a variety of expressive languages, forms and techniques;
- the safety of structures, styles and time limits;
- the protection of acting a role in someone else's story;
- a chance to rehearse alternative behaviours safely;
- exploration of the social context, as well as the individual;

- ways of exploring distressing experiences without exposing personal vulnerabilities;
- a basis for including 'real' feelings in working towards consensus about sensitive issues;
- opportunities for less forthcoming students to make a full contribution;
- a model of working practice which is implicitly anti-bullying.

Good practice – a checklist

In choosing, using and adapting published drama materials on bullying – whether plays, videos, excerpts or exercises – a school might like to bear in mind the following questions:

- Does the material try to do justice to the full range of experiences: emotional, physical and psychological?
- Is the material accessible in terms of languages, language level and other special needs?
- Is the material 'closed' or 'open' in the way it allows people to use and interact with it?
- Are cultural differences and differences of value and belief being respected?
- Is the material suitable on its own? As part of a course? After a recent incident?
- How might the material become part of the curriculum (Health Education, PSE . . .) or part of a school initiative on dealing with bullying?

A workshop approach

The aim of my consultancy training work is to show in practice how participatory drama can be an effective tool for working on issues that impact on young people's mental health, especially bullying, but also grief and self-esteem. Through a variety of non-specialist drama and video techniques I hope to give participants an awareness of, and confidence in, some active learning methods well adapted to a Health Education or PSE curriculum approach, as well as useful for direct work with those bullying or bullied.

To do this I adopt a workshop approach, using exercises, roleplays and powerful video drama extracts to reawaken the full, dramatic reality of bullying as it affects all those involved in physical, emotional and psychological ways. The message of this is that any practice or intervention, however well intentioned, which does not address the difficult feelings, numbing ambivalences and sometimes buried horror of the bullying situation cannot hope to achieve lasting positive change. The workshop is substantially the same as that for young people, but with more analytical discussion of ways and means.

A workshop begins with brief exercises, designed both as warm-ups for the group and pointers to the way even the shortest and most artificial games can have a bearing on promoting an anti-bullying ethos. Partners then use each other as mirrors to get ready in front of and to see their feelings reflected. In another exercise, partners conduct a dialogue consisting only of yes and no. The results of these games are fed back to the whole group, and it soon becomes clear that links can be made with issues around bullying.

In the next exercise groups form – one by one but without prior discussion or allocation of roles – into frozen pictures of 'some aspect of bullying'. These pictures are considered in turn: What can be seen to be going on? What roles are involved? – a process which brings with it the suggestion that bullying is a behaviour each of us is capable of engaging in, and one which occurs in a social group. By means of adopting different roles, participants also get an experience of how far their own behaviour is chosen, and how what they do affects the group.

In developing this exercise I use a technique called 'Feelings Balloons' whereby an advocate from among the spectators goes up to one character in the frozen picture, stands behind them and articulates the emotion or thought being experienced (often acutely) at that moment. There is a safety factor here as well as a liberation: feelings can be expressed which it would be difficult to say on one's own. By this stage of the workshop the debriefing often includes remarks on how accurate and sensitive the advocates have been. One further development of these frozen pictures is for a spectator to intervene and make one small change to one character's gesture or posture – and then to test out how the group responds.

Another roleplay technique I use is called 'Dilemmas'. Following a video extract showing a bullying situation, three participants enact the drama of a character's inner conflict: one in role and the others as two opposed, alternating 'voices'. The drama is most effective if the 'voices' position themselves a little behind the person in role, out of sight but not out of mind as it were. The person in role says what their dilemma is, but can then let the voices express and test all the conflicting feelings and thoughts and worries it entails; those watching the dilemma can also contribute suggestions. In the case of the character getting bullied these voices could be one of fear and one of anger; the inner conflicts of the person bullying, the sidekick, the witness, the teacher etc, are also dramatised.

'Dilemmas' brings out the mental anguish bullying can cause, but can also be used to show who (among the many roles involved) might be in the position to make a decision, to begin a resolution. Again debriefing from the exercise can make these links – it is also important for participants to come out of role.

And in this spirit the active part of the workshop always ends with a group 'deroling' exercise to gather and rechannel the energy in a positive direction. Such intense and interactive drama work can release powerful feelings, and a responsible workshop, I feel, needs to locate these within a relatively whole experience.

Drama work with young people

These exercises derive from my work as Education Officer with the Neti-Neti Theatre Company, especially the time when, a few years ago, I was working on ways of supporting the play – and then video – *Only Playing, Miss*. Written by Penny Casdagli, this play about bullying is performed multilingually in English, Sign Language and Bengali and is aimed mainly at Years 7 to 9.

Initially my work was exploratory and aimed at developing writing work for the project. I approached bullying as a type of behaviour actual or potential in most people's lives, and sought to embed it within themes of feelings and empathy, power, communication, friendship, ethical choice and consensus.

These workshops were small-scale, practical and participatory. They began with drama, acting games and roleplay, with a record being kept on tape, in writing or on video. They first explored individual feelings of powerfulness and vulnerability before moving on to social relations and the dilemmas caused by abuses of power. The issue of bullying was then isolated from this context, looked at in its various guises at home and in school, and broken down into its constituent parts: name-calling, teasing, exclusion, intimidation, assault etc.

Other workshops had the specific goal of making a *Help and Advice Pack* for new pupils. Everything achieved in the workshop in discussion, on paper, or on tape was put together and presented as the group's consensus. We made a video to show to the rest of the year group. In this way one workshop of 15–18 students, drawn from different classes, could pass on their experience and conclusions.

Later work was more direct in tackling the dynamic within the group. Such workshops tried to create an atmosphere in which pupils could be honest about their experiences and tell their stories without fear of ridicule – not always easy if there was bullying within the group. Consensus about what bullying is, let alone what can be done about it, cannot be assumed from the start: a group works slowly towards admitting that certain behaviour – such as teasing or 'blanking' – is really bullying. Individuals gradually open up as they feel supported.

Only Playing, Miss

The play takes as its subject the story of Eugene Hickey who returns to his class following the death of his father. His behaviour is seen by some of his classmates as out of order, and one of them, David Rant, begins to bully him. In this he is joined by Sam, who also turns her friends against Becky, Eugene's ally.

The cycle of ritual violence and cruel taunting continues, despite the efforts of Eugene's wise friend Jo, until Becky gets the others to help her tell their teacher, Mrs Richards. The audience witnesses Mrs Richards confronting the bullies, but only later learns of her work with the respective parents. It is only in the final scene that Eugene and his friends find the courage to stand up to David Rant, and Rant to share the story of his own bereavement with Eugene.

This story, presented in varied dramatic ways as narrative, naturalistic action and song, can be seen as the *content* of the play, with meanings readily accessible to the school audience. But the full impact of the play owes much to Neti-Neti's *practice* as a company.

Multilingual presentation by a mixed and fully integrated cast of differently abled actors adds a particular resonance to a story about bullying, which often has its roots in the fear of difference. With black, Asian and deaf performers playing substantially positive roles, *Only Playing, Miss* implicitly challenges those racist and ablist attitudes which bullies often exploit.

Only Playing, Miss is only a play. It offers no easy solutions, but uses the real-life nature of the story to make an impact, and all the resources of drama to break the silence which bullying relies on.

Initially within the play there is much that is familiar to those watching. The school depicted is mixed and multicultural; there's an unsympathetic teacher as well as a supportive one; the main incident of bullying occurs in an unsupervised changing room; the boys are more physical than the girls; the girls behave and talk more as a group. Anyone watching who has themselves been bullied immediately recognises Eugene's or Becky's situation and feelings.

At the same time, though, there are elements in the dramatic world of the play which are not at all familiar – or rather operate in a different context. The songs, for instance, which punctuate the action, allow for a much greater expression of individual feeling than could be found in the school playground.

In fact all the language of the play is rather special. In the fictional school of the play all pupils and teachers use Sign as well as English; some of them also speak Bengali with the Bengali-speaking character, Hashi. It appears (as is the case with the performers) that one pupil and one teacher are deaf; and they sometimes use their first language BSL (British Sign Language). Communication between pupils and with teachers then, provided the will is there, is not only possible but *abundant*. In contrast, when the action moves to

147

Rant and Eugene's homes, the characters are restricted to only one language, English.

There is a message in this about the problems and possibilities of communication which is reinforced by the events of the play. Eugene's silence and complicity in the bullying is challenged by Jo, who speaks from his own history and shares what he has learned; the silence of the whole class is broken by Becky when she unites the girls and informs Mrs Richards; and David Rant's silence over the death of his mother finally cracks as Eugene and friends stand up to him.

It is the value of friendship which emerges as the strongest motivation for change: more powerful in the end than the assaults of the toughest bully. Affection between boys is shown in a confirming way, as is the expression and sharing of strong feelings which friendship allows.

In *Only Playing, Miss* the loss of a parent and the grief this causes have to stand for all the other vulnerabilities that bullying behaviour latches on to. These, however, can be talked about in workshops or follow-up classes.

Using the video

I have found that the video and script of *Only Playing, Miss* can be used in many fruitful ways in workshops as a stimulus to acting, discussion and decision-making:

- scenes can be acted out before viewing and then compared;
- scenes can be interrupted so that predictions can be made or acted out;
- key moments can be acted in slow motion or with 'forum' techniques;
- the viewpoints of different characters can be traced;
- the changes in characters can be assessed from the beginning to end;
- scenes or characters can be compared with real life etc.

Working in pairs or small groups the students could concentrate on a different character in the play, answering questions such as:

- What is Eugene like at the start? By the end?
- How does he feel about himself?
- What does he think of Rant?
- What do you think is the turning point for him?
- How has he changed by the end?
- How has the group changed?

And at this stage the focus can move from the play to the young people's own experience, with questions such as:

- In this school what are people who bully like?
- And people who get bullied?
- And people who see bullying going on but don't do anything – what are they like?

In each case the questionnaire could give a range of options to circle in agreement: honest/tough/scared/mentally strong/sensitive/babyish/brave/ weak/unlucky/like any ordinary person/cowardly/good at making friends/ in need of help/don't trust teachers.

The next task would be an exercise asking the pair or group to imagine that their friend is being bullied with questions such as:

- How do you feel about your friend?
- How do you feel about the bully/bullies?
- What do you do?
- Who helps you?
- What problems do you have?
- What happens in the end?

Working on this scenario the students offer their own strategies for dealing with bullying in their school. The workshop leader may advise and, if necessary, challenge fantasy or violent 'solutions'.

Spokespeople from each of the work groups could then report on their opinions and strategies in the plenary session. If the workshop has gone well there is often a high degree of consensus both about the character in the play and the most effective ways of dealing with the problem of bullying in the school.

The plenary session *now* functions as a reunion of the characters in the play at the point where the bullying drama has been resolved – resolved because in each of the characters there has been some change: an insight, a decision, an access of courage, a new valuing of friendship.

But it also offers an enlightening and perhaps surprising opportunity to see a problem approached from different perspectives producing a more or less consensus outcome.

In each case, at the plenary, students hear the same message coming from their peers. Bullying is bad for everyone. Speaking out and stopping it is good for everyone. And preventing it is a job for everyone – parents, teachers, support staff, managers and every pupil in the school.

Sources

Only Playing, Miss: Video, 1990, director Penny Casdagli, Neti-Neti. A video drama in English, Sign Language and Bengali, performed by the original cast. VHS 56 mins.

Only Playing, Miss: Playscript/Workshops in Schools, 1990, Penny Casdagli and Francis Gobey, Trentham Books, Stoke-on-Trent. Contains the script, young people's writings and an account of the workshops.

Contact Neti-Neti Theatre Company, George Orwell School, Turle Road, London N4 3LS (Tel: 0171–272 7302 voice, fax and minicom).

16

■ ■ ■

What do teachers need to know?

ASTRID MONA O'MOORE

All I can remember is being hit and called names and never getting a chance to learn anything. When I told the teachers, they just told me to stand up for myself.

(*Observer*, 19 March 1989)

Hopefully, the days are numbered when teachers can so easily dismiss bullying behaviour. In the British Isles, teachers can hardly have failed to notice the growing awareness of the problems of bullying which has developed since the first European Teachers' Seminar on Bullying in Schools which was held in Stavanger, in August 1987 (*see* O'Moore, 1988). Several books, for instance, have since been published in Great Britain (Besag, 1989; Roland and Munthe, 1989; Olweus, 1993; Tattum, 1993; Smith and Sharp, 1994). Moreover, there have been regular newspaper reports, television programmes and six national conferences (Kidscape, 1989–1996) devoted to the subject of bullying. Indeed, parent pressure groups have been founded whose aim is to introduce an anti-bullying ethos into all schools in the British Isles. (The UK founder is Janet Perry and in Ireland the founder is Vivette O'Donnell. The present author has developed an anti-bullying research and resource centre in Trinity College, Dublin.)

The above publications and media reports have all highlighted the fact that bullying is more widespread than most parents and teachers realise. Although there is now increased awareness of bullying in the British Isles recognising the intense suffering, humiliation and stress among schoolchildren of all ages and social classes, there is still a need for more empirical data. The delegates at the first European Seminar on Bullying in Schools concluded that in order to implement effective preventative and treatment measures, more detailed and well controlled cross-cultural research is needed. Initially our understanding of victimisation and bullying has been largely limited to pioneering studies emanating from the Nordic countries (Pikas, 1975; Olweus, 1978; Bjorkvist *et al.*, 1982; Lagerspetz *et al.*, 1982; Roland, 1989). However, in the last ten years there has been a steady growth in high-quality research projects in Europe and from other parts of the world. This has added significantly to the knowledge of bully/victim problems in schools (Boulton and Underwood, 1992; Pepler *et al.*, 1993; Whitney and Smith, 1993; Neary and Joseph, 1994; Siann *et al.*, 1994; Slee, 1995). The object of the present chapter is therefore to elucidate further our present understanding of bullying by presenting empirical data from a study of victimisation and bullying carried out in Dublin.

The study

The study comprised a total of 783 children (285 boys and 498 girls) aged between 7 and 13 years. They were drawn from 30 classes in four 'state-run' national schools in Dublin. The schools chosen in the study were typical of national schools in Dublin and were not chosen on the basis of any particular problems. All the children were tested in class by their own teachers. The extent to which children bully others or are themselves bullied was assessed by the self-report questionnaire used in Norwegian studies (Olweus and Roland, 1983). Before distributing the questionnaire to the children, the teachers first explained in their own words what was meant by bullying. They were guided by the definition of bullying used in Scandinavia, namely 'bullying is longstanding violence, mental or physical, conducted by an individual or a group and directed against an individual who is not able to defend himself/herself in the actual situation'.

The children answered the questions anonymously although each question-naire had a bar code so that pupils could be identified for the purpose of further analysis of psychological data that were to be gathered at a later date.

The questionnaire was conducted throughout each school at the same time. This was to ensure that the children would not have any prior knowledge of the questionnaire through contacts with other respondents, thereby eliminating opportunities for intimidation or conspiring to 'fake good'.

The Piers-Harris Self-Concept Scale (Piers, 1984), a self-report questionnaire, was used to examine the self-esteem of the children in the study. Also, teachers rated the behaviour of the children using the well-known Behaviour Questionnaire (Rutter, 1967).

Results of the study

Incidence: children with special needs

A detailed account of the incidence of bullying among children in our study has already been reported (O'Moore and Hillery, 1989b). Perhaps the most surprising of all the findings in relation to the incidence of bullying was the high level of bullying and victimisation reported by children who were either attending remedial classes or were full-time in special classes. For example, of the 109 children who received remedial tuition at the time of assessment, 38 of them (34.9 per cent) reported that they had been occasionally bullied and a further 19 (17.4 per cent) said they had been frequently bullied, that is once a week or more often. In comparison only 5.6 per cent of 639 non-remedial children were frequently bullied. Similarly more remedial children were bullies than non-remedial children. The respective percentages were 35.8 per cent and 26.5 per cent. There were no frequent bullies among the 'remedial children'.

Of the 35 children who attended special classes 17 (48.6 per cent) of them reported that they had occasionally behaved as bullies and two of them (5.7 per cent) stated that they had bullied other children frequently. The percentage of children in special classes who were victims was even higher than that of bullies. Namely, there were 14.3 per cent frequent victims and another 51.4 per cent occasional victims.

These results suggest that children who attend either remedial classes or full-time special classes are particularly prone to being frequently involved in bullying either as victims or bullies.

Pupils with low achievement have repeatedly been found to have low self-esteem (Burns, 1982). This was also found to be true of children in the present study. The remedial children, in particular, had the lowest mean score on the self-concept scale. In comparison to non-remedial children, they perceived their behaviour as more difficult. They also felt more inadequate in relation to their intellectual and school status and they were more unhappy and dissatisfied.

These findings, which have been given further support by subsequent research (Ní Irghile, 1992, and Smith and Sharp, 1994), have obvious implications not only for remedial education but also for the treatment and prevention of bullying in all schools. This will be discussed later.

Incidence: bully/victims

Another difference between the present results and earlier empirical studies which might have implication for the treatment and prevention of bullying is the higher percentage of children whom we found both bully and in turn are bullied. This is due to the fact that they have been found to be a particularly problematic and vulnerable group. Stephenson and Smith (1989), however, found only 6 per cent of children in their sample of final year primary school children were both bullies and victims (i.e. bully-victim). Olweus (1985) found that approximately 18 per cent of those children who are bullied occasionally also bully others and that only 6 per cent of those who are bullied frequently bully others. Roland (1989) reported an incidence of 20 per cent of victims who bully others. In contrast, we found of the 330 victims in our sample as many as 151 (45.9 per cent) had engaged in bullying others. Of the 269 who had been occasional victims, 115 (42.8 per cent) of them reported they had also been occasional bullies and another nine (3.3 per cent) had been frequent bullies. Furthermore, out of the 60 children who were frequent victims, 24 (40.0 per cent) stated that they had acted as bullies occasionally and a further three (5.0 per cent) stated that they had bullied others frequently.

Similarly, when we focused on the 228 self-confessed bullies in our study, it was found that out of the 214 children who bullied others occasionally at school, 115 (53.7 per cent) had been occasional victims and a further 24 (11.2 per cent) had been frequent victims. Moreover, of the 14 children who were serious bullies, nine (64 per cent) said that they had been bullied occasionally and a further three (21.4 per cent) reported that they were also frequent victims.

Thus while it is often assumed that children are either bullies or victims, we found that only 32.8 per cent of bullies in our study could be described as pure bullies in that they had never been victimised. Similarly, 54.4 per cent of all the victims in our study can be classified as pure victims, that is they say they had not bullied anyone. Yet even among this group of pure victims, teachers reported that 25 of them (14.0 per cent) had in fact engaged in bullying others.

Later in the discussion it is shown that the above distinctions of pure victim, pure bully and bully-victim have important predictive value in relation to self-esteem and behaviour.

Teachers' estimates of bullying

Teachers' estimates of the incidence of bullying behaviour among school-children in the study suggest that teachers greatly underestimate the amount of bullying that goes on in their schools. For example, teachers identified only 17 (22.1 per cent) of the 77 self-confessed pure bullies and 38 (25.2 per cent) of the 151 bully-victims. Thus only 24 per cent of the total number of bullies were identified by their teachers.

One can only speculate as to why teachers are so unaware of bullying. Indeed 23.1 per cent of all children in the present study reported that their teachers did not know that bullying goes on.

There are undoubtedly many reasons. It might be because of the covert nature of bullying and the subtle manner which bullies use to intimidate their victims. Moreover, it might reflect the taboo on telling tales. Obviously much valuable information is lost to teachers as a result of pupils' reluctance to inform teachers about bullying incidents that they have witnessed, though it must also be pointed out that many teachers are unsympathetic to pupils telling tales.

In the study as many as 33.6 per cent of children stated that they would not tell their teacher if someone was rough with them or bullied them in school. An even higher percentage of children (50.8 per cent) said they would not tell their teacher if someone bullied them on their way to or from school. In contrast only 14.9 per cent of children said they would not tell someone at home if they were bullied in school or on the way to or home from school. It was also noted that 55.3 per cent of the children would not tell if they saw someone else from their own class being bullied in school or on the way to school. The reasons given by the children were that it was wrong to tell tales (45.7 per cent) and they'd be afraid that the bully might pick on them (54.3 per cent). However, it was interesting to learn that no one reported that 'Teacher gets cross when I tell tales.'

Besag (1989) provides a very useful list of other reasons which might explain why children are reluctant to tell tales. Among the possible reasons offered is that children have no confidence in the adults' ability to help. However, only 2.3 per cent of the children in our study were of the opinion that teachers never do anything to stop bullying (see Table 16.1).

Table 16.1: Children's responses to the question, 'What do the teachers in your school do to put an end to bullying?'

Responses	Frequency	
	No.	%
They never do anything to stop bullying	18	2.3
They do try occasionally	66	8.4
They do try often	105	13.4
They try almost all the time	369	47.1
They do not know that it goes on	181	23.1
Missing cases	44	5.6
Total	783	100.0

The results shown in Table 16.1 suggest that efforts are being made by teachers to stop bullying. However, in view of the fact that there were 48 per cent of children engaging in bullying behaviour at the time of assessment, 10.5 per cent of whom were involved in serious bullying, this suggests that there is an urgent need to improve strategies for coping with bullying.

Indeed, preliminary results from the present authors' nationwide study of bullying behaviour in Irish schools, sponsored by the Department of Education and Calouste Gulbenkian Foundation, indicate that the reluctance to tell both at home and at school increases steadily as the pupils advance through primary and post-primary school (O'Moore, 1994). However, the results on the incidence of bullying suggest that the increased efforts over the recent years by the Department of Education, teacher unions, National Parents Council, individual schools, teachers and parents are being rewarded. For example, the incidence of victimisation during primary school children as reported by O'Moore and Hillery (1989b) has dropped in Dublin from 42 per cent to 33 per cent. However, the incidence of children bullying other children has only dropped by 2 per cent (from 29 per cent to 27 per cent). Thus, while there is cause for optimism on the one hand, there is no room for complacency. Continuous and increased attention must be given to prevent and counter the ill effects of bullying behaviour.

It has been pointed out that to implement measures which are most effective in preventing or combating bullying greater effort must be made to understand more fully the psychological make-up of children involved in bullying (O'Moore, 1988).

Self-esteem: victims

Analysis of the data in relation to self-concept and behaviour of the children in the study produced many significant differences.

When children who reported that they had been victims were compared with those who reported that they had never been victims, it was found that victims had a significantly lower self-esteem ($F = 11.22$, $P = < 0.001$). Analysis of the six 'cluster scales' of the Piers-Harris Self-Concept Scale suggested that victims saw themselves as more troublesome ($F = 6.40$, $P = < 0.01$), more anxious ($F = 11.24$, $P = < 0.001$), less popular ($F = 15.51$, $P = < 0.001$) and less happy and satisfied ($F = 6.81$, $P = < 0.001$). The greater the frequency with which children were victimised the greater were the feelings of inadequacy. These findings confirm much of what is known about the victim (Olweus, 1984; Besag, 1989; Roland, 1989; Neary and Joseph, 1994). However, when only the pure victims were compared with the controls (children who have neither ever bullied or been bullied) it was found that the pure victims had come closer to the ordinary children. While they had a lower global self-concept than the controls the difference between them did not reach statistical significance. However, statistically significant differences were found between the two groups in relation to behaviour, anxiety and popularity. Namely, the pure victims viewed themselves as more troublesome and anxious and less popular.

The results in respect of victims who bullied indicated that they had even lower self-esteem than pure victims. It can be seen from Table 16.2 that the victims who bully have more unhealthy psychological qualities than the pure victims. They behave less well, they have poorer intellectual and school status, and above all they are less happy and satisfied.

Teacher assessment of behaviour: victims

A similar pattern of results regarding the 'self-concept' was found in relation to the teachers' assessment of the children's behaviour. Namely, teachers rated the pure victims as less well behaved than the controls, the respective mean scores

156

Table 16.2: Comparison of mean cluster and total scores on the Piers-Harris Self-Concept Scale for pure victims and victims who bully

Scale	Pure victims n = 178	Victims/ occasional bully n = 139	Victims/ frequent bully n = 12	F ratio
Behaviour	12.93	11.32	10.50	11.73***
Intellectual and school status	12.34	11.19	10.90	4.25**
Physical appearance and attributes	9.13	8.67	8.70	.89
Anxiety	9.56	9.14	9.30	.68
Popularity	8.55	8.34	7.50	.86
Happiness and satisfaction	8.68	8.07	7.70	4.43*
Total	59.71	55.38	53.10	5.54**

* = $P < 0.5$, ** = $P < 0.01$, *** = $P < 0.001$

being 5.68 and 3.15 (F = 36.05, $P < 0.001$). However, the victims who bullied were in turn significantly worse behaved than the pure victims (F = 4.95, $P < 0.01$). Victims who were occasional bullies obtained a mean score of 6.73 whereas victims who were frequent bullies had a mean score of 10.83. A score of nine and more indicates that there is a conduct disorder (Rutter, 1967). From Table 16.3 it can be seen that 91 (27.7 per cent) out of the 329 victims had a conduct disorder. The conduct disorders were mostly antisocial in nature. It is of note that victims who bully frequently were the most antisocial of victims.

Table 16.3: Teachers' ratings of the frequency and nature of conduct disorders for victims and controls

Children	No.	Type of behaviour disorder						Total	
		Anti-social		Neurotic		Undiff.*			
		No.	%	No.	%	No.	%	No.	%
Controls	376	21	5.5	14	3.7	2	0.5	37	11.5
Pure victims	178	26	14.5	8	4.5	6	3.4	40	22.5
Victims/occ. bully	139	32	23.0	8	5.8	4	2.8	44	31.7
Victims/freq. bully	12	6	50.0	1	8.3	0	0.0	7	58.3

* Undifferentiated means that the total score on the antisocial and the neurotic clusters are the same.

Self-esteem: bullies

The total group of bullies had a statistically lower self-esteem than children who had not bullied (F = 11.20, $P = < 0.001$). Analysis of the individual cluster scales indicated that the 'bullies' perceived themselves to be (a) less well behaved (F = 28.05, $P = < 0.001$), (b) to have a lower intellectual and school status (F = 28.05, P = < 0.001), (c) to be less popular and (d) to be less happy and satisfied (F = 11.10, P = < 0.001). Indeed 49.6 per cent of the bullies reported that they hated school and 46 per cent stated that they were often sad.

These self-perceptions from the 'bullies' do not conform to the stereotype so often described in the literature, namely of a tough, confident, reasonably popular character (Olweus and Roland, 1983; Besag, 1989).

The pure bullies, however, came closer to the stereotype. While they had a lower global self-concept than the controls the difference was not statistically significant. The respective means were 59.22 and 61.59 (F = 2.64, P = 0.10). Nevertheless, analysis of the cluster scales indicated that the 'pure bullies' saw themselves as more troublesome than the controls (F = 34.62, P = < 0.001). They also were less happy and satisfied than the controls (F = 11.10, P = < 0.001).

From Table 16.4 it can be seen that bullies who have also been victims harbour significantly more feelings of inadequacy than 'pure bullies'. They regard themselves, as compared to pure bullies, as being more troublesome, more anxious, less popular and more unhappy and dissatisfied.

Table 16.4: Comparison of mean cluster and total scores on the Piers-Harris Self-Concept Scale for pure bullies and bullies who are victims

Scale	Pure bullies n = 77	Bullies/ occasional victim n = 124	Bullies/ frequent victim n = 27	F ratio
1. Behaviour	11.65	11.63	9.70	3.65*
2. Intellectual and school status	11.62	11.38	10.26	1.26
3. Physical appearance	9.62	8.72	8.44	2.23
4. Anxiety	10.30	9.54	7.48	9.04***
5. Popularity	9.65	8.55	7.15	10.95***
6. Happiness and satisfaction	8.32	8.25	7.15	3.34*

* = P < 0.5, *** = P < 0.001

Teacher assessments of behaviour

The teachers' assessments of the children's behaviour were again in close agreement with the children's self-perceptions. In other words, teachers rated the total group of bullies as more disturbed than those who did not bully. The respective means of children who bullied occasionally and who bullied frequently as compared to those who did not bully were 6.62, 11.79 and 3.97 (F = 31.87, P < 0.001). The higher the score the more difficult is the behaviour.

When the different subgroups of children who bullied were examined, it was found that pure bullies were rated by their teachers as having significantly more undesirable qualities of conduct than controls. The respective means were 6.69 and 3.15 (F = 36.6, P = < 0.001). However, the situation was even worse for bullies who were victims. There was a tendency for teachers to rate them as more troublesome, with frequent victims being even more difficult than those who were occasional victims. However, the differences did not reach statistical significance.

In all, 73 (32 per cent) of all 228 bullies in the study had conduct disorders. Table 16.5 shows the frequency and type of behaviour disorder for 'pure bullies', 'bully/victims' and controls. It can be seen from this table that there were among 'bullies' as there were among 'victims' more antisocial than neurotic conduct disorders.

Table 16.5: Teacher ratings of the frequency and nature of conduct disorders for bullies and controls

Children	No.	Type of behaviour disorder						Total	
		Anti-social		Neurotic		Undiff.*			
		No.	%	No.	%	No.	%	No.	%
Controls	376	21	5.5	14	3.7	2	0.5	37	11.5
Pure bullies	77	18	23.4	2	2.6	2	2.6	22	28.6
Bully/occ. victim	124	29	23.4	9	7.3	4	3.2	42	33.9
Bully/freq. victim	27	9	33.3	0	0.0	0	0.0	9	33.3

* Undifferentiated means that the total score on the antisocial and the neurotic clusters are the same.

Discussion

The results from the present study indicate that there is a strong relationship between feelings of poor self-esteem and bullying behaviour. The relationship was particularly strong among children with special educational needs. In contrast to studies involving Swedish and Australian children (Olweus, 1984; Rigby and Slee, 1992), the results reported in this chapter indicate that bullies share with victims feelings of low self-worth. They share perceptions of themselves as being more troublesome, less popular with peers and of being more unhappy and dissatisfied than children who have not been involved in bullying, either as victims or bullies. However, bullies in contrast to victims expressed strong feelings of unworthiness in relation to intellectual and school status. Victims, on the other hand, were distinguishable from bullies with regard to their higher levels of anxiety, with the exception of bullies who were frequent victims.

Preliminary analysis of the present authors' recent nationwide study of Irish schoolchildren reflects an even stronger relationship between self-esteem and bullying behaviour. In relation to the 6328 randomly selected primary school children (aged 8 to 13) the results indicated that, whether the children bullied others or were bullied or indeed were 'bully-victims', they all had significantly lower global self-esteem than the children who were not involved in bullying behaviour. A similar trend was found for the sample of 5401 children attending post-primary schools (aged 11–18). Thus it becomes increasingly difficult to share the strong view of Olweus (1996) that 'bullies' do not 'suffer from poor self-esteem'.

It may be, of course, as has been argued earlier, that the controversy is not so much one of difference but of semantics (O'Moore, 1995). Thus, it may be that children who bully may not necessarily have 'poor' self-esteem but rather that their self-esteem is poorer than children who are not involved in bullying behaviour. However, our concern should be to determine the antecedents to the 'lower' self-esteem of children who bully. Home factors undoubtedly play a significant part (Roland, 1988; Bowers et al., 1992; Olweus, 1993). However, the role of the school is more contentious.

Olweus (1996) believes that aggressive behaviour of bullies cannot be explained as a consequence of frustrations and failures in school. However, the present results indicate that feelings of inadequacy (such as were expressed in relation to their academic and school status and their popularity among peers) could be a strong contributory factor in their behaviour as bullies (e.g. 49.6 per cent of bullies reported, 'They hated school'). Rigby and Slee (1992) have also found that pupils who bully are less happy than most students and dislike school more.

How children react to feelings of low self-esteem will depend on the temperament of the child. If children are inclined to extroversion, they are more likely to compensate and fight back at the source of frustration. On the other hand, if introverted by temperament, the child is more likely to demonstrate shy timid behaviour (Lawrence, 1978). Data on the personality of children in the study, which has been reported on in more detail (O'Moore, 1995), indicated that children who bully are indeed more extroverted than pure victims.

Thus the stereotype of the bully as confident and tough might be a 'cover' for feelings of inadequacy. By making others feel helpless and isolated he makes himself out to be powerful and in control. Such a show of strength, particularly if he is also physically strong, disguises the fact that he actually has low feelings of self-worth.

It is to be expected that as long as the factors contributing to the low self-esteem or threatened egoism of bullies remain (Baumeister et al., 1996), the compensatory behaviour will not cease. Olweus (1987) did a follow-up study of bullies and found that their aggressive behaviour was quite stable over time. Olweus interpreted the insignificant change which he found in the bullies' aggressive behaviour as an indication that aggression was a stable trait. However, since he retested the children while they were still at school, their situation may not have changed. For example, the same sources of frustration which might have contributed to their initial behaviour, such as a heavy emphasis on competition and pressures from teachers to achieve academically, might also have been operating at the time of retesting. Thus it could be argued that the aggressive behaviour was not so much an indication of a stable trait as situation-specific. Indeed, Pollack *et al.* (1989) have recently found evidence to support the hypothesis that aggressive behaviour will depend on the circumstances in which a child finds himself at a particular time.

There has been some lively discussion on the cause and effect of victimisation on the self-concept (Olweus, 1984; Roland, 1989). Does low self-esteem in children contribute to their victimisation by their peers or is it an effect of peer rejection? Might the same question now be asked of bullies? Obviously this discussion cannot be settled until more longitudinal studies are carried out. However, Rigby and Slee (1992) have speculated that 'bullying others may serve as a means of gaining a sense of power through dominating others and have the effect of restoring self-esteem.' If that were the case might one not expect to find higher self-esteem among children who bully others frequently as compared to those who only bully occasionally? Results from the authors' national study on bullying behaviour finds the opposite to be true. Namely, both primary and post-primary pupils who reported they bullied others 'once or twice' or 'sometimes' had a statistically significant higher self-esteem that those who bullied 'once a week' or 'several times a week'.

Another of our findings that might have important implications for the treatment and prevention of bullying is the high incidence of children who both bully and are bullied (i.e. bully-victims). It was found that these children had more unhealthy psychological qualities than either the pure victims or pure bullies. The bully-victims in the study shared the characteristics of the small number of bully-victims in the study of Stephenson and Smith (1987). However, they also had much in common with the other small subgroups of victims and bullies which have been identified, namely anxious bullies (Stephenson and Smith, 1987), 'hangers on' (Olweus and Roland, 1983) and provocative victims (Olweus, 1984; Roland, 1989). For example, it was found that bullies who were frequent victims were the most anxious and unpopular of all bullies, thus sharing qualities with 'anxious bullies' and 'hangers on'. Similarly, victims who bully were found to be emotionally less stable, more excitable, expedient and frustrated, thus having much in common with 'provocative victims'.

It is tempting, therefore, to speculate whether these subgroups comprise children who are all involved in bullying in the capacity of both victim and bully.

In any event schools will need to take account, in the short term at least, of the fact that there might be a considerable number of children who may need psychological intervention above and beyond that which an anti-bully policy can provide.

What can be done?

In the light of the findings from the present study there is absolutely no doubt that teachers hold the key to the successful prevention and treatment of bullying.

Essentially, bullying and victimisation is not a normal phase of development through which children pass unscathed. On the contrary, it is symptomatic of social and emotional difficulties which require attention if the welfare of the children is at heart. For school authorities to say 'There's no bullying here', as Terrill (1989) was repeatedly to hear when he approached schools for an open and honest discussion on bullying, is to behave irresponsibly. All current research has shown that no school is immune to bullying. Thus initiating an anti-bully policy in schools should not be seen as an admission of failure, or as a poor reflection on the school, but instead it should be viewed as a positive step in creating education in an environment of mutual support and caring. Social, emotional and academic growth is optimised in a supportive environment that is free from feelings of humiliation, distress and despair. Thus to allow bullying to go unchallenged is effectively to deprive children from realising their full potential which is after all the aim of education.

There is at present no shortage of valuable suggestions and guidelines for creating a school ethos and organisation which repudiates bullying (Besag, 1989; O'Moore, 1989a; Roland and Munthe, 1989; Tattum and Herbert, 1990; Besag, 1992; Dept of Education, Ireland, 1993; Elliott, 1993/94, 1994; Scottish Council for Research in Education, 1993; HMSO, 1994).

However, many of the recommendations are of short-term value. Robin Chambers, one of the pioneers of an anti-bully policy, gave some evidence of this when after strenuous efforts at challenging bullying in his school, he commented that he was working against the tide. He stated, 'If you take your eye off it for two days, well, it's like a weed. You keep having to pluck it out, and always will, so long as we've got the society we've got' (St. John Brooks, 1985).

The present author believes that in order to effect any real change in bullying behaviour one must tackle the root cause of the problem. From our results we have reason to believe that low self-esteem is a contributory factor in bullying. Indeed, this lends support to the existing strong body of evidence which indicates that self-esteem is the single most influential factor in determining behaviour (Burns, 1982). Thus the emphasis in the alleviation and prevention of bullying should be on enhancing the self-esteem. Self-esteem begins in the family, and before entry to school each pupil is, to quote Burns (1982), 'invisibly tagged, some enhancingly by a diet or nourishing interest and affection, and others crippled by a steady downpour of psychic blows from significant others, denting, weakening and distorting their self-concepts'. However, once at school peers and teachers take precedence over parents. In schools even more evaluation takes place than the child has already experienced at home. There is daily appraisal of academic work, of sporting ability and of social behaviour. This is particularly true of schools where there is a heavy emphasis on competition. Thus the majority of pupils experience daily reminders of their potential and limitations. They are constantly being ranked and evaluated. Frequently the superior achievement of one child is used to debase the achievements of others. Thus for every child whose self-esteem is boosted there is another whose feelings of self-worth is potentially diminished. Whereas a few successful or unsuccessful experiences may not have a major effect on the self-concept, it is the frequency and consistency of feelings of adequacy or inadequacy over a period of years which leaves its mark on the self-concept.

It has been repeatedly shown that whether or not children come to school with a firm picture of their self-worth, teachers have the potential to employ the academic and social learning experiences of school to either reinforce or reteach children a positive view of themselves. This includes competence, worth and belonging (Thomas, 1980; Burns, 1982; Lawrence, 1987; Wheldall and Merrett, 1989).

All too often, however, schools overlook the emotional needs of the child in their efforts to achieve academic results. For example, it is not uncommon to hear teachers express the view that 'due to curricular and examination pressure we have no time to spend on the social and emotional problems of students.' Yet, self-concept contributes positively towards both academic success and social and emotional adjustment. There is considerable evidence to indicate that reported self-concept of ability is a better predictor of academic success than is the intelligence quotient (Thomas, 1980).

It is a terrible indictment on schools when school leavers report that the post-school period was a time when they recovered from the emotional and devaluing effects of schools (Burns, 1982).

It should be noted that teachers with high self-esteem have been found to produce pupils with high self-esteem. The converse has also been found to be true (Burns, 1982; Lawrence, 1987). For example, Lawrence reports that in addition to qualities of empathy, acceptance and genuiness, teachers of high self-esteem are (a) able to delegate routine jobs, (b) are able to find time to relate personally to pupils, (c) are tolerant of pupils' conversations and (d) are generally relaxed in teaching. This implies that they are able to present a high self-esteem model with which the pupils identify. Lawrence further explains that this process of identification with the teacher is strongest where the pupils perceive the teacher as establishing a 'growth-producing atmosphere'.

It is, therefore, timely to reconsider the stimulating view held by Thomas (1980) that 'only by seeing teaching as one of the helping professions and less an elitist procedure for purveying knowledge, can we encourage a positive sense of worth not only in our pupils but in ourselves.'

To conclude, it must be stressed that by placing so much emphasis on the school with teachers holding the key to the alleviation and treatment of problems in schools is not to deny the influence of the home, as has been demonstrated by both Olweus (1984) and Roland (1989). However, there is clear evidence to show that the incidence of behavioural difficulties has a stronger association with the quality of the teacher–pupil relationships in a school than with the pupils' socioeconomic background (Rutter *et al.*, 1979; Weissbourd, 1996). In other words, schools do make a difference. Thus it is no longer justifiable for schools when faced with behavioural difficulties such as bullying or victimisation to apportion all the blame on the child's home background. The evidence is clearly in favour of the view that a positive school ethos does contribute significantly to the good behaviour of pupils.

References

Baumeister, R. F., Smart, L. and Boden, J. M. (1996) 'Relation of threatened egotism to violence and aggression: the dark side of high self-esteem', *Psychological Review*, Vol. 103, No. 1, pp. 5–33.

Besag, V. E. (1989) *Bullies and Victims in Schools*, Milton Keynes, Open University Press.

Besag, V. E. (1992) *'We don't have bullies here!'*, London, Calouste Gulbenkian Foundation.

Bjorkqvist, K., Ekman, K. and Lagerspetz, K. (1982) 'Bullies and victims: their ego picture, ideal ego and normative ego picture', *Scandinavian Journal of Psychology*, No. 23, pp. 307–13.

Boulton, M. J. and Underwood, K. (1992) 'Bully/victim problems among middle school children', *British Journal of Educational Psychology*, Vol. 62, pp. 73–87.

Bowers, L., Smith, P. K. and Binney, V. (1992) 'Cohesion and power in the families of children involved in bully/victim problems at school', *Journal of Family Therapy*, Vol. 14, pp. 371–87.

Burns, R. B. (1982) *Self-concept Development and Education*, London, Holt-Rhinehart & Winston.

Byrne, B. (1994) *Bullying: A Community Approach*, Dublin, Columba.

Department of Education (1993) *Guidelines on countering bullying behaviour in primary and post-primary schools*, Stationary Office, Department of Education, Ireland.

Elliott, M. (1988) *Keeping Safe, A Practical Guide to Talking with Children*, Hodder & Stoughton.

Elliott, M. (1993/94) *Booklet for parents and children and material for teachers*, Kidscape, 152 Buckingham Palace Rd, London SW1W 9TR.

HMSO (1994) *Bullying: Don't suffer in silence, an anti-bullying pack for schools*, Her Majesty's Stationery Office, London.

Kidscape (1989–96) Annual National Conferences on Bullying, London.

Lagerspetz, K., Bjorkqvist, B. and King, E. (1982) 'Group aggression among school children in three schools', *Scandinavian Journal of Psychology*, No. 23, pp. 45–52.

Lawrence, D. (1987) *Enhancing Self-Esteem in the Classroom*, London, Chapman.

Neary, A. and Joseph, S. (1994) 'Peer victimization and its relationship to self-concept and depression among school girls', *Personality and Individual Differences*, Vol. 16, pp. 183–6.

Ní Irghile, M. (1992) *'Bullying and the special class'*, unpublished. BEd dissertation, Trinity College, Dublin.

Olweus, D. (1978) *Aggression in Schools: Bullies and Whipping Boys*, Washington DC, Hemisphere.

Olweus, D. (1979) 'Stability of aggressive reaction patterns in males: A review', *Psychological Bulletin*, No. 94, pp. 852–75.

Olweus, D. and Roland, E. (1983) *Mobbing, bakgrunn og tiltak*, Oslo, Kirke og Undervisnings-departementet.

Olweus, D. (1984) 'Aggressors and their victims: bullying at school', in N. Frude and H. Gault (eds), *Disruptive Behaviour in Schools*, London, Wiley.

Olweus, D. (1985) '80,000 Elever innblandet i mobbing', *Norsk Skoleblad*, No. 2, pp. 18–23.

Olweus, D. (1993) *Bullying in Schools: What We Know and What We Can Do*, London, Blackwell.

Olweus, D. (1996) 'Bully/victim problems in school', *Prospects* (Paris, UNESCO), Vol. 26, No. 2, pp. 331–59.

O'Moore, A. M. (1988) *Bullying in Schools*, Council of Europe Report, DECS-EGT (88) 5-E, Strasbourg, Council for Cultural Cooperation.

O'Moore, A. M. (1989a) 'Bullying in schools in Britain and Ireland', in E. Roland and E. Munthe (eds), *Bullying: An International Perspective*, London, Fulton Press.

O'Moore, A. M. and Hillery, B. (1989b) 'Bullying in Dublin Schools', *The Irish Journal of Psychology*, Vol. 3, No. 10, pp. 426–41.

O'Moore, A. M. and Hillery, B. (1991) 'What do teachers need to know?', in M. Elliott (ed.), *A Practical Guide to Coping for Schools*, London, Longman.

O'Moore, A. M. (1994) 'Bullying behaviour in children and adolescents', *Journal of the Irish Association for Counselling and Therapy*, Vol. 1, No. 30, pp. 23–30.

O'Moore, A. M. (1995) 'Bullying behaviour in children and adolescents in Ireland', *Children and Society*, Vol. 9, No. 2, pp. 54–72.

Pepler, D., Craig, W., Ziegler, S. and Charach, W. (1993) 'A school-based anti-bullying intervention: preliminary evaluation', in D. Tattum (ed.), *Understanding and Managing Bullying*, Oxford, Heinemann.

Piers, E. V. (1984) *Piers-Harris Children's Self-Concept Scale*, California, Western Psychological Services.

Pikas, A. (1975) *Sa stopper vi mobbing*, Stockholm, Prisma.

Pollack, G., Gilmore, C., Stewart, J. and Mattison, S. (1989) 'A follow-up of aggressive behaviour in children', *Educational Review*, No. 41, Vol. 3, pp. 263–70.

Randall, P. (1996) *A Community Approach to Bullying*, London, Trentham Books.

Rigby, K. and Slee, P. (1992) 'Dimensions of interpersonal relations among Australian children and implications of psychological well-being', *Journal of Social Psychology*, Vol. 133, No. 1, pp. 33–42.

Roland, E. (1989) 'Bullying: the Scandinavian research tradition', in D. P. Tattum and D. A. Lane (eds), *Bullying in Schools*, London, Trentham Books.

Roland, E. and Munthe, E. (eds) (1989) *Bullying: An International Perspective*, London, Fulton Press.

Rutter, M. (1967) 'A children's behaviour questionnaire for completion by teachers: Preliminary findings', *Journal of Child Psychology and Psychiatry*, No. 8, pp. 1–11.

Rutter, M., Maughan, B., Mortimore, P. and Owston, J. (1979) *Fifteen Thousand Hours: Secondary schools and their effects on children*, London, Open Books.

SCRE (1993) *Supporting schools against bullying*, The Scottish Council for Research in Education.

Sharp, S. and Smith, P. K. (1994) *Tackling Bullying in Your School: A Practical Handbook*, London, Routledge.

Siann, G., Callaghan, M., Glissov, P., Lockhart, R. and Rawson, L. (1994) 'Who gets bullied? The effect of school gender and ethnic group', *Educational Research*, Vol. 36, No. 2, pp. 123–34.

Slee, P. T. (1995) 'Peer victimization and its relationship to depression among Australian primary school students', *Personality and Individual Differences*, Vol. 18, No. 1, pp. 57–62.

Smith, P. K. and Sharp, S. (1994) *School Bullying: Insights and Perspectives*, London, Routledge.

Stephenson, P. and Smith, D. (1987) 'Anatomy of a playground bully', *Education*, 18 September, pp. 236–7.

St. John Brooks, C. (1985) 'The school bullies', *New Society*, 6 December, pp. 262–65.

Tattum, D. P. and Herbert, G. (1990) *Bullying: A Positive Response*, South Glamorgan Institute of Higher Education.

Tattum, D. P. and Herbert, G. (1990) *Bullying: A positive response: Advice for parents, governors and staff in schools*, Cardiff Institute of Higher Education.

Tattum, D. P. (1993) *Understanding and Managing Bullying*, Oxford, Heinemann.

Terrill, C. (1989) 'Beating the bully', *The Listener*, 30 November.

Thomas, J. B. (1980) *The Self in Education*, Slough, NFER.

Weissbourd, R. (1996) *The Vulnerable Child, What Really Hurts. America's children and what we can do about it*, New York, Addison-Wesley.

Wheldall, K. and Merrett, F. (1989) *Positive Teaching in the Secondary School*, London, Chapman.

Whitney, I. and Smith, P. K. (1993) 'A survey of the nature and extent of bullying in junior/middle and secondary schools', *Educational Research*, Vol. 35, No. 1, pp. 3–25.

17

■ ■ ■

Why some schools don't have bullies

PETER STEPHENSON AND DAVID SMITH

Introduction

We have defined bullying, in our research, as an interaction in which a more dominant individual or group intentionally causes distress to a less dominant individual or group.

This definition makes explicit the unequal nature of the interaction which is a key feature of bullying. The bully has higher dominance and will inevitably be the victor. The victim has lower dominance and will inevitably be the loser. Bullying is, essentially, the abuse of power.

It is helpful, in practice, to classify bullying behaviour as either verbal or physical and as either direct or indirect. Evidence of direct verbal bullying might be name-calling or a verbal attack, whereas examples of direct physical bullying might be exclusion or a physical attack. Indirect verbal bullying might take the form of spreading rumours or belittling victims in their absence whereas indirect physical bullying might take the form of hiding or defacing possessions or setting 'booby traps'. In our definition we stress that bullying behaviour may take a wide variety of forms.

It is the intention behind the act rather than the act itself which is important. A mere 'look' or 'gesture' or a refusal to reply becomes bullying if the behaviour is intended to and does in fact cause distress. Parodying a person's speech or behaviour is not bullying if the intention is to please rather than to cause distress to the other person. Similarly, verbally or physically attacking another person is not bullying if, for example, the intention is to defend property or territory rather than to cause distress.

One final observation. The majority of research on bullying has been carried out in the Scandinavian countries and studies carried out in this country, including our own, owe a considerable debt to this work. We note, however, that in the Scandinavian research, bullying is often defined as repeated acts of aggression. It is assumed that it is the repetition of the behaviour that defines it as bullying. We would like to query this. We do not state that child abuse has to be repeated to be classified as 'child abuse'. Why should we in the case of bullying? If only a single incident of bullying takes place, it is still important to take action to stop it. There is evidence that children themselves do not consider the behaviour needs to be repeated in order to be considered as bullying (La Fontaine, 1991; Madsen, 1996).

The Cleveland research study

In a survey, we asked the teachers of final-year primary school children in 26 schools to provide information on all the children in their classes. Among other things, we enquired about bullying. Altogether we collected information on over 1000 children in the 26 schools. The schools were chosen so that they were a representative sample so far as the catchment areas of the schools were concerned.

A main finding was that bullying was reported to be a common occurrence. About a quarter of the children were involved as either bullies or victims. Another finding was that the bullying was reported to persist.

In about 80 per cent of cases it was said to have been going on for a year or longer. There was no evidence that it sorted itself out. Bullying was reported to be more common among boys than girls. The boys were reported to use mainly direct physical or a combination of direct verbal and physical techniques whereas the girls were reported to use mainly verbal and indirect forms of bullying. All these findings have been replicated in research carried out in 16 primary schools in Sheffield in which information was obtained directly from the children. In this study 27 per cent of the children were found to be involved in bullying (Whitney and Smith, 1993).

We also found that there were five groups of children involved in the bullying – not just a group of bullies and a group of victims. The situation was more complex than we had anticipated.

About 10 per cent of the children in the sample were reported to be bullies and the majority of these were described as being active, dominant children. They were not rated as being insecure or unpopular with other children. They appeared to be children who enjoyed exercising power over others. A number of them might well be successful in their chosen careers when they left school.

We did find that a small number of these children – 18 per cent of the 112 bullies – had different characteristics. They were rated as being insecure, as lacking self-confidence, as being unpopular and as being behind in schoolwork, and were more often reported to have difficulties at home. These children appeared to be more like the traditional stereotype of the bully who is said to compensate for feelings of inadequacy by bullying. We called these children 'anxious bullies', borrowing the term from the Scandinavian researcher, Dan Olweus (1978).

About 7 per cent of the children in the sample were reported to be victims. The majority of these children were said to be passive individuals who lacked physical prowess, had low self-confidence and were unpopular with other children. They were very much children who would have difficulty in coping with being bullied.

We again found that a small number of these children – 17 per cent of the 73 victims – had different characteristics. These children were said to actively seek out aggressive situations and appeared to precipitate the bullying to which they were subjected. Whereas the main group of victims seldom told their teachers that they were being bullied, the group of 'provocative victims' frequently told their teachers. The term 'provocative victim' is again borrowed from Dan Olweus.

Finally, there was a group of children who were both bullied and who themselves bullied other children. There was a surprisingly high number of these children – 6 per cent of the total sample. These children, whom we refer to as 'bully/victims', were rated as being the least popular with other children of all the groups identified and appear to have some of the characteristics of both anxious bullies and provocative victims. The psychological well-being of the anxious bullies, provocative victims and bully/victims is of particular concern. Very little research has been carried out that has investigated the characteristics of anxious bullies or of bully/victims but other studies do provide confirmation that provocative victims are a particularly vulnerable group of children (Smith *et al.*, 1993).

School factors

We investigated factors that might have contributed to the bullying and found that a variety of factors play a role, including the personalities and the home backgrounds of the children.

Of particular interest in the present context, bullying was reported to be very much more common in some schools than in others. In three of the 26 schools, 30 per cent or more of the children were said to be involved. In one school over 50 per cent of the year group was said to be involved.

It may be significant that two of the three schools in which there was said to be no bullying at all were unusually small schools, both of which employed cross-age grouping of pupils. A teacher at one of these schools expressed the view that cross-age grouping encourages a more caring, less competitive ethos among children and that this discourages the emergence of bullying. If children of the same age are grouped together, issues of dominance are perhaps more likely to arise.

Generally speaking, bullying was reported to be more frequent in schools located in more socially deprived areas. There also tended to be rather more bullying in the larger schools with larger classes though this finding was not statistically significant. A difficulty here was that some schools in the more deprived areas were also smaller schools with smaller classes so that it was difficult to disentangle the operation of the two factors. There is some suggestion that size of school and size of class was a more significant factor as regards schools located in the more deprived areas.

The Sheffield study also found that bullying was more common in disadvantaged schools but there were no significant correlations between the incidence of bullying and either school or class size (Whitney and Smith, 1993).

It needs to be added that in our study there were exceptions to the general rule that there was more bullying in schools in more deprived areas. In some schools there was more bullying than expected and in other schools there was less than expected. In fact, one school located in one of the most socially deprived areas and which also had large classes had one of the lowest levels of bullying. Initially we were suspicious of this finding but enquiries suggested that there was in reality very little bullying at the school which had a very caring ethos.

We did also look in more detail at the six schools with the lowest and the six schools with the highest levels of bullying. A difference that emerged is that the head teachers in the low bullying schools tended to express articulate, considered views on bullying and attached importance to controlling and preventing its occurrence.

How to encourage bullying

Thus the evidence suggests that the incidence of bullying does vary from school to school and this suggests that while social, family and personality factors are probably important, the effect of the school upon the level of bullying must be examined. Bullying is a highly complex behaviour, difficult to define and often near impossible to witness. We have no doubt that the factors contributing to bullying are equally complex and difficult to identify. Certainly we are not suggesting that schools alone cause bullying but the evidence suggests that they may contribute to it, or that at the very least they sometimes provide an environment which makes dealing with bullying more difficult.

In looking at which aspects of school life might contribute to bullying we decided first to imagine that we wished to create a school which prided itself upon its bullies and which fostered the bully ethos. Imagine, for instance, that a management consultant has been asked to design a school to meet these requirements. Perhaps his report might contain some of the following suggestions.

Management consultant's report

1 The school should have many areas which are difficult for staff to supervise. These areas should include the entry and exit points to the school, playgrounds as well as toilet and washing areas.

2 The children should be placed in these areas at times of least supervision. This should include break times and lunch times, as well as at the beginning and end of the school day. However, on wet days the school should arrange for all children to remain inside the school building, perhaps restricting them to classroom areas with again little or no supervision.

3 The school should ensure that if some supervision is provided at lunch time it is by untrained and underpaid staff. These supervisors will then have little authority and should enjoy only minimal respect from teachers and pupils alike.

4 The school day should be arranged so that the whole age range of the school arrives at, and leaves, the school at the same time. Similarly the whole age range could be thrown together on three occasions each day. There should be no designated places of respite for children and the majority of the areas where the children congregate should be dominated by fast and furious games (apart, of course, from the area behind the bicycle shed). No constructive activities should be encouraged and few, if any, seats should be made available.

5 The school should establish a firm rule that any child seeking to leave these areas by entering the school or leaving the school premises should be penalised.

6 Wherever possible arrangements should be made by the school which contribute to large numbers of children having to move around the school in different directions at the same time. Thus the timetable could be designed so that virtually the whole school has to move from one lesson to the next simultaneously, several times a day. Children should be asked to travel different distances between lessons but to get there in the same length of time. All children should use the same corridors.

7 The school should be designed so that the corridors used at changeover times are narrow. Perhaps lockers could be placed down one wall of the corridor thereby increasing congestion as children try to get things in and out of the lockers. In addition we recommend swing doors at the end of each corridor which can be pushed in either direction.

8 Again we envisage little supervision being provided at these times. Staff would either be preparing for the next lesson or moving themselves hurriedly to the next classroom.

9 We would suggest that classrooms should be designed with little or no thought as to how they might affect children's behaviour. There will usually be only one door into and out of the classroom. Many classrooms should be sited on the first or second floors and have windows facing out but not inwards. The only means of supervision from outside of the classroom should be via a small window in the door. This should encourage children who are left unsupervised in the class to feel that they are unlikely to be observed.

10 We should ensure that materials and equipment are in short supply so that children have to share. The majority of resources should be allocated to children with the fewest educational problems. This should indicate to the pupils the priorities of the school.

11 Teachers should be encouraged to arrive late at lessons whenever possible. This could be facilitated in a number of ways. The staffroom should be sited a long distance from the majority of classrooms, perhaps in the separate administration block. Ideally the school should be organised on a split site with those involved in drawing up the timetable taking little or no account of distances teachers need to travel from one lesson to the next. Staff meetings could be organised before school with an agenda which is bound to overrun. Teaching arrangements could be made or altered without regard to where the materials required for the lesson might be kept.

12 The school should be organised so that there is little or no liaison between subject departments and the pastoral system. Subject departments should view their remit as solely concerning academic issues with no formal arrangement for linking with the objectives of the pastoral system.

13 There should be no agreed, clear and consistent way of recording incidents. Whether, and how, a bullying incident is reported or recorded should be a matter for the individual teacher to decide.

When incidents are recorded they should not include details of the actions taken and outcomes. Teachers should not be told who to pass such records to.

14 Teachers should feel free to adopt patterns of behaviour for themselves that they would not accept from pupils and should see no link between the ways in which they behave and the ways in which children behave. They should feel free to employ bullying tactics in controlling children.

15 There should be a lack of rewards available for teachers to use in school which combined with many of the factors already mentioned should encourage teachers to use threats and sarcasm as their main means of control.

16 There should be a lack of any clear and agreed policy on the use of sanctions. Similar pupil behaviour should lead to wide variations in teacher responses from one teacher to the next. This should confuse pupils as to what is and what is not acceptable and appropriate behaviour.

17 We recommend that whenever bullying does occur in the school this should be viewed as part of the 'normal growing-up process', and as 'helping children to learn how to stand on their own two feet' and 'giving them backbone'. Children who are victims or bullying should be viewed as 'asking for it' and/or as 'inadequate'.

18 The school should encourage the view that high achievement rather than relative achievement or effort is valued. This should ensure that for many children school life has little to offer and that they feel inadequate. We should ensure that lessons are not differentiated sufficiently to meet the needs of children.

19 We should ensure that curriculum space is filled as far as possible by academic subjects with little or no time for pastoral issues and that these are dealt in an insular rather than in a cross-curricular fashion.

20 Finally we must at all costs avoid developing anything that vaguely resembles a whole-school policy on bullying.

If the school agrees to follow these recommendations in full we have little doubt that an ethos will be created in which bullying behaviour will flourish.

Yours sincerely

Keith (Flashman) W.

How to discourage bullying

We have described above action that might be taken to encourage bullying. The description given is not dissimilar to the way some schools are organised at the present time. We will now stand these recommendations on their head. How would we organise schools to discourage bullying?

School ethos

Our first recommendation is that action should be taken that contributes to the development of a school ethos that encourages 'non bullying' behaviour and views bullying as unacceptable. Whatever is done in response to bullying should have the goal of bringing about a situation in which a non-bullying ethos is created – one in which relationships are based on mutual respect, trust, caring and consideration for others rather than on power and strength. If an ethos is created which promotes these qualities bullying will be marginalised – children will not even consider the option of engaging in bullying.

It is often assumed that bullying is an inevitable fact of life – it is just one of those things. In fact, as indicated by our research, bullying is very much more common in some schools than in others and this does not just reflect the catchment areas of the schools. Schools are able to make a difference.

In present-day society generally, strength tends to be admired and weakness despised. Whatever the difficulties, we are all expected to be able to cope. If we are having a rough time, we are expected to keep quiet about it and just put up with it. Children are told to 'take it like a man'. This thinking needs to be challenged. Children subjected to bullying are the very children least able to cope with it. Both victims and other children should be encouraged to report bullying. Reporting incidents of bullying should be viewed as taking responsible action rather than as 'telling tales'.

It is likely that, on at least some occasions, part of the motivation for bullying is to impress other children – to impress bystanders. If an appropriate ethos is established, children will not in fact define themselves as 'bystanders' but will take steps to stop the bullying and will report it to a teacher.

There is some evidence that bystanders are more likely to help victims of aggression if they know what to do and have been given training on what to do. The implication here is that children should be given training in helping skills and be given the opportunity to practise them.

We suggest that the school behaviour policy should underwrite the non-bullying school ethos. If staff and children are engaged in the development of the policy, they are more likely to actively support it. The policy is of little value if staff and children are not committed to it. The Sheffield study showed that if school anti-bullying policies are developed in this way, they do have a significant impact in reducing the incidence of bullying (Smith and Sharp, 1994).

The policy should stress the need to prevent and not just control bullying. It is not enough to tell the bully off and to offer support to the victim. As well as dealing with the immediate situation, it is necessary to ask why the bullying has taken place and to take appropriate measures.

Supervision and monitoring

Staff need to be aware of signs that may indicate that a child is being bullied and need to be alert to the possibility of bullying taking place. There should be adequate supervision arrangements, particularly at times and in places where bullying is likely to take place. Spot checks might be regularly carried out on a random basis in places where bullying is likely to occur. In this context, ensuring that children are not regularly unattended in classrooms and cutting down the number of children moving round the school at any one time, for example by staggering the school day, are steps that might be taken. If pupil surveys of bullying are carried out on a regular basis, this not only provides a check on the occurrence of bullying, but helps maintain awareness of bullying as a problem.

There also needs to be an adequate system for recording incidents of bullying which ensures that there is good communication between staff, and that no divisions exist between the academic and pastoral departments. In all cases reports of bullying should be taken seriously, enquiries should be made and the outcome fed back to those involved. The effectiveness of action taken to stop the bullying should also be monitored and fed back to those involved. Unless such steps are taken bullying will be seen to be condoned.

Playgrounds and school buildings

Playgrounds tend to be a focus for bullying. Their design should encourage a diversity of constructive, creative play. In reality they are often barren wastelands, and ways of redesigning and zoning the physical space need to be explored. Bullying is likely to flourish in unstructured, unsupervised situations given over to boisterous play. Playground rules and procedures should be developed.

It is often assumed that the physical appearance of school buildings is unimportant. There is in fact evidence that there is a relationship between standards of behaviour in schools and how well cared for the school buildings are, e.g. whether they are free from graffiti and rubbish. Surveys have been carried out in which children have been asked what they like and dislike about school. The responses suggest that children have difficulty in coping with features of school life such as smelly, unhygienic toilets which offer only limited privacy and noisy, crowded dinner-halls.

The status and role of playground supervisor in managing behaviour and facilitating play should also be acknowledged and appropriate training offered. A number of psychological services are now offering Inset packages to playground supervisors.

Teaching and classroom management skills

The relationship between teachers and children should be characterised by mutual respect and trust so that the children feel able to tell teachers if they are being bullied or if they witness bullying.

Teachers should be aware that children sometimes model their behaviour on the behaviour of adults they admire. They should, therefore, be careful to avoid engaging in bullying themselves. Emphasis should be placed on praising good behaviour rather than on the use of sanctions and there should be positive expectations of pupil behaviour. Teachers should make every effort to arrive on time and be well prepared, and senior management should give priority to punctuality.

Overcoming bullying is not easy. Teachers require time, patience and skill to deal with children involved in bullying and their parents. In this context adequate support should be made available to teachers, especially those new to the profession.

Children should be encouraged to participate in the management of the class and the school. There is evidence that this leads to improved pupil behaviour and is, in part, the rationale behind approaches such as Kidscape and Teenscape.

Curriculum matters

We found in the Cleveland study that many of the children involved in bullying were behind educationally, particularly the anxious bullies. It is important that an appropriate curriculum appropriately delivered is offered to children. Non-academic as well as academic achievement and cooperative as well as competitive learning should be valued.

In addition discussion of bullying should be incorporated in both the academic and PSE curriculum. Techniques such as social and friendship skills training should also be incorporated in the PSE curriculum.

Help for bullies and victims

As regards bullies we suggest it is necessary to take action which communicates unambiguous disapproval of the bullying. We stress that the disapproval should be aimed at the behaviour of the child and not the child itself. At the same time action should be taken which encourages the development of caring, responsible behaviour on the part of the bully, for example through peer tutoring. The aim is to channel the dominance of the bully into more productive and fruitful activities. There is some evidence that counselling-based approaches which focus on solving the problem rather than on apportioning blame have some success (Pikas, 1989; Duncan, 1996).

As regards victims, and to some extent all children involved in bullying, steps should be taken to improve their self-confidence, self-esteem and social skills. There is evidence that assertiveness training, victim support groups and peer counselling approaches help empower these children (Arora, 1991; Smith and Sharp, 1994).

Bystanders, as well as the children immediately involved in bullying, should be offered support and help, and immediately after a bullying incident all those who have witnessed it should be debriefed.

The role of parents, the local community and other agencies

Parents should be kept informed if their child is involved in bullying and should be encouraged to work with the school to overcome the problem. Parents should also be made aware of the complaints procedures.

Traditionally schools and parents have tended to be wary of each other and have tended to blame each other for behaviour difficulties presented by children. It is now much more widely accepted that schools should aim at establishing a genuine partnership with parents.

This partnership should also include school governors, the local community, the LEA support services and other agencies. Bullying is too large a problem for schools to be able to deal with on their own.

Conclusion

Many schools do now acknowledge that bullying exists and are making efforts to deal with it. However, recognition and ownership of the problems still remain an issue in other schools. Some schools remain unaware of, or deny, the serious impact that bullying has upon the lives of a significant proportion of pupils.

For those schools which recognise that bullying is a problem which needs to be tackled but are not sure what action to take we conclude with a set of questions they may wish to address and a set of guidelines they may wish to adopt.

Bullying – some question for schools

1 Is bullying seen as a problem by staff in your school? Do they recognise that it occurs? Do they think anything should be done about it?

2 Do the physical characteristics of the school contribute to bullying? If so, how could they be altered?

3 How and by whom are rules determined in your school? How are rules communicated? Are they applied consistently by members of staff?

4 Is there an efficient communication system between different parts of the school organisation?

5 Are topics such as bullying looked at in PSE or tackled in a cross-curricular fashion?

6 Are incidents of bullying and how they are dealt with recorded, discussed and evaluated by staff?

7 Are there agreed procedures for dealing with bullying? Are they followed?

8 Does the school inform parents of bullying incidents? How is this done?

9 Are children encouraged to 'tell' if they have been bullied or have witnessed bullying?

10 If the school has a whole-school policy on discipline, is bullying mentioned specifically?

Guidelines on dealing with bullying

1 Ensure that action taken contributes to the development of a school ethos that encourages non-bullying behaviour and that views bullying as unacceptable.

2 Ensure that the school behaviour policy underwrites this ethos and stresses the need to prevent, not just control, bullying.

3 Ensure that all staff are actively committed to the behaviour policy and the ethos that underlies it.

4 Ensure that steps are taken to publicise the policy to children and parents and to enlist their support.

5 Seek to bring about the situation in which children themselves actively discourage bullying and view reporting incidents of bullying as being responsible rather than as 'telling tales'.

6 Ensure that staff are alert to the possibility of bullying taking place.

7 Ensure that there are adequate supervision arrangements particularly at times and in places where bullying is likely to take place.

8 If there are narrow corridors or inaccessible corners, ensure that special supervision arrangements are made.

9 Operate a system of 'spot checks'.

10 Cut down the number of children moving round the school at any one time.

11 Ensure that children are not regularly left unattended in classrooms.

12 Ensure that there is an adequate system for monitoring and recording incidents of bullying.

13 Ensure that there is good communication between staff in monitoring and managing bullying problems.

14 Carry out pupil surveys to monitor the occurrence of bullying.

15 Ensure that the design of playgrounds and the use made of them encourage a diversity of constructive, creative play.

16 Ensure that the status and role of playground supervisors in managing behaviour and facilitating play are acknowledged and appropriate training offered.

17 Ensure that the playground and school buildings are well cared for and free from graffiti and rubbish.

18 Ensure that the relationship between teachers and children is characterised by mutual respect and trust so that children feel able to tell teachers if they are bullied.

19 Ensure that teachers model non-bullying behaviour – ensure that methods of teaching and or control do not endorse bullying tactics.

20 Ensure that there is emphasis on praising good behaviour rather than on the use of sanctions and that there are positive expectations of pupil behaviour.

21 Ensure that teachers arrive on time for lessons and are well prepared.

22 Ensure that the curriculum encourages non-academic as well as academic achievement and cooperative as well as competitive learning.

23 Ensure that discussion of bullying is incorporated in both the academic and PSE curriculum.

24 Encourage children to participate in the management of classes and the school.

25 Ensure that techniques such as social and friendship skills training are incorporated in the PSE curriculum.

26 Ensure that adequate support is made available to teachers, especially teachers new to the profession, in handling bullying problems.

27 If children or parents report bullying, the report should be listened to, taken seriously and appropriate enquiries made.

28 The outcome of enquiries should be made known to those involved.

29 The effectiveness of action taken to stop bullying should be monitored and discussed with those involved.

30 Ensure that action is taken which communicates unambiguous disapproval of bullying to bullies and that additional action is taken which encourages caring responsible behaviour.

31 Take steps to improve the self-confidence, self-esteem and social skills of victims and, to a lesser extent, the others involved in bullying.

32 Ensure that 'bystanders' as well as the children immediately involved are offered support and help.

33 In serious cases, inform the children's parents and seek their involvement and cooperation in resolving the bullying.

34 Ensure that there are procedures for dealing with parental complaints about bullying.

35 Enlist the cooperation of parents and the local community in dealing with school bullying problems.

36 Make effective use of LEA support services in tackling bullying.

37 Enlist the support and advice of school governors in dealing with bullying.

References

Arora, C. M. J. (1991) 'The use of victim support groups', in P. K. Smith and D. Thompson (eds), *Practical Approaches to Bullying*, London, David Fulton Publishers.

Duncan, A. (1996) 'The shared concern method for resolving group bullying in schools', *Educational Psychology in Practice*, Vol. 12, No. 2, July.

La Fontaine, J. (1991) *Bullying: The Child's View*, London, Calouste Gulbenkian Foundation.

Madsen, K. C. (1996) 'Differing perceptions of bullying and their practical implications', *Educational and Child Psychology*, Vol. 13, No. 2.

Pikas, A. (1989) 'The common concern method for the treatment of mobbing', in E. Roland and E. Munthe (eds), *Bullying – An International Perspective*, London, David Fulton Publishers.

Smith, P. K. and Sharp, S. (1994) *School Bullying – Insights and Perspectives*, London, Routledge.

Smith, P. K., Bower, L., Binney, V. and Carde, H. (1993) 'Relationships of children involved in bully/victim problems at school', in S. Duck (ed.), *Learning About Relationships*, Sage.

Whitney, I. and Smith, P. K. (1993) 'A survey of the nature and extent of bully/victim, problems in junior/middle and secondary schools', *Education Research*, Vol. 35, No. 1, pp. 3–25.

18

■ ■ ■

The study, diagnosis and treatment of bullying in a therapeutic community

L.F. LOWENSTEIN

Allington Manor is a residential school and therapeutic community for children in need of special assistance. The school accepts girls and boys between the ages of 11 and 16 with a range of learning, emotional and behavioural difficulties. The emphasis of the school is on rehabilitation for the child, socially, emotionally and educationally.

Introduction to the problem

Patrick and Robert (names have been changed) were two boys with serious problems who were admitted to Allington Manor. Their main disturbing behaviour was bullying other children and the distress this produced in the bullied children and the community as a whole. Patrick and Robert bullied through a combination of verbal threats and unprovoked sadistic and physical attacks on those children who were in fear of them. Naturally, this produced stress and frustration in the tormented children who already had their own problems, which necessitated their being placed in a therapeutic community for schooling, care and treatment.

Thus the problem of aggressive, sadistic, bullying behaviour affected the whole community and reinforced the negative behaviour of the two boys. It was vital to intervene, both for the sake of the two boys and the community as a whole, and in particular the victims of bullying.

As can be imagined many methods for dealing with Patrick's and Robert's bullying had been tried in the past with little or no positive results, hence their placement at Allington Manor.

As will be seen from the background history which follows, both boys had experienced a considerable amount of bullying themselves from parents, siblings and other children. They had therefore taken for granted that the world consisted essentially of two types of individuals: bullies and the bullied. Having themselves experienced the distress and pain of being the victims of bullying, they had chosen now that they were stronger and older to be the perpetrators instead of the victims of aggression.

While this obviously satisfied *their* needs it was causing serious problems to the victims and to the community as a whole. It was equally not in the long-term best interest of the perpetrators of bullying to be allowed to continue to behave in this way.

The goal was to create a feeling of awareness in the two boys that what they were doing was wrong because it was causing distress to others. It was also the aim to develop some positive feelings of care towards others and hence to promote kind behaviour rather than sadistic behaviour. It was the aim also to help them form personal relationships along alternative lines with all children. This would, of course, constitute an asset for the compulsive bully and the therapeutic community as a whole.

The background history of Patrick

Patrick had come from an extremely disturbed background where a considerable amount of violence had taken place in the home, mostly by the father physically attacking the children and his wife from time to time, usually under the influence of alcohol. Patrick therefore suffered from child abuse at a very early age. Both parents had been in care themselves.

Even at the age of 4, bruising was frequently noted while Patrick attended school and an NSPCC office was notified. There were many subsequent injuries and eventually Patrick was removed from the home at the age of 8 to a place of safety. Patrick's father was convicted of assault about the same time. There were many subsequent changes in placement for Patrick, but he was returned home on a trial basis at the age of 14.

This broke down less than a year later. He had gone missing several times from home. He was finally rejected from home by his parents because of his abusive behaviour towards his mother and also his threatened violence. No contact with home has been made since that time and Patrick has no desire to seek any contact whatsoever.

The social worker described Patrick as: 'a difficult and quite damaged boy who is capable of producing some quite bizarre behaviour. A return home in the foreseeable future is unlikely and this leaves him with no real aim for his future.'

Patrick also had great difficulty in relating to the school situation. He was frequently quite uncooperative and even when tested by the psychologist refused to perform in certain of the test items. He was totally uncooperative in most lessons and not expected to do anything that could be loosely termed academic. He frequently even refused to go to school, and once there tended to run away. He was also disruptive and abusive to both staff and other children. He gave the impression of hating and despising all around him. He always had a surly, aggressive look on his face and was very uncouth in every way and lacking in manners, grasping at everything, self-centred and uncaring. He seemed to be going out of his way to make everybody hate him.

His relationship with his peer group was poor and almost non-existent, but so was his relationship with adults. Patrick's first reaction to requests was an ignorant 'Hmph' and often uncooperative behaviour, ignoring what was being said. When disciplining measures were taken he would often become stubborn and argue, saying he was being victimised and 'picked on'. A great deal of pressure had to be exerted before he would comply to any sort of structure.

The background history of Robert

Robert's personal history before he attended the therapeutic community was described as 'verbally and physically aggressive'. Outbursts were directed towards peer groups and staff in general. Community homes in most of Wales where he was placed were unable to contain him. He was also noted to be hyperactive. He was of slim build but very energetic and strong, height five feet one inch and seven stone.

At a case conference held shortly before his coming to the therapeutic community a number of the staff felt considerable reservations about Robert's long-term prognosis due to his difficult behaviour, disrespect for staff, and also his temper with a high degree of aggression following.

Robert comes of a Welsh background and could converse equally well in Welsh and English. The results of the testing indicated that his ability was in the low average range. Further reports by the psychologist who investigated him clearly showed that there was a lack of emotional bonding between himself and his parents. Robert was described as being very much like a 'demanding, egocentric three year old'.

Robert was placed in care at the age of 3 due to home difficulties in managing him. He was also placed with foster parents but this only lasted three months before he was placed in a children's home with elder twin brothers. He was then returned home but this again broke down when Robert was aged 8.

There were no sleep problems and his appetite was good. He appeared to need some form of firm control over him for as soon as it was removed he would become insecure and aggressive. His behaviour was described prior to coming to the therapeutic community as moody and unpredictable. At the same time there was a considerable warm, helpful and caring side to his personality. He expressed affection through hostility and could be very affectionate towards adults especially when he wanted something. He accepted discipline and punishment but only if he himself considered it fair.

Although he frequently expressed the view that he would like to be at home with his mother, to whom he claimed to be close, he found it difficult to live in that environment due to her lack of control over him.

In the peer relationship in his younger years he was considered to be the 'group clown' and scapegoat and was frequently in conflict with other children due to his attention-seeking toward the staff and the stressful interaction this caused with the others. Robert tended to be a major source of irritation to the group.

His relationship with adults varied considerably. He appeared to be more relaxed with staff who were able to control him and who, in a sense, could be in charge of him but he was abusive to those he felt weak. He related superficially to many people and appeared on the whole to be self-centred.

Robert was one of five illegitimate children. Mother was, at the time, cohabiting with the same person she has been with for six years. The problems within the family were chronic and long-standing and this had been damaging to Robert. As already mentioned, the prognosis for Robert was not good and there was some possibility that he might become involved in crime. This crime was likely to be of a violent nature because of his temper outbursts against people and objects.

In the therapeutic community his behaviour continued very much as previously. His behaviour was very challenging, demanding, violently provocative, bullying and threatening.

Treating or dealing with the problem

In dealing with the problem of bullying, a number of specific treatment measures were simultaneously instituted. These were at least in part based on the specific problems and diagnosis carried out earlier. Useful methods were also gleaned from such theoretical bases as rational emotive therapy.

Let us look at a summary of some of the strategies used to remedy or eliminate the process of bullying:

1   creating awareness in the community and in the individuals involved, i.e. in the bully and the victim, and making certain bullying is discovered every time or most of the time;

2   making certain that bullying can never be used successfully to gain ends since it results in the victim suffering distress;

3   making certain that the community as a whole is against the bullying and takes actions against such behaviour by reporting it and acting against it in any way necessary;

4   making certain that bullying is punished;

5   providing alternative socially acceptable ways towards which habitual bullies can turn and use to achieve their ends if this does not conflict with the rights and welfare of others;

6   drawing attention to the model of non-bullying behaviour and encouraging such alternative behaviour. This may be done by shaping improved behaviour;

7   rewarding non-bullying type behaviour with tokens, praise and through extrinsic reinforcement;

8   physically restraining the bully in the midst of his physically aggressive behaviour, causing him to experience similar pain, distress and frustration to that which he is foisting on his victim, albeit this method must be used sparingly.

It will be noted that all these aims are simultaneously used and are methods of combating bullying and similar antisocial behaviour. They will be discussed individually in detail despite the fact that they are interrelated.

Creating awareness of the bully in the community

It is an important role for the leader of the therapeutic community to create an awareness and a conscience within the community concerning the dangers of bullying. Similarly, the individual or individuals carrying out the activity of bullying must be made aware how they are affecting others, be it through verbal threats or physical aggression.

This is done via individual encounters with Patrick and Robert as well as through group meetings. Here all members of the community are encouraged to have the confidence to express their feelings about the bullies, knowing their protection is ensured by the staff and the other children. In a group, individuals who are victims of bullying are encouraged to express what has happened and how it is affecting them emotionally and behaviourally.

In this way, three things happen concurrently:

1   the victim gets rid of his pent-up feelings of fear, anxiety, aggression and frustration;

2   the bully is made aware of how the victim feels as a human being through his sadistic behaviour. Bullies on the whole tend to de-humanise their victims;

3   the victim receives support from the group while the group condemns the actions of the bully.

All this brings pressure on the bully to stop his cruel behaviour. It may also provide the bully with the opportunity to release his or her own tensions and frustrations concerning his or her past experiences in other than bullying behaviour. Frequently, bullies will report having suffered a great deal in the past themselves and how this accounts for their present behaviour. This, in itself, provides the bully and the community with insight into why such behaviour occurs.

Sometimes it is necessary to conduct a 'poll' within the group anonymously by asking them as a body to write on a piece of paper whom they regard as the biggest bullies and victims of bullying in the group. The result is then collated and a bar graph is drawn, which is discussed by the group and hung up in a public place for everyone to see. The same poll is then repeated after a sufficient period of time has elapsed and changes, for the better or worse, noted. Then the bully is either praised or punished in some manner depending on the outcome of the group assessment. On the whole, these two assessments show virtually always an improvement in behaviour of the bully. This is possibly due to the fact that the bully himself feels ashamed of being thus noted for his antisocial behaviour and seeks to make amends for it.

Making bullying an unsuccessful way of gaining satisfaction

Bullies appear to gain some gratification from the sadistic act of threatening and/or actually carrying out acts of aggression against the victim. This in itself acts as a reward and encourages future acts of bullying. The inflicting of pain appears to trigger off satisfaction. It is for this reason that the behaviour must be halted for the sake of the perpetrator as well as the victim.

This is because, for the victim, it becomes immediate as well as a lasting source of torment, which has its effects long after the bullying has passed. For the bully, it is a maladaptive pattern which eventually brings him into conflict with society and the law. Behaviour such as assault, grievous bodily harm, mugging and violence towards wife, children and others is likely to follow with the anticipated consequences that such behaviour must be terminated or reduced in any way possible.

These are but some of the reasons why the bully must be totally unsuccessful in his behaviour. Lack of success must also be engendered through the punishment that follows such behaviour. This will be discussed in greater detail later on.

Obtaining the support of the community (staff and children) in combating bullying

Allington Manor School and Therapeutic Community exists in part in order to produce a miniature society and one which, through the interaction of its members, seeks to produce change in those members who require it in positive and desired directions. The support of all or most of the membership, therefore, is vital in order to effect the optimum change in bullying behaviour.

The leader of the therapeutic community has a vital role in seeking to unify the group in condemning the cruel activities of bullies. In part, this is achieved by creating an awareness that the problem not merely exists, but that something definite must be done about it. Knowing that the leader feels as he does and knowing that others can become victims of bullying, the membership is likely to back the goals and the other procedures that have been adopted in order to attain these goals.

Numerous group, as well as individual, meetings with children and staff create a climate which suggests the importance of each and everyone standing up against bullying and showing a positive care for others. This works from the top down suffusing every member of the community, including new members who join it.

It is of course important to seek up-to-date information from the community to check on the bullying behaviour, such as whether it has changed for the better or worse. Such information is also important to the bully who obtains the appropriate reinforcement (negative or positive) based on his own behaviour during the interim period. It certainly makes the bully aware that he is being observed and checked and that reports are being provided. The victim can also act as reinforcer by his responses. It incidentally also provides the victim and others with the view that the staff and other children of the therapeutic community as a whole care about their welfare.

Ensuring that the bully is punished

Whenever punishment is used, ethical considerations come into play despite the suffering of the victim of the bully in this particular case. Any behaviour that is encouraged or even tolerated by a community is likely to continue, especially if it is rewarding to someone. If certain behaviour is considered 'outlawed' and is subsequently punished, there is every likelihood that it will in time be inhibited. It will occasionally reappear, unless substitute behaviour is found which takes the place of the maladaptive bullying behaviour.

In the first instance there may be the need to lower one's aim rather than expect a total inhibition of bullying. One way of decreasing problem behaviour is through differential reinforcement of other behaviour (DRO). This may be the avoidance of bullying without any truly friendly or warm relations towards

187

victims of bullying. It may be accomplished by keeping the bully busy doing other things which he enjoys. Bullying behaviour is therefore less likely to occur.

Such methods may work for a time but stress and frustration experienced by the bully sooner or later will lead to a resuming of his negative behaviour. Therefore, other more severe ways must be found to combat bullying including the physical restraint of the individual, which will be discussed in the final section.

Whenever possible, the victim of bullying must be kept from the bully, since victims act almost as a trigger for the outlet of the bully's pent-up frustrations which then lead to aggression. Somehow, however, the bully always 'finds' the victim. For this reason certain areas of the school and community must be made 'no-go areas' for the bully. Places like the communal television room, music room or dining room may have to be made inhospitable to the bully. In so doing there is a strong element of punishment since this constitutes a deprivation of privileges. It constitutes also a 'time-out' procedure. Having to eat alone constitutes an escalation in the ostracism by the staff and the community as a whole of the individual who is bullying.

The bully is in fact first warned of the impending 'natural time-out' procedure that will be adopted.

1 If you cannot stop bullying you will no longer be permitted to use the TV room, music room and eventually you will not be allowed to eat in the dining room with all the other members of the community.

2 If bullying continues, the threat is put immediately into operation.

3 This eventually affects the bully, though he may not show it for a time and may become even more aggressive in his bullying. It certainly affects the community and makes clear the standards expected of the therapeutic community. It also reduces the peer attention received by the bully.

4 Once the target behaviour of non-bullying has a chance of being reached, this 'time-out' procedure is reduced and then eliminated altogether. This acts as a positive reinforcement of non-bullying and eventually caring behaviour may follow.

5 It is important to reintroduce all the sanctions if the bully has a relapse and it is sensible to expect that he will. Then the process of punishment and removal of punishment must continue until the bullying behaviour is extinct.

6 Extinction of bullying within the community means that such behaviour is less likely to occur outside the community.

7 Finally, the aim of the therapeutic community is to encourage 'over-correction' in the bully. This means the bully will eventually be required to

make amends to the victim. This alternative behaviour is reinforced, first by the fact that there are no aversive repercussions and second by the fact that such behaviour is reinforced extensively by tokens, pocket money, privileges, etc. Ultimately, the alternative behaviour is likely to continue even when more obvious reinforcement ceases.

Providing opportunities to behave positively

As already mentioned, changing behaviour through aversive methods works best when combined with learning or conditioning in a positive direction. The objective therefore is to discourage and, if possible, to eliminate maladaptive behaviour that is harmful to others and eventually to oneself. The individual is also encouraged to substitute attitudes and behaviour. Behavioural changes occur under optimum learning conditions, i.e. critical learning times, traumas, through practice leading to a new habit, and of course the individual's cooperation with such changes is important.

A good part of the work must be done by the individual himself to promote his capacity for self-control and redirection of behaviour. For this to occur he must be encouraged or induced over a long period of time to accept suggestions to change. Much depends on a combination of the suggestibility of the individual and the skill of the therapist or director.

Eventually, the influence of the therapist must take second place to the behaviour of the individual and his ability to use his own resources adaptively. Initially, the bullier should do all he can to avoid being in the vicinity of the victim of his bullying, since in this way, he reduces the temptation element to bully. Later, however, to be truly over the need to bully, he must be able to interact in a neutral way or benevolently with his potential victim.

In the case of Patrick and Robert, suitable incentives or rewards were offered if, in the short term, bullying was reduced and if, in the final analysis, they would desist from bullying altogether. In the case of Patrick, the reward was a cigarette, given even for a slight improvement. For Robert it was the opportunity of having sweets and, if successful, being able to spend a week with a member of staff and her family, something he enjoyed very much.

Eventually Patrick and Robert became aware how much more pleasant life was when the rights of others were respected. They also became aware of the pressures upon them to change. This encouraged a more favourable attitude generally and this was ultimately also manifested by their behaviour. Much of this was achieved through the individual and group therapy sessions. The token system which will be described later, was also useful in reinforcing the other methods currently in use to reduce antisocial and asocial behaviour such as bullying. It meant eventually greater acceptance of the bullies by the other members of the community.

189

Perhaps one of the greatest difficulties for the two boys was to overcome the intrinsic reinforcement which they received from their bullying of others. Only a combination of punishment for this with positive reinforcement for socialised behaviour could dislodge eventually the gratification they got from their maladaptive action. It required the following:

1 a commitment towards change in the desired direction;

2 a lengthy period of practice of the new pattern of behaviour, with appropriate reinforcement being given;

3 the feeling that one was rewarded or at least not punished by the change in behaviour.

Encouraging modelling (imitation) of non-bullying behaviour

As has already been established, individuals who bully have not merely frequently suffered from the effect of bullying themselves, but have also identified and now imitate modes of bullying behaviour. It is therefore necessary when changing behaviour to find a model or models who can act as substitute for such identification. It must be a model worthy of imitation, i.e. strong, benevolent, sympathetic and attractive.

More often than not, new behaviour needs to be shaped gradually by the method of successive approximations. This means initially reinforcing behaviour which falls far short of the standards one ideally wishes to inculcate. Hence, initially, one aims to bring about a lessening of the bullying behaviour rather than its total stoppage.

This inculcating of socialised behaviour is done through the model or direction which is received and continually reinforced through pressure from all directions. Factors which enhance modelling (imitation of behaviour) are the similarity of sex, age, race, attitude, prestige, competence, warmth and nurturance of the directing model.

It should be remembered that the modelling approach should be seen merely as one approach to help the bully. Frequently, it is best to combine this technique with other methods and to use it as part of a total approach.

Reinforcing non-bullying and alternative behaviour

It is vital to reward non-bullying behaviour. This includes rewarding a neutral position of non-involvement by the former bully with victims. Later the expression of favourable comments and actions towards the real or potential victim must be reinforced. Hence, if the bully can actually learn to display caring and helping behaviour towards his former victim, then treatment may be said to be almost successful. Total success is achieved when this attitude and behaviour generalise to other individuals elsewhere outside the community.

Equally, bullying behaviour must never be reinforced but the reverse attitude must be taken. It must be punished and discouraged in every possible way. One very useful method which has long been used is the Token Economy Programme (TEP), evaluated as being useful in modifying a number of disorders and maladaptive or unsocialised patterns of behaviour.

Tokens are conditioned reinforcers that are given immediately or as closely as possible to a response or behaviour which is deemed desirable. It is therefore reinforced or rewarded because it is socialised and hence desirable. There is then the expectation that non-bullying behaviour will recur with greater and greater frequency. The tokens, although symbolic in the first instance, can be spent 'to buy' or 'be exchanged for' extrinsic rewards such as sweets, privileges, cigarettes or even money.

Equally, failing to behave appropriately leads to minus tokens being awarded which places the individual into a kind of 'behavioural debt'. These minus tokens need to be 'worked off' before any kind of positive reward or privileges are provided. TEP need not and should not be continued once the improvement or total cessation of bullying has occurred. Gradually, the TEP method can be reduced.

Imposing physical restraints

In some cases where all the positive and aversive methods have been unsuccessful in reducing or stopping bullying behaviour, a final method must be contemplated. This consists of physically curtailing the negative behaviour of the bully directly and decisively. It may also be necessary to use this method when the punitive aspects already described are circumvented or ignored by the bully.

Obviously, the method of physical restraint should be used sparingly for optimum results, but when it is used, it must always be considered as one step, the next of which must lead to a positive direction. This might be illustrated when the action of restraint actually occurs.

A bully found in the act of viciously bullying another child should be firmly restrained by being forced to lie on the floor. This minimises injury to himself and to the member of staff, and also reduces the likelihood of damage to property. The bully must be gripped firmly and at the same time he must be told what is happening, i.e. his behaviour is being controlled because he is unable to do so on his own.

Frequently, the bully will claim, while he is being physically controlled, that the adult himself is a bully just like himself. This claim must quickly be discounted by the adult with a statement such as, 'I am not doing what you are doing. You're enjoying your threats and physical attacks against your victim. I don't enjoy what I have to do. I must do this and hold you because you are bullying other people. As soon as I know you will stop this behaviour, initially by your giving me your assurance, I will stop holding you. There is therefore a big difference between what you do and what I am doing. If you fail to keep your promise and bully again, I will be forced to do this again in order to protect your victim as well as yourself.'

Hence, while being physically restrained, the bully is actually forced to listen and gain information, possibly in a way which will make an impact. He benefits from the physical restraint and verbal communication simultaneously. It will of course be argued that 'treatment' thus carried out must be done by a reasonably fit and strong individual who will not abuse his own power. Such an argument is absolutely correct. In the right hands, this method is very effective and often 'gets through' the message while other approaches will fail, because they are insufficiently basic or reality orientated.

Conclusion

The main object of these eight steps is to help the children develop the self-confidence and the independence to deal with problems which will arise in life. If we give these children a clear message that bullying behaviour is not acceptable and that there are more positive ways of dealing with their anger, then other children will be spared the pain of becoming their victims.

19

■ ■ ■

A whole-school approach to bullying

MICHELE ELLIOTT

Bullying makes life more difficult for teachers. Dealing with the aftermath of a bullying case means seeing the bully, the victim and perhaps the parents, and then having to be on the alert for the revenge that will surely follow. In a day fraught with demands on the teacher's time, bullying is just one of a thousand things. No wonder it goes on. But life would be so much easier for everyone in the school if there were less bullying. With a little bit of effort, it is possible to substantially reduce bullying. In fact, by spending just a few hours dealing with the problem at the start of the school year, school staff could save hundreds of hours of aggravation later.

The most effective way to deal with bullying is to have a whole-school programme and policy (Foster, Arora and Thompson, 1990; Olweus, 1993; Elliott and Kilpatrick, 1994; Besag, 1995). The initiative for this can come from staff, parents or the children themselves. Once it is in place, it is difficult for bullying to go on as the combined force of the school and community will ensure that it simply is not tolerated – in any way, shape or form.

In setting up a whole-school policy, it is a good idea to find out the extent of the problem in the school. The following steps have been taken by many schools and are presented here as a possible model.

Steps to take

1. Survey

Ask students to fill out an anonymous questionnaire about bullying. Either make up your own or use the one at the end of this chapter (Model 19.1). This will give you an indication of what is happening. Although some schools ask for the names of those who bully, this could affect the veracity of the children and invites abuse. ('If I find out anyone's put down my name, I'll thump 'em'.) What you are trying to find out in the survey is if the students find bullying a problem. If the classroom teachers compile their own survey, it will not take long to put all the results together. Otherwise, ask a trusted parent-volunteer to compile the survey.

2. Staff meeting

Meet with the staff to share results and discuss the implications of the survey. Decide on how to share with the students. A whole-school assembly takes less time, but a discussion brings out more information.

3. Class rules

Ask each class to put together five or ten 'Rules' they would like everyone to live by in the school. You may wish to extend these beyond bullying. To protect those students who are shy or may be victimised, you could have the rules written and passed in. Ask a student to compile them.

4. School rules

With the students (perhaps the Student Council) put together a list of rules using the class rules as a guideline. Limit the number so that you don't end up with a manifesto which is impossible to live with. One group of teenagers compiled a list which would have done the Spanish Inquisition proud.

5. Staff approval

If you had a teacher meeting with the students in Step 4, then this stage may be eased through. Either ask the teachers who were involved to present the list to the staff or invite in the students or a combination of both. The problem, of course, with a combined meeting is time and sometimes the resistance of staff. However, a combined meeting helps to establish a more solid student/teacher response to bullying.

6. Student approval

Either refer the school rules back to the students for a vote if there are dramatic changes to the original proposal or skip this stage if there are few changes. Make the ballot secret if you have a real problem with bullying. If not, a school assembly with a show of hands speeds up the process.

7. School contract

From the rules which are agreed, draw up a common contract which will be signed by each student. The contract works best if also signed by the parents, so that no one can later say, 'I didn't know anything about the rules!' The contract should be run off on coloured paper, funds permitting, and kept in each student's file. Of course, you will need parental and governor support for this (*see* Model 19.2).

8. School governors

Depending upon your school, this stage may be the first. Most governors, however, will be able to make a more informed decision with the survey results and the proposed rules. Otherwise, you may spend time debating if you have a problem and then have to have another meeting.

9. Parents

By now some of the parents will have heard something about bullying. You may want to send a letter home at an early stage to say you are looking into the problem. This could lead to hundreds of telephone calls from parents anxious tell you about their child's problem or parents of bullies ringing to ask if you are starting a vendetta. If you want to send a preliminary letter home, there is an example (Model 19.3) at the end of this chapter.

Another approach would be a meeting of parents, perhaps as part of the normally called meeting. Have the students present the rules and ask for questions and concerns.

One school just sent home a letter saying that the rules had been agreed and asked concerned parents to get in touch. They only had six calls in a school of 180 children, so this would seem to be the most time-efficient method depending upon the verbosity of your parents.

Parents are usually only too pleased that the school is taking this initiative and most parents sign the contract and agree the rules with no problem.

10. Local authority

Since the rules will be part of your policy, the local education authority should be informed. If you are part of an enlightened local authority, they may use your efforts as a model for other schools. Alternately the local education authority may have suggestions from other schools or from their policy department which may be useful.

Reducing bullying

Once aware of the extent of bullying, and once the contracts have been signed by parents and students, there are, of course, many things teachers can do to reduce bullying on the playground and in the school building itself (*see* Chapters 5 and 17).

How do you continue to implement the policy once it has been agreed? The main strategies to employ follow.

School assemblies

During school assemblies, remind the students that yours is a 'telling' school and that everyone has the responsibility to tell if they see bullying happening. If the students are still worried about reporting, then you can install a box to put in notes anonymously. This rather defeats the purpose of open communication, but may be necessary in your school setting.

Rules

The agreed school contract should be posted on bulletin boards throughout the school.

Supervision

Although it may surprise some, teachers cannot be in all places at all times. Bullying tends to happen when there is no supervision or when the supervisors are untrained, but willing, volunteers. To decrease the possibility of bullying, invite these supervisors to the meetings on bullying, ensure that they know the rules and that they have a clear idea of what to do and who to tell if something happens. If you are unfortunate enough to occupy one of those buildings designed to enhance bullying, rotate student monitors, get in parent-volunteers, vary movement of classes by a few minutes if possible (*see* Chapter 17) and lobby your local authority for more funds for supervision. Structure the playground time with games or activities (*see* Chapter 5). Ask all the staff to keep a friendly eye on things as they pass by groups of students and places of known difficulty.

Posters

Have a poster contest and award prizes to those who best capture the ways to deal with bullies. Get a local business to give prizes and invite the local media to cover the story (Pavey, 1990).

Curriculum

Sometimes children do what a bully tells them because they are frightened or just don't know what to do. We can help children with strategies by introducing programmes in school which deal with bullying. The Kidscape programmes for the under 5s, 5–11s and teenagers all have lessons on bullying based upon stories, roleplays and discussion (*see* the Resources section at the end of the book). At the end of this chapter are examples of 'What if?' questions for discussion (Model 19.4). For teenagers, try giving them a scenario and asking them to make up their own roleplays. The Teenscape programme has specific suggestions for teenagers.

Any work that it is possible to squeeze into the curriculum on self-esteem and assertiveness also helps. As Valerie Besag mentions in Chapter 5, the staff/pupil relationship is important in helping children to develop self-esteem, which helps prevent them from becoming both bullies and victims.

Transition

Ragging and initiation rites of passage have institutionalised bullying in many schools in the past. Hopefully, these practices have been stamped out, but children do still fear the transition periods from primary to secondary. In a survey of 200 primary children in 1995 (Elliott, 1996), 64 per cent were worried that they might be bullied or picked on when they got to secondary school. Most good teachers are aware of children's concerns about this transition period. Children are invited to spend a morning in their new school during which questions and worries are addressed. Perhaps we can go one step further, as some schools have done, and assign the new students an older student to show them around and ease the way.

Since much bullying comes from slightly older children, this might also help to change the attitude of the older children to one of protection instead of harassment.

Bystanders

If it is part of the school policy that there are no bystanders, it will be the responsibility of everyone to stop bullying (Elliott, 1994).

Intervention

The prevailing attitude, 'Let the kids sort it out themselves', plays right into the hands of the bully. It allows him or her unfettered power and this will be used to inflict misery. When bullying is identified, immediate intervention is crucial. This gives a clear message that bullying at any kind will not be tolerated and that action will be taken. After the initial action, it is important to consider help for the bully and victim (Chapters 9 and 11). If it is a serious bullying situation, the parents should be informed and the bully may face suspension (*see* Chapter 3).

Consequences

As part of the school policy, there should be consequences or punishments meted out to those who break the rules. If these are clearly spelled out, perhaps as a letter home such as Linda Frost includes in Chapter 3, it lessens the hassle when teachers have to enforce the rules. These consequences can be posted along with the rules or explained to the children in class or in assembly.

If there are no consequences to their actions, bullies will learn that bad behaviour is rewarded. One of the first consequences should be that the bully apologises and in some way makes up for his or her behaviour.

No blame

The 'no blame' approach was originated in Sweden by Anatol Pikas and called 'common concern'. The idea of this approach is to get the bullies and victims to work together to try to figure out a mutually agreeable way to deal with the bullying. It is based upon the assumption that the bullies actually want the bullying to stop. The adult who intervenes avoids blaming anyone for the problem. This approach can work in less serious cases of bullying when the bully and victim may have previously been friends but have fallen out with each other. It is unlikely to work if the bullies are picking on children they don't know or care about and if the patterns of bullying are so well established that the bullying itself has become a reward for the bullies.

Bully courts

In some schools, as part of the consequences for breaking rules, children are liable to come before a court of their peers. These courts can only work in schools which have established a caring atmosphere and in which the school contract is firmly in place (*see* Chapter 7).

Bully gangs

The only effective way to break up bully gangs is to meet with them separately and break down the group identity and ethos which encourage bullying. The following suggestions for dealing with gangs come from various teachers and staff who have successfully dealt with the problem of bully gangs (Elliott, 1993).

Breaking up bully gangs

1 Meet with the victim or victims separately – have them write down what happened.

2 Meet with each member of the gang separately – have them write down what happened.

3 Agree with each member of the gang separately what you expect and discuss how s/he has broken the contract about guidelines for behaviour (*see* Chapter 7).

4 Meet with the gang as a group and have each state what happened in your individual meeting; ensure that everyone is clear about what everyone else said. This eliminates the later comment, 'I really fooled him' since everyone has admitted his/her part in front of the group.

5 Prepare them to face their peer group – 'What are you going to say when you leave here?'

6 Decide whether to involve the bully court – this will depend upon what you have agreed with the students.

7 Whatever is decided, reiterate to all students that they are all responsible if anyone is being bullied – there are no innocent bystanders.

8 Talk to parents of all involved – show them written statements.

9 Keep a file on bullying with all statements and penalties.

10 Teach victim strategies (as in Kidscape lessons).

11 Do not accept false excuses (*see* Chapter 2).
   - If the bullying was an accident, did the children act by helping the victim or getting help or giving sympathy?
   - If it was just for a laugh, was everyone laughing?
   - If it was a game, was everyone enjoying it?

12 If a child is injured, take photographs of the injury.

13 If gangs of bullies from outside your school appear, take photographs – they tend to run when they see the camera.

14 If there is serious injury, contact the police.

By setting up a whole-school approach to eliminating bullying, you are sending signals to the children that you do care about their welfare. This approach assumes good pupil–staff relations and creates an atmosphere which continues to foster those relationships. Involving parents and the community will help to change attitudes which encourage bullying.

The ultimate goal of all schools is to make bullying unthinkable.

MODEL 19.1

Kidscape bullying questionnaire

1. Do you consider that you have ever been bullied?
   Yes ☐ No ☐

2. At what age? under 5 ☐ 5–11 ☐ 11–14 ☐ over 14 ☐

3. When was the last time you were bullied? today ☐
   within the last month ☐ within the last 6 months ☐
   a year or more ago ☐

4. Were you bullied: once ☐ several times ☐ almost every day ☐
   several times a day ☐

5. Where were you bullied? at home ☐ going to or from school ☐
   in the playground ☐ at lunch ☐ in the toilets ☐ in the classroom ☐
   other ☐

6. Did/do you consider the bullying to have been: no problem ☐
   worrying ☐ frightening ☐ so bad that you didn't want to go out or
   to school ☐

7. Did the bullying: have no effects ☐ some bad effects ☐
   terrible effects ☐ make you change your life in some way (e.g.
   change schools or move out of a neighbourhood) ☐

8. What do you think of bullies? no feeling ☐ feel sorry for them ☐
   hate them ☐ like them ☐

9. Who is responsible when bullying continues to go on? the bully ☐
   the bully's parents ☐ the teachers ☐ the head ☐ the victim ☐
   children who are not being bullied, but do not help the victim ☐
   others ☐

10. Please tick if you are a: girl ☐ boy ☐

11. Was the bully (bullies) a: girl ☐ boy ☐

12. If you have ever been bullied, was the bullying: physical ☐
    emotional ☐ verbal ☐ (you may tick more than one)

13. What should be done about the problem of bullying?

14. Have you ever bullied anyone? Yes ☐ No ☐

Source: Elliqtt (1995).

MODEL 19.2

Contract

1. We will not tolerate bullying or harassing of any kind.

2. We will be tolerant of others regardless of race, religion, culture or disabilities.

3. We will not pass by if we see anyone being bullied – we will either try to stop it or go for help.

4. We will not allow bullying or harassing going to or from school, either on the school bus or public transport or walking.

5. We will allow a quiet area in the playground for those who do not want to run around or be in games.

6. We will use our 'time-out' room if we feel angry or under pressure or just need time to calm down or work out what is wrong.

7. We will not litter or draw on school property (walls, toilets, books, etc.).

8. We will be kind to others, even if they are not our friends, and will make new students feel welcome.

9. On school journeys we will act in a way which brings credit to our school.

10. We will have a discussion group once a week in class to talk about any problems that are bothering us.

11. We will be honest when asked about anything that we have done or are supposed to have done.

12. We will cooperate with and abide by the findings of the school court.

MODEL 19.3

Letter to Parents

Dear

There has been much national media attention recently about the problem of bullying. As far as we are aware our school does not have a particular problem with bullying, but we would like to ensure that this is the case. We know that children learn better when they are happy and not worried.

Having talked with the children, we have decided that an anonymous survey about bullying might be helpful. We will be giving the children the enclosed questionnaire (Model 19.1) and thought that you would like to see a copy. We will obviously keep you informed of the results and value your support.

We are giving the children the survey on   . If you have any questions, there will be a brief meeting for parents on   .

If you could keep any questions until this meeting, we would greatly appreciate it, as we are so busy at the moment with the start of the school year.

Thank you for your support.

Yours sincerely,

MODEL 19.4

What ifs?

The suggested answers are for discussion only – the students may have ideas which will work just as well or better.

1. You are walking to school and a gang of older bullies demands your money? Do you:
    (a) fight them?
    (b) shout and run away?
    (c) give them the money?

    A: Give them the money – your safety is more important than the money.

2. You are on the school playground and someone accidentally trips you?
    Do you:
    (a) hit the person hard?
    (b) give him or her a chance to apologise?
    (c) sit down and cry?

    A: Give the person a chance. If it was an accident, then he or she should say 'sorry'.

3. You are in the school toilet and an older student comes in, punches you then tells you not to do anything or 'You'll get worse'. You know who the person is and you have never done anything to him/her.
    Do you:
    (a) wait until the person leaves and then tell a teacher?
    (b) get in a fight with him/her?
    (c) accept what happened and don't tell?

    A: You didn't deserve to be punched and the bully was wrong to do it. If you don't tell, the bully will just keep on beating up other kids.

4. You are walking into the lunch room and someone yells out a negative comment directed at you. Do you:
    (a) ignore it?
    (b) yell back
    (c) tell?

    A: You can either ignore it (if it is the first time and that's all that happens) or tell if it really bothers you. People should not yell out negative comments directed at you.

5. You are continually harassed by bullies calling you names, making rude comments about your mother and generally making you miserable. Do you:
    (a) tell them to bug off?
    (b) get a group together and make comments back?
    (c) if possible, get a witness and then tell?
    (d) it isn't really bullying so just live with it?

    A: Name-calling which makes you miserable is bullying and should not go on. Tell even if you don't have a witness.

6. You see someone you hardly know being picked on by a bully. Do you:
    (a) walk by and be thankful it isn't you?
    (b) immediately rush to the defence of the victim and push the bully away?
    (c) get help from other kids?
    (d) tell someone on the staff?

    A: If possible solve the problem with other kids, but be careful not to fight the bully. Then tell what happened.

7. You are walking in your neighbourhood on a Saturday morning. A kid you know from school comes by you, pushes you and grabs your money before running off. Do you:
    (a) tell your parents?
    (b) tell your teacher?
    (c) tell the police?
    (d) chase after him?

    A: Tell the police. This is a crime. You will also need to tell your parents. Be wary of chasing him – you could be hurt and possessions are not worth your safety. As for the school this has nothing to do with it as it happened away from the school grounds. You may wish your teacher to know, but it is not his/her responsibility to do anything about it.

8. Your sister (brother) bullies you all the time. Do you:
    (a) thump her (him)?
    (b) sneak up behind her (him) and dump a bucket of water over her (his) head?
    (c) ask your parents for a family meeting to discuss ways to stop the bullying?

    A: The sensible thing to do is (c), even though you may wish to do(a) and (b). The problem is that acting like that might make the situation worse.

9. Your teacher continually bullies you. Do you:
    (a) tell your parents?
    (b) talk to the teacher?
    (c) tell the head teacher?
    (d) put up with it?

    A: It is best to start with your parents, though it will be necessary to tell the head teacher. Talk with the teacher if you think he/she doesn't realise it is bothering you, but whatever you do don't put up with it.

10. Your father (mother) bullies you. Do you:
    (a) tell your teacher?
    (b) tell a favourite aunt (gran, uncle, etc.)?
    (c) do nothing as telling might make it worse?

    A: If you have a relative to confide in, start there. Perhaps your other parent could help. Doing nothing is one way out, but it won't stop the bullying.

References

Besag, V. (1995) *Bullies and Victims in Schools*, Milton Keynes, Open University Press.

Elliott, M. (1993) *Stop Bullying* (booklet), London, Kidscape.

Elliott, M. (1994) *Keeping Safe, A Practical Guide to Talking with Children*, Hodder Headline.

Elliott, M. (1995) *Teenscape*, Health Education Authority.

Elliott, M. (1996) 'Primary School Survey', unpublished, London, Kidscape.

Elliott, M. and Kilpatrick, J. (1994) *How to Stop Bullying: A Kidscape Training Guide*, London, Kidscape.

Foster, P., Arora, T. and Thompson, D. (1990) 'A whole-school approach to bullying', *Pastoral Care in Education*, September.

Olweus, D. (1993) *Bullying at School: What We Know and What We Can Do*, Oxford, Blackwell.

Pavey, J. (1990) 'Bullying: more serious than we thought?' *Crime Prevention News.*

Help organisations
■ ■ ■

Books

Mail-order booksellers with up-to-date catalogues on bullying and disruptive behaviour are as follows:

Abbey Books
4 Bank View Road
Derby
DE3 1EL
Tel: 01332 290021

Forum Bookshop
86 Abbey Street
Derby
DE22 3SQ
Tel: 01332 368039

Advice and information

Anti-Bullying Campaign
Tel: 0171–378 1446
Support service for parents and children: 9:30 a.m. to 5:00 p.m. Mon. to Fri.

ChildLine
Tel: 0800 1111
24-hour freephone helpline for children and young people.

Commission for Racial Equality
Tel: 0171–828 7022
Information and advice regarding racial bullying.

Kidscape
152 Buckingham Palace Road
London SW1W 9TR
Tel: 0171–730 3300: 10.00 a.m. to 4.00 p.m. Mon. to Fri., parent helpline
Send a large SAE for copies of three free booklets about bullying and information about training courses.

Samaritans
Tel: 0345 909090
24-hour helpline for anyone with problems.

Youth Access
1A Taylor's Yard
67 Alderbrook Road
London SW12 8AD
Tel: 0181 7729900
Gives information about local counsellors for young people.

Legal advice

Advisory Centre for Education (ACE)
1B Aberdeen Studios
22 Highbury Grove
London
N5 2EA
Helpline: 0171–354 8321 2.00 p.m. to 5.00 p.m. Mon. to Fri.
Gives free advice for parents and publications for parents and professionals about education law.

Children's Legal Centre
Advice line: 01206 873820 2.00 p.m. to 5.00 p.m. Mon. to Fri.
Provides free legal advice regarding children and the law.

Education Law Association (ELAS)
29 South Drive
Ferring
Worthing
West Sussex BN12 5QU
Tel: 01903 504949
Gives names and addresses of solicitors throughout the country who deal with education law.

Scottish Child Law Centre
Lion Chambers
170 Hope Street
Glasgow
G2 2TU
Tel: 0141–226 3737 10.00 a.m. to 4.00 p.m. Tues. to Fri.
Provides free legal advice about children and Scottish law.

Advice on home education

Education Otherwise
Tel: 0891 518303
Answerphone with a list of local contact numbers.

Home Education Advisory Service
Send large SAE for comprehensive information pack to:
PO Box 98, Welwyn Garden City, Herts AL8 6AN.

Advice on playground design

Learning through Landscapes
Third Floor, Southside Offices
The Law Courts
Winchester
Hants
Tel: 01962 846258
Information, books and videos on improving playgrounds.

Advice on school phobia

No Panic
93 Brands Farm Way
Randlay
Telford
Shropshire
TF3 2JQ
Helpline: 01952 590545 10.00 a.m. to 4.00 p.m. Mon. to Fri.
Information and advice for all types of phobias.

Resources

■ ■ ■

Programmes for schools and training

The following materials are available from Kidscape (*see* address and telephone number in Help section).

Kidscape Under Fives Programme
52-page manual includes lessons for 3- to 5-year-olds and children with special needs about bullying, stranger danger and keeping safe.

Child Protection Programme
278-page manual and videos with lessons and follow-up activities about bullying, touching, stranger danger and other personal safety issues for 5- to 11-year-olds and children with special needs.

Teenscape
168-page guide for teaching teenagers about issues such as bullying, crime, abuse, saying no, gambling addiction and other safety topics.

How to Stop Bullying: Kidscape Training Guide
262-page manual with over 90 practical anti-bullying exercises to use with students. It also has sections to use to train professionals about the issues involved in bullying, as well as a sample whole-school anti-bullying policy.

Books for professionals

Assertion Training: How to be who you really are
Authors: S. Rees and R. Graham
Publisher: Routledge
ISBN: 0-415-01073-X

Bullies and Victims in Schools
Author: Valerie Besag
Publisher: Open University Press
ISBN: 0-335-09542-9

Bullying: An Annotated Bibliography, of Literature and Resources
Author: Alison Skinner
Publisher: Youth Work Press
ISBN: 0-86155-143-5

Bullying: A Community Approach
Author: Brendan Byrne
Publisher: The Columbia Press
ISBN: 1-85607-103-0

Bullying: An International Perspective
Editors: Erling Roland and Elaine Munthe
Publisher: David Fulton Publishers
ISBN: 1-85346-115-6

Bullying at School: What We Know and What We Can Do
Author: Dan Olweus
Publisher: Blackwell
ISBN: 0-631-19241-7

101 Ways to Deal with Bullying
Author: Michele Elliott
Publisher: Hodder & Stoughton
ISBN: 0-340-69519-6

Coping with Bullying in Schools
Author: Brendan Byrne
Publisher: Cassell
ISBN: 0-304-33071-X

Don't Pick on Me: How to Handle Bullying
Author: Rosemary Stones
Publisher: Piccadilly Press
ISBN: 1-85340-159-5

Helping Children Cope with Bullying
Author: Sarah Lawson
Publisher: Sheldon Press
ISBN: 0-85969-683-9

A Positive Approach to Bullying
Author: Eve Brock
Publisher: Longman
ISBN: 0-582-21490-4

Positive School Discipline
Authors: Margaret Cowin *et al.*
Publisher: Longman
ISBN: 0-582-08713-9

Practical Approaches to Bullying
Authors: Peter Smith and David Thompson
Publisher: David Fulton Publishers
ISBN: 1-85346-159-8

Some Approaches to Bullying
Author: Des Mason
Available from: Governors Support Unit, South Glamorgan Council

Teenscape
Author: Michele Elliott
Publisher: Health Education Authority (also available from Kidscape)
ISBN: 1-85448-069-3

Turn Your School Round
Author: Jenny Mosley
Publisher: LDA
ISBN: 1-85503-174-4

'You Know the Fair Rule'
Author: Bill Rogers
Publisher: Longman
ISBN: 0-582-08672-8

We Can Stop It
Author: Hilary Claire
Publisher: Islington Safer Cities Project

We Don't Have Bullies Here
Author: Valerie Besag
Publisher: Calouste Gulbenkian Foundation

Free booklets

For one free copy of the following, send a large SAE to Kidscape (*see* Help section for address).

Stop Bully!
20-page booklet including 'what if?' questions and general information about bullying.

You Can Beat Bullying! A Guide for Young People
20-page booklet with information for teenagers about how to cope with bullying.

Preventing Bullying! A Parent's Guide
24-page booklet for parents, includes advice about helping victims and bullies, as well as how to work with the school or make a complaint if necessary.

Books on reducing bullying in the playground

'Can I Stay in Today Miss?'
Authors: Carol Ross and Amanda Ryan
Publisher: Trentham Books
ISBN: 0-948080-42-6

Children's Games in Street and Playground
Authors: Iona and Peter Opie
Publisher: Oxford University Press
ISBN: 0-19-281489-3

The Outdoor Classroom
Editors: Brian Keaney and Bill Lucas
Publisher: Scholastic
ISBN: 0-590-53034-8

Using School Grounds as an Educational Resource
Author: Kirsty Young
Available from: Learning Through Landscapes (Tel: 0962 846258)
ISBN: 1-872865-04-6

Videos

Bullying: Face It, Stop It, How
20 mins. 10 years to teens, with accompanying notes (32 pages).
Produced by: Cumbria Education Service with the Alfred Barrow
School, Barrow-in-Furness, Cumbria (Tel: 01229 827355).

Kicks and Insults
20 mins. 11 years and up.
Produced by: Educational Media Film & Video Ltd, Harrow, Middx
(Tel: 0181–868 1908/1915).

Bullying
50-min. BBC documentary. Teens and professionals.
Peer counselling - this video follows the progress of four student counsellors.
Produced by: HopeLine Videos, PO Box 515, London SW15 6LQ.

Only Playing, Miss
56 mins. Playscript also available. Teens.
Produced by: Neti-Neti Theatre Company, London (Tel: 0171–272 7302).

Sticks and Stones
20 mins. 11–16-year-olds.
Produced by: Central Television in association with Kidscape.
Available from: Kidscape (Tel: 0171–730 3300).

Books for children

Books for younger children

The Anti Colouring Book   Age: 4+
Authors: Susan Striker and Edward Kimmel
Publisher: Hippo
ISBN: 0-590-70011-1

The Bad Tempered Ladybird   Age: 3+
Author: Eric Carle
Publisher: Picture Puffin
ISBN: 0-14-050398-6

Being Bullied   Age: 5–8
Authors: Kate Petty and Charlotte Firmin
Publisher: Bracken Books
ISBN: 1-85170-955-X

Bill's New Frock   Age 7–9
Author: Anne Fine
Publisher: Mammoth
ISBN: 0-7497-0305-9

Boy on a Bus   Age: 7–11
Author: Dermot McKay
Publisher: Grosvenor Books
ISBN: 1-85239-009-3

The Bullies Meet the Willow St Kids   Age: 7–11
Author: Michele Elliott
Publisher: Piccolo (also available from Kidscape)
ISBN: 0-330-32800-X

Bully   Age: 3–6
Author: David Hughes
Publisher: Walker Books
ISBN: 0-7445-2169-6

Bully for You   Age: 4–7
Publisher: Child's Play
ISBN: 0-85953-365-4

Calling Tracy   Age: 6–9
Author: Clare Cherrington
ISBN: 0-241-13276-2

Feeling Happy Feeling Safe   Age: 2–6
Author: Michele Elliott
Publisher: Hodder & Stoughton (also available from
Kidscape – *see* Help section for address)
ISBN: 0-340-55386-3

Feeling Left Out   Age: 5–8
Authors: Kate Petty and Charlotte Firmin
Publisher: Bracken House
ISBN: 1-85170-954-1

I Won't Go There Again   Age: 3+
Author: Susan Hill
Publisher: Walker
ISBN: 0-7445-2091-6

Making Friends   Age: 5–8
Authors: Kate Petty and Charlotte Firmin
Publisher: Bracken Books
ISBN: 1-85170-956-8

Playing the Game   Age: 5–8
Authors: Kate Petty and Charlotte Firmin
Publisher: Bracken Books
ISBN: 1-85170-953-3

Rhyme Stew   Age: 6+
Author: Roald Dahl
Publisher: Jonathan Cape
ISBN: 0-224-02660-7

Rosie and the Pavement Bears   Age: 4+
Author: Susie Jenkin-Pearce
Publisher: Red Fox
ISBN: 0-09-972090-6

The Twits   Age: 6+
Author: Roald Dahl
Publisher: Puffin
ISBN: 0-14-031406-7

Sally-Ann in The Snow   Age 4+
Author: Petronella Breinburg
Publisher: The Bodley Head
ISBN: 0-370-01809-5

The Trouble with the Tucker Twins   Age: 4–6
Authors: Rose Impey and Maureen Galvani
Publisher: Picture Puffins
ISBN: 0-14-054089-X

Books for older children and teens

The Bailey Game   Age: 12–Teen
Author: Celia Rees
Publisher: Piper
ISBN: 0-330-33326-7

Bullies   Age: 12–Teen
Author: Ed Wick
Publisher: Kingsway
ISBN: 0-85476-406-2

Bully   Age: 10–Teen
Author: Yvonne Coppard
Publisher: Red Fox
ISBN: 0-09-983860-5

The Bullybusters Joke Book   Age: 9–Teen
Author: John Byrne
Publisher: Red Fox
ISBN: 0-09-960981-9

Chicken   Age: 9–12
Author: Alan Gibbons
Publisher: Orion Children's Books
ISBN: 1-85881-051-5

The Chocolate War   Age: 9–13
Author: Robert Cormier
Publisher: Lions, Tracks
ISBN: 0-00671765-9

Don't Pick On Me   Age: 10–Teen
Author: Rosemary Stones
Publisher: Piccadilly
ISBN: 1-85881-053-1

The Fish Fly Low   Age: 10–Teen
Author: Steve May
Publisher: Mammoth
ISBN: 0-7497-1410-7

Lord of the Flies   Age: 12–Teen
Author: William Golding
Publisher: Faber & Faber
ISBN: 0-5710-8483-4

The Present Takers   Age: 12–Teen
Author: Aiden Chambers
Publisher: Mammoth
ISBN: 0-7497-0700-3

The Trial of Anna Cotman   Age: 10–Teen
Author: V. Alcock
Publisher: Mammoth/Octopus
ISBN: 0-7497-0978-2

Whose Side Are You On   Age: 9–12
Author: Alan Gibbons
Publisher: Orion Children's Books
ISBN: 1-85881-053-1

Index